Write Here

Online Materials for Instructors

This text has a companion site with resources for instructors.

Please visit:
sites.broadviewpress.com/ write-here/

Access code: **whd34221**

Instructor site resources include assignment ideas, teaching tips, discussion questions to prompt deeper understanding of concepts, and suggested answers to the exercises in each chapter.

Write
Here

Developing Writing Skills in a Media-Driven World

Randi Brummett de Leon
and Brooke Hughes

broadview press

BROADVIEW PRESS – www.broadviewpress.com
Peterborough, Ontario, Canada

Founded in 1985, Broadview Press remains a wholly independent publishing house. Broadview's focus is on academic publishing; our titles are accessible to university and college students as well as scholars and general readers. With 800 titles in print, Broadview has become a leading international publisher in the humanities, with world-wide distribution. Broadview is committed to environmentally responsible publishing and fair business practices.

Library and Archives Canada Cataloguing in Publication

Title: Write here : developing writing skills in a media-driven world / Randi Brummett de Leon and Brooke Hughes.
Names: Brummett de Leon, Randi, author. | Hughes, Brooke, 1981- author.
Description: Includes bibliographical references and index.
Identifiers: Canadiana (print) 20200262475 | Canadiana (ebook) 20200262483 | ISBN 9781554814770 (softcover) | ISBN 9781770487277 (PDF) | ISBN 9781460406830 (EPUB)
Subjects: LCSH: English language—Rhetoric—Study and teaching (Higher) | LCSH: English language—Composition and exercises. | LCGFT: Textbooks.
Classification: LCC PE1408 .B78 2020 | DDC 808/.0420711—dc23

Broadview Press handles its own distribution in North America:
PO Box 1243, Peterborough, Ontario K9J 7H5, Canada
555 Riverwalk Parkway, Tonawanda, NY 14150, USA
Tel: (705) 743-8990; Fax: (705) 743-8353
email: customerservice@broadviewpress.com

For all territories outside of North America, distribution is handled by Eurospan Group.

 Broadview Press acknowledges the financial support of the Government of Canada for our publishing activities.

Edited by Tania Therien
Book Design by Em Dash Design

PRINTED IN CANADA

Contents

1

Welcome to *Write Here*

- - - - - - - - - - - - - - - - - - - -

DEVELOPING WRITING SKILLS IN A MEDIA-DRIVEN WORLD

"We have more media than ever and more technology in our lives. It's supposed to help us communicate, but it has the opposite effect of isolating us."

—Tracy Chapman

FACT OR FICTION?
The media are entertainment. There is no connection between the media and reading/writing.

FICTION.
Many forms of media include written text that must be read and understood. We do not just absorb the information provided by media; we also participate in the media. Just as the media affect and change us, we can change others by sending our thoughts, feelings, and creations through media. Imagine you are reading a blog you follow regularly. The most recent post is about a small, local farm that has been devastated by flooding. Moved, you tweet out your support. After talking to a few friends, you decide to start a crowd-sourced fundraiser for the farm and promote your efforts with a persuasive post on Facebook.

MEDIA are forms of communication that reach many people. Radio, television, newspapers, magazines, advertisements, websites, and social media are all included within the broad term *media*. Media are all around us. Most of us will experience several forms of media before we even get to school or work: advertisements on billboards and buses call out for our attention, social media accounts nudge us with push notifications, and radio stations sneak in news between songs. We are immersed in media, but we also react and contribute to media. Imagine when the alarm clock on your phone goes off, and you are drawn to check your Twitter account before you get out of bed. On your feed, you

see that the *New York Times* tweeted an article about women in the entertainment industry who have accused Harvey Weinstein, a film producer and studio executive, of sexual harassment. Stunned, you chat with friends and classmates about the news. After watching Dr. Phil interviewed about Weinstein on *The Late Show with Stephen Colbert*, you vlog about it on YouTube, sharing your opinions and thoughts with your followers. About a week later, you see Alyssa Milano's tweet calling those who have experienced sexual harassment to reply #MeToo, reviving an awareness movement. Since you are following the hashtag conversation on both Facebook and Twitter, you see how many people are affected and feel compelled to write your research paper for class about sexual harassment.

Being aware of various forms of media—social media and television in this case—can connect you to others and encourage you to be more engaged. Media can act as a catalyst for your critical thinking skills. You can receive multiple points of view, connect with people from all around the world, and even interact in thoughtful discussions.

As you've seen from the previous example, media are inescapable in our lives. Many of us are aware and accepting of the increasing role media play; we must not make the mistake of assuming media are here only for our entertainment. Media help us understand what's going on around us in the news, allow us to relate to others through television shows, provide opportunities for us to express ourselves via social platforms, and convince us that we want and even need certain products. Additionally, the process of analyzing media helps us sharpen our reading, writing, and critical thinking skills. Just like a written message, such as a newspaper article or academic essay, each media message is carefully constructed by the author/speaker and is designed to have a specific and powerful effect on the reader/listener.

Imagine you are in a grocery store shopping for pasta. You may be initially attracted to a particular box of pasta by the packaging, price, or the brand name. Because you are a cautious and responsible shopper, you evaluate and analyze the product more before you put it into your cart. You check the ingredients, the amount of pasta in the box, and the expiration date. You even compare it to other similar items on the shelf before you feel confident that you will buy the pasta. While you may not realize it at the time, you are analyzing media while shopping for pasta.

Media messages are made to be consumed by an audience, much like products. Each feature and word on the box was carefully chosen to attract the attention of a specific audience and persuade them to purchase the pasta. For instance, a red box with the phrase "just like grandma used to make" would emotionally appeal to shoppers who loved pasta as a child or want something authentic. While we would like to think that we make our purchases objectively, advertisers know that this is not always the case. A savvy shopper can find and evaluate the messages from advertisers. Other messages in the media should be carefully evaluated in the same way.

Various forms of media affect our buying habits, such as the branding of a box of pasta; they also influence what we think is important, what we consider normal, and the way in which we interpret the behavior of others. Think about the programming meant for children. *Sesame Street*, like other educational programs, teaches children about their world and culture. Children are encouraged to learn social norms like being polite and concepts like diversity. Since media permeate our lives, we are often unaware of how we decipher, sort, and evaluate information we receive from various types of media.

Critical reading and writing skills are important in every academic discipline. No matter what program or career path you choose, communicating will be an essential tool. For instance, in a psychology course, you might be asked to read several case studies and then write a paper demonstrating that you can apply concepts you learned in class to the studies you read. In order to do this, you must be able to analyze the readings, organize the information, and present your thoughts in a written format. This kind of assignment may take time and practice to perfect, but the essential reading and writing skills you learn in this textbook will help to prepare you for a variety of such assignments across disciplines.

A New Perspective: *Write Here: Developing Writing Skills in a Media-Driven World*

This textbook is designed to teach you essential reading and writing skills, using media examples to help explain academic concepts and provide opportunities for practice. You will be asked to analyze and respond to many types of media, including music videos, advertisements, pictures, and television shows. Four specific types of media are highlighted in individual chapters: social media (Chapter 10), advertisements (Chapter 11), news (Chapter 12), and television (Chapter 13).

SOCIAL MEDIA Connect (through an Internet-based means of communication) groups of people with shared interests and allow users to create social or professional contacts **EXAMPLES**: Facebook, Twitter, Snapchat, LinkedIn, TikTok, and Instagram	**ADVERTISEMENTS** Help us choose what products to buy, but they can also ask for our support for organizations and political candidates **EXAMPLES**: Print ads, television commercials, billboards, radio ads, branding, and social media sites
NEWS Provides audiences with information about local, regional, national, and world events **EXAMPLES**: Radio broadcasts, newspapers, magazines, press releases, television shows, and websites	**TELEVISION** Gives us a broad array of programs to choose from and helps fulfill some of our needs, such as a need for education and a need for entertainment **EXAMPLES**: Comedies, children's programming, reality television, dramas, and news

Write Here encourages self-assessment. Within each chapter, you'll find features that will help you get the most out of your learning experience. Discovering Key Points provides a list of what you can expect to learn in a chapter. Since the Discovering Key Points highlights important content, you can use this feature to direct your focus as you work through each chapter. At the end of each chapter, you will find more help in the sections entitled Assessing Your Knowledge and Deepening Your Understanding. Assessing Your Knowledge allows you to review and evaluate how well you have understood the material. Deepening Your Understanding offers you related topics to investigate if you would like more information. Together, these features allow you to focus and assess your own learning, helping you get the most out of the textbook and improve your reading and writing skills.

This textbook embraces the idea that we live immersed in media. As a result, you may be surprised to find yourself watching a movie for homework in preparation for a formal essay or analyzing an advertisement that will be included in an oral presentation. This textbook reintroduces and reinforces concepts from the reading and writing chapters (Chapters 2 through 9) using specific examples from media-themed chapters (Chapters 10 through 13). For example, you will learn about Aristotle's rhetorical appeals when reading an article or writing an essay. Later, you will be asked to apply this knowledge about rhetoric to a television show, such as *Good Eats*, by watching a clip and providing a thoughtful and developed answer. The second half of the textbook will teach you to craft a research paper utilizing sources (Chapters 14 through 16) and then to refine your writing (Chapters 17 through 26).

Assessing Your Knowledge

KEY POINTS	REMINDER	HOW WELL DID YOU UNDERSTAND THIS MATERIAL?	PAGE(S)
Identify types of advertisements	There are many types of advertisements: print ads found in magazines, radio commercials, television commercials, social media advertisements, billboards, political advertisements, and other ads, such as those found on buses.	☐ I've Got It! ☐ Almost There ☐ Need More Practice	pp. 170–71
Recognize rhetoric used in advertisements	Successful advertisements use all three rhetorical appeals—**ethos** (making their brand/product trustworthy), **logos** (presenting facts/statistics), and **pathos** (evoking an emotion from the audience).	☐ I've Got It! ☐ Almost There ☐ Need More Practice	pp. 171–72
Identify target audience and placement in advertisements	The **target audience** for an advertisement is the specific group it is selling the product to. The **placement** is where that ad could be found. These two elements work hand in hand as well, because where the advertisement is placed will tell you a good deal about the target audience.	☐ I've Got It! ☐ Almost There ☐ Need More Practice	pp. 172–74
Identify techniques used in advertisements	**Techniques**, such as the "cool" factor and sex appeal, are used to evoke emotion, or pathos, in the audience. These techniques help the advertisement become more effective.	☐ I've Got It! ☐ Almost There ☐ Need More Practice	pp. 174–75

Deepening Your Understanding

If you would like to go beyond the material in this chapter, explore additional connections, and get more practice, check out these related topics:

- **Adjectives:** Advertisements use descriptive words to explain what the product is like to the viewer. These expressive words are known as adjectives.
- **Using Precise Language:** Companies know that using the right words is important in advertisements. Choosing the right words can affect the ethos of the product and company.
- **Argumentation:** All advertisements argue or persuade us to buy the product. Ethos, logos, and pathos all influence whether or not the advertisement is argumentative or how argumentative it is.
- **Description:** Advertisements rely heavily upon description, as they must communicate what the product is, does, and looks like. An advertisement without detailed, specific description is not an effective advertisement.

GRAMMAR LESSON: SINGULAR OR PLURAL?

Many now consider it entirely acceptable to use *media* as a collective noun. In other words, when the word is presumed to be acting as a single entity for various media outlets, it's acceptable to use the noun with a singular verb. However, it is still acceptable to use *media* with a plural verb in all circumstances. If you are uncertain whether *media* should be singular or plural in your written work, treat it as a plural noun, as this is always accepted. In *Write Here*, we will be using *media* as a plural noun; however, some of the essays in the book may present *media* as singular.

Singular	In some cases, it feels as if the <u>media has tried and convicted</u> the accused even before the trial begins.	All forms of media are acting as a unified group.
Plural	In some cases, it feels as if the <u>media have tried and convicted</u> the accused even before the trial begins.	The plural form is always accepted.

An Academic Response to Media

This textbook includes readings, but it also incorporates visuals and hands-on projects. As you learn about reading and writing concepts, you will be asked to apply them to media before you practice with a more traditional assignment. While your responses to the media will sometimes be casual (taking notes), you will also be asked to craft responses that are required to be more formal and organized. You may be asked to write a journal, compose an essay, participate in a discussion, or even create a video as a response to media messages. Before you can respond in a clear and reasoned way, you will need to critically view the message and to analyze it.

Step 1: Read or view the media piece critically. Pay attention to the details of the message. Ask the following questions: Who is the author? What is it about? Why was it created?

Step 2: Analyze and evaluate the media piece. Think about choices the author/speaker has made. Does the author express emotion? Does the author use facts or opinions? Are strong words or visuals used? If so, why do you think they are used? What was your first response to the message?

Step 3: Respond to the media piece. First, write a brief and organized summary. Then offer a clear statement that explains your understanding and interpretation of the work, with examples to support your statements.

> **STUDENT EXAMPLE**

Oded is asked to watch "Regifting (Web Exclusive): *Last Week Tonight with John Oliver*." His teacher has asked that he record his observations and findings as he views, analyzes, and responds to the media example (shown below).

Read/View	Read or view the media piece critically. Pay attention to the details of the message. Who is the author? What is it about? Why was it created?
	This clip from Last Week Tonight with John Oliver is about regifting. Regifting is the practice of giving gifts you receive to others, usually without admitting that the gift was originally intended for you. While probably created just to entertain the audience, Oliver does give practical advice on how to do this successfully.
Analyze	Analyze and evaluate the media piece. Does the author express emotion? Does the author use facts or opinions? Are strong words or visuals used? If so, why do you think they are used? What was your first response to the message?
	My first response was to laugh, since he is talking about a light subject with a serious demeanor. His message relies heavily on examples of gifts he feels are disappointing and humorous analogies, rather than facts.

Respond	Respond to the media piece. Write a brief and organized summary. Then offer a clear statement that explains your understanding and interpretation of the work, and provide examples to support your statements.

John Oliver gives a brief and humorous description of regifting. He also gives guidelines for successfully regifiting: never regift to someone who knows the item was originally for you, personalize the regift with a note, rewrap the gift being regifted, and only regift once per person. For comedic purposes, Oliver treats regifting with the same tone and level of seriousness as global warming and overseas sweatshops. However, some people feel that regifting is rude and dislike the practice. I haven't thought too much about it, but with his helpful tips, it seems like a fun challenge. |

YOUR TURN

Search online for the Pepsi commercial featuring Nicki Minaj. Record your observations and findings as you view, analyze, and respond to the media example.

Read/View	Read or view the media piece critically. Pay attention to the details of the message. Who is the author? What is it about? Why was it created?
Analyze	Analyze and evaluate the media piece. Does the author express emotion? Does the author use facts or opinions? Are strong words or visuals used? If so, why do you think they are used? What was your first response to the message?
Respond	Respond to the media piece. Write a brief and organized summary. Then offer a clear statement that explains your understanding and interpretation of the work, and provide examples to support your statements.

Participating in and Responding to the Media

We do not just absorb the information provided by the media; we also participate in the media. We can change others by sending our thoughts, feelings, and creations through the media. For example, we use the media to form and express our identities on Facebook, Twitter, Instagram, and YouTube. The media allow us to gather and share the information we acquire on blogs and websites. Our responses to media are sometimes casual, much like the examples just offered. Other times, our responses to the media are required to be more formal and organized, like they are in the classroom.

1. What type of media do you see and experience daily? Describe each type.

2. What cartoons did you watch when you were a child? What lessons or values did they try to teach you?

3. Many college campuses use media to reach students, faculty, and the community. Think of the ways in which your campus communicates information about sports scores, club events, or student elections. Create a list of the types of media utilized by your campus. Compare your list with a classmate's. Did your classmate have any items that you did not?

4. Should people be held responsible for what they post on their social media accounts? Explain your answer.

Deepening Your Understanding

If you would like to go beyond the material in this chapter, explore additional connections, and get more practice, check out these related topics:

- **The Writing Process**: The reading process closely mirrors the writing process. When you understand the writing process fully, you can apply that knowledge to the reading process and ultimately become a better reader and writer.

- **Vocabulary**: You can't understand what you read if you don't know what the words mean. The more advanced essays you read, the more developed vocabulary you will need.

- **Parts of the Essay**: No matter what type of essay you read or where you found the essay, understanding what an essay looks like and recognizing the parts is important to the reading process. Identifying these parts of the essay allows you to better understand where to find an essay's main point and how it is organized.

- **Essay Introductions, Conclusions, and Titles**: You can find prereading clues just by looking at the title of each essay. The introduction and conclusion can provide clues about the main idea and the writer's tone.

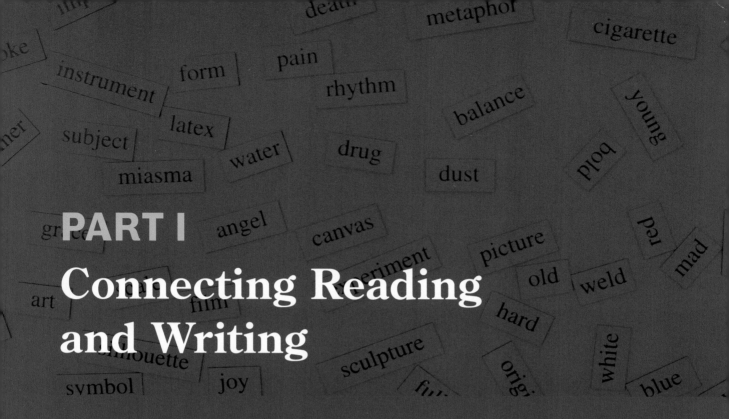

PART I
Connecting Reading and Writing

READING AND WRITING are inevitably connected. Stephen King once said, "If you don't have time to read, you don't have time to write. Simple as that." Reading regularly will help you build your vocabulary, understand the language, develop your own style, and inspire your own writing. Just as before we ride a bike, we watch others riding bikes to see how it's done, one of the best ways to learn about writing is to read others' writing. Reading is just another form of watching.

Many students don't feel they are strong readers or writers. All of us (yes, even teachers and professionals) have struggled at some point as readers and writers. We are not born amazing writers or close readers. Reading and writing skills develop over time. We must practice these skills, in order to become better, and we must practice them every day. For example, you may have sat down to write an essay and stared at a blank screen. This issue is frequently referred to as writer's block. This can be easily solved by writing every day. Practicing reading and writing every day helps boost your creativity and increases your confidence, and with enough practice, you won't fear the blank screen when you sit down to write.

A good reader reads closely, takes notes, asks himself or herself questions, and makes guesses while reading. You do this naturally when you read in your daily life. For example, imagine you and your friends agree to see a movie this weekend. They ask you, "Hey, what movie sounds good?" When you read the synopsis of each film, you are reading a short summary of the plot, but you are also guessing what type of film it might be. You question whether the film might be good based on the plot summary. You might also make a guess as to how good the film is just by seeing who the director is or looking at the list of actors.

A good writer is descriptive, clear, and to the point. These are also skills you use in your everyday life. For example, when you write a tweet, you have to keep in mind that you have a 280-character limit that you cannot exceed. It can be very difficult within that limit to choose your words and language wisely so as to be expressive while also making sure your followers understand your tweet. When your writing is sarcastic, serious, or funny, your use of expression is a choice you make. That's the same whether you are writing a tweet or a research paper.

Before You Read

Before you read the chapters in Part I, answer the following questions:

1. Create a list of what you read and write in a normal day. How much do you read or write? Did anything you logged surprise you? Compare your list to a classmate's. How are the lists similar? How are they different?

2. Describe an instance when you were told or felt that you weren't a good writer or reader. How did that make you feel? What did you do to improve?

3. Think of two ways in which you think writing and reading are alike. Then think of two ways in which they are different.

Reading

"Do not read, as children do, to amuse yourself, or like the ambitious, for the purpose of instruction. No, read in order to live."

—Gustave Flaubert

FACT OR FICTION?
I only need to read an essay once through to understand it.

FICTION.
The act of reading has many steps, including prereading, reading, rereading, and postreading. These steps allow you to connect to the reading and understand it better.

Discovering Key Points

- Learn about and understand the reading process
- Understand and practice prereading strategies
- Understand and practice annotating and reading strategies
- Understand and practice rereading strategies
- Understand and practice postreading strategies

The average North American reads 7,000 words a day. From the texts we receive on our phone to the road signs on our way to work, reading is a part of our everyday lives. We read a recipe when we want to make a chocolate cake. We read song lyrics to understand what a musician is singing about. We Google and read through websites when we want to know more about a person, place, or idea.

We learn to read at an early age, and reading remains an important part of our lives. Reading is all-encompassing; it affects our lives in many ways. And the more we read, the better we are likely to be able to write. Writing becomes easier when you are a frequent reader. As you read, your vocabulary grows. You learn new words and you can then apply them to your own writing. And reading is empowering: the more we read, the more we are informed of what is going on around us. Reading even allows us to learn more about ourselves. Finally, reading can inspire us and fire our imaginations.

Reading is also vitally important in everyday life. If you don't read directions for how to handle chemicals, you may injure yourself or others. If you don't read signs on the road, you break the law. If you don't read the job application instructions, you might not fill out the application correctly and thus might not get the job.

Reading an essay is different from instructions or signs—but arguably it is just as important. Reading essays allows us to exercise our brains, learn new vocabulary and sentence structures, be entertained, and develop faculties such as creativity and empathy. When we read essays, we learn about the world and ourselves.

Like the writing process, **the reading process** has multiple stages. Here are four stages in the reading process:

Want to know more about the writing process? See Chapter 3.

- Prereading
- Reading
- Rereading
- Postreading

You can think of the actions you need to take for each stage with the acronym PECC (see table below). When we eat a meal, we shouldn't devour it quickly but rather savor each bite. The same goes for reading. Rather than try to "swallow" an essay in one bite, we should take it slowly, or "PECC" at the reading.

Prereading	**P**redict: Make educated guesses about what is to come in the essay.
Reading	**E**nvision: Generate pictures in your head of the words and ideas.
Rereading	**C**onnect: Connect the ideas presented in the essay to what you already know and what you have experienced.
Postreading	**C**onfirm & Critique: Look at your initial predictions and decide whether you were correct, and why. Then you can make an overall assessment of the essay.

Prereading [PECC = Predict]

The act of **prereading** happens before you read. Prereading is important because it provides clues about the reading and allows you to make a connection with the essay by looking only at a few key areas and making predictions, or guesses, about the rest of the essay. When you preread and make these predictions, you are bringing what you know and your own personal experiences to the essay. This affects how you read the essay and how well you connect with it. For example, if you are reading an essay titled "How *The Voice* Affects Music Sales on iTunes," and you are a fan of the television show, you are going into the reading process with knowledge of the show. If you are unaware of what *The Voice* is, you are at a disadvantage when you are prereading because you do not have that prior knowledge, but you can still make predictions about the essay based on clues in the title alone. Even if you knew nothing about either *The Voice* or iTunes, you could still infer from the essay title that both *The Voice* and iTunes had something to do with music.

What Should I Look for When I Preread?

- **The Title**—Are there keywords in the title that clue you into what the **subject** of the essay is or what the writer's argument is? The subject is the matter being discussed or described in the essay. Usually, the subject is a word or phrase.
- **The Writer**—Do you know anything about the writer of the essay?
- **The Place Published**—Was the essay published in a magazine, newspaper, or book? What does the placement tell you about the essay itself? (For example, an essay published in a neuroscience journal will tell you that the essay is probably difficult to read and meant for medical professionals or scientists.)
- **The Date Published**—When was the essay published? Is it current (published within the last two years)? If it was published many years ago, how have developments in the years since changed things? (For example, an essay about Friendster is out of date, as that social media site is rarely used. Now people use Twitter, Facebook, reddit, TikTok, or other social media sites.)

We make inferences every day. We may infer that a novel is a romance when examining the title (*The Springtime of Love*), the cover (with two people embracing each other), and the color scheme (pastels). If someone says "what a horrible year!" with a grim expression, we may use those facts to infer that they are not happy. We infer what a DVD will be like based on the title, DVD cover, and cast. Notice that word *infer* above; these sorts of preliminary interpretations we make about things we don't know for sure are called **inferences**. When you preread, you want to make inferences about the essay. Ask yourself these questions:

> Still don't understand inference? See Chapter 5 for more examples and practice.

- Based on the title, what is the subject of the essay? How do you know?
- Based on the title, can you tell anything about the writer's opinion/argument?

- Can you tell anything about who might be the target readers based on the newspaper, book, or magazine the essay was published in?
- Do you know anything about the writer and his/her background with the subject?
- Overall, what do you think this essay is going to be about? Why did you make this inference?

MEDIA EXAMPLE OF PREREADING

Prereading isn't found just in essays. It can also be found in the media. Find a clip from *Tosh.o* tiled "Guess What Happens Next?"

What did you think was about to happen? What clues allowed you to make that guess? Were you right or wrong?

STUDENT EXAMPLE

Dalton's instructor asks him to do some prereading for an essay titled "Our Zombies, Ourselves: Why We Can't Get the Undead Off Our Brains," written by James Parker in *The Atlantic Monthly*'s April 2011 issue. As Dalton answers the prereading questions, he makes inferences, or predictions.

1. Based on the title, what is the subject of the essay? How do you know?
   I think this essay will be about zombies. I think this because of the keywords "zombies" and "undead."

2. Based on the title, can you tell anything about the writer's opinion/argument?
   Based on the title, I think the author also thinks that zombies are popular.

3. Can you tell anything about who might be the target readers based on the newspaper, book, or magazine the essay was published in?
   The Atlantic Monthly sounds like a magazine for the East coast. My guess is that the readers are mostly from the East coast states.

4. Do you know anything about the writer and his/her background with the subject?
   I don't know anything about this author. But based on the name, I can infer that the author is male (most people named James are men).

5. Overall, what do you think this essay is going to be about? Why did you make this inference?
   I think this essay is about how popular zombies are since the author titled the essay "we can't get" them "off our brains," which sounds like we can't forget

them. I think he will probably talk about zombies in movies or television, since zombies aren't real.

YOUR TURN

Answer the prereading questions for the following essay, based only on the information below.

"*Crazy Rich Asians* Has Survived Impossible Representation Standards," by Steven Nguyen Scaife in the August 28, 2018, issue of *The Verge*.

1. Based on the title, what is the subject of the essay? How do you know?

2. Based on the title, can you tell anything about the writer's opinion/argument?

3. Can you tell anything about who might be the target readers based on the newspaper, book, or magazine the essay was published in?

4. Do you know anything about the writer and his/her background with the subject?

5. Overall, what do you think this essay is going to be about? Why did you make this inference?

Reading [PECC = Envision]

During your first **read** through, you should be reading to get through the essay. Before you even begin reading, make sure that you set aside enough time for the length of the essay. An essay that is two pages long will take you less time to read than a twelve-page essay. Also be sure that you are in an environment you can read comfortably in. For some people, this means finding a place with total silence. For others, it includes background music. Location is important as well. Some like to read outside, others in bed or at their desk, and still others at their local coffee shop. Find what works best for you and your learning style. Can you read with distractions? Do you need total silence? Do you mind if others are around you while you read?

When you read an essay for the first time, begin to envision, or imagine, what is going on in the text. Let the essay paint a picture in your mind. When the writer describes something in the essay, do your best to imagine what he or she is referring to.

Annotation

Think of annotating as communicating with the essay as you read. Annotation is more than just highlighting or underlining. It is thinking about the essay as you are reading. This practice allows you to interact with the essay on a deeper level than just reading and trying to memorize.

Formal annotation for a book or essay is the process of writing footnotes or endnotes. Informal annotation is simply the process of making brief notes about what you are reading. When you annotate, you'll want to do it right on the page, rather than have a separate page of notes. This way, you can see the exact spot where you wrote in your comments or notes. When you annotate, you are reading and writing comments, notes, and explanations in the margin or between the lines. You may even annotate on Post-it Notes that you stick to the essay. This approach to note-taking makes going back to your notes later easier than if you wrote them in a separate notebook or piece of paper.

As you read in this chapter about reading, rereading, and postreading, you will be provided with annotation strategies for each stage.

MEDIA EXAMPLE OF ANNOTATING

Annotating isn't done only for essays. It can also be found in the media. *Pop-Up Video* "annotates" music videos with fun facts and other information about the song and musician.

As a class, watch a Pop-Up video together; while you watch the video, annotate it with your own personal comments, questions, and experiences. Then get into small groups and share your annotations. What annotations were similar among the group? Which were different?

What Should I Do When I Read?

- **Keep Predicting**—During prereading, you inferred something of what the essay was about. Now that you are reading, you need to keep making inferences. If the essay is telling a story, try to predict from what you have already read what is likely to happen next. If the essay is making an argument, try to predict from what you have already read the direction that argument will take. Write in the essay itself, in the margin, or on a Post-it Note stuck to the essay what you think will come later.
- **Mark Confusing Areas**—Are there any sentences, paragraphs, or ideas that are confusing or unclear? If so, mark them with an X. You can look them up before your second reading.
- **Look Up Unfamiliar Vocabulary**—Are there words or vocabulary that you don't recognize or understand? Circle those unknown words as you find them. First, try to guess what the word means based on how it is used in the sentence. Then check if your guess is right by looking the word up in a dictionary.
- **Discover How the Essay Was Written**—Which of the nine modes of writing (see below) are being used? Remember that more than one mode can be used at the same time.
  - **Illustration** (provides examples)

- **Description** (captures visually a person, place, event, etc.)
- **Narration** (tells a story)
- **Definition** (defines a topic)
- **Comparison/Contrast** (shows similarities and differences)
- **Cause/Effect** (explains reasons and consequences)
- **Division/Classification** (separates a single item into multiple components OR categorizes multiple items into groups)
- **Argumentation** (persuades readers)
- **Process Analysis** (describes "how to")

ⓘ Need more practice with the modes of writing? See Chapter 6.

- **Find the Subject**—What is the essay about? Look for repeated words and phrases for clues about the subject. Also look at the title of the essay; it should provide clues as to what the subject is.
- **Detect the Main Idea**—What is the writer's **main idea** or argument in the essay? The main idea is the point or argument the author is trying to make. Note that the main idea can be stated or implied. **Stated** means the main idea is expressed directly in the essay. You, the reader, can pull out one or two sentences that clearly sum up the main point(s) of the essay. **Implied** means the main idea is not directly stated in the essay, but rather suggested or hinted at. If the main idea is implied, you, the reader, will need to figure it out—to infer the main idea from what has been written.

Let's look at an example of an opening paragraph in which the main idea is implied, rather than stated openly:

> On the face of it, a basic income (also known as a guaranteed annual income) seems like an attractive idea. People who support the idea of a basic income say that replacing the many different types of financial support for the disadvantaged that are currently available with a guaranteed annual income for everyone would be a fairer, a more efficient, and even a less expensive way of helping those who need it. But we all have some experience of schemes that seem too good to be true. Let's look more closely at how a basic income scheme would actually work—and at how much it would really cost.

Notice that the writer doesn't state directly in this opening paragraph whether the essay will argue for or against a basic income. But there are several clues. Notice the expression *on the face of it* (meaning *on the surface, superficially*) with which the passage opens—and notice too the verb, *seems*. When writers use expressions such as *on the face of it* together with a verb such as *seems*, you can infer that they are likely to argue that the reality is different from how things may appear on the surface.

This writer says that a basic income "seems like an attractive idea." But then the writer appeals to the reader's experience: "we all have some experience of schemes that seem too good to be true." The writer does not directly state that the concept of a basic income is too good to be true, but that is what is implied. Then notice the words *actually* and *really* in the paragraph's final sentence. With those words the writer suggests more strongly still that, in reality, a basic income scheme would not work well and would be very expensive.

It would be quite possible to rewrite this paragraph so that the main point is stated directly and plainly:

> Some people argue that we should replace the many different types of financial support that we now provide for the disadvantaged with a guaranteed annual income for everyone. They say a basic income would be a fairer, a more efficient, and even a less expensive way of helping those who need it. I disagree. Although a basic income sounds attractive in theory, a closer look suggests that—in practice—it likely would not work very well and would be very expensive.

There are many reasons why writers often choose to imply their main point(s) rather than state them directly. Writing that suggests and implies (rather than always makes bald statements) can be more interesting—and more persuasive to readers. But it may take some time for those with little experience of such writing to learn how to infer the writer's meaning.

Outline the Essay—While you read for the first time, you may want to outline its most important points on paper. Jot down a phrase or sentence summary of each paragraph. This will help you later try to figure out which mode(s) of writing the writer was using, as well as how the essay was organized.

ⓘ
Want to practice tone and see more examples? See Chapter 5.

Recognize the Writer's Tone—The writer's attitude or feeling toward the subject is called **tone**. The writer may choose to use a formal tone or an informal tone. For example, a writer may say, "Before the debate, all of the candidates were hanging out behind the scenes" or "the candidates were assembled together before they attended the presidential debate." Both sentences have the same meaning, but the first is more informal in tone. The writer may also choose to be funny, sarcastic, or serious; if you chuckle when reading an essay, that could be one obvious sign that the writer was trying to be humorous. But clues to tone are often difficult to detect. When you read an essay, it can help to underline any words or phrases that may hint toward the writer's tone.

Look, for example, at this sentence from a movie review of *Grace of Monaco* that appeared in the May 14, 2014, issue of *The Guardian*, a British newspaper: "It is a film so awe-inspiringly wooden that it is basically a fire-risk." Normally the word *awe-inspiringly* should be taken to mean that the film so described is remarkable or impressive. Is that the case here? There is a clue that suggests it isn't—that the writer is in fact using the word in a negative way, intending to suggest that *Grace of Monaco* is *not* a film worth watching. The word that follows awe-inspiringly is *wooden*, a word that means dull or emotionless.

Looking at an author's tone is quite important, as it can help you understand the author's meaning. Sometimes, tone can be easy to detect, while other times, you must examine each word carefully to see if there is an underlying meaning.

MEDIA EXAMPLE OF READING

Reading isn't found only in essays. It can also be found in the media. Check out online the music video for the song "We Are Young" by fun., featuring Janelle Monáe.

What is the "main point" of the song? Is there any vocabulary you are unfamiliar with? If so, which words, and what are their definitions? Which areas of the song did you find confusing?

STUDENT EXAMPLE

Dalton now begins to read the essay, focusing first on one paragraph. While he reads, he annotates the essay by doing the following:

- Predicting what will happen next.
- Looking for key words or phrases that suggest the author's tone about the subject.
- Highlighting the main idea of the paragraph.
- Placing an X by sentences or ideas that are confusing.
- Circling unfamiliar words, then writing the definition next to the word.
- Writing comments or questions in the margin.

"Our Zombies, Ourselves: Why We Can't Get the Undead Off Our Brains," by James Parker

The Atlantic Monthly, April 2011

I've seen this show. It's great!

The author's tone is excited. He uses the word "gladness" and says the zombies "never looked better."

I think the next paragraph of the essay will discuss specific examples about The Walking Dead.

Sometimes a zombie is just a zombie. Strike that: a zombie is *always* just a zombie. The blow-'em-all-away success of *The Walking Dead* is no mystery: the show, and the comic-book series by Robert Kirkman on which it's based, mark a triumphant return to zombie orthodoxy, to the non-galloping zombie and his icons. Once again, and with great gladness, we see shotguns, frantically tuned radios, smoke pillars of apocalypse on the horizon—the full zombie opera. The zombie himself has never looked better, dripping with wounds, full of conviction. With his dangling stethoscope, or his policeman's uniform, or his skateboard, he exhibits the (pathos) *"feeling of pity or sadness"* of his ex-personhood. He flaps and sighs. He crookedly advances. He's taking his time. X But he'll get there.

X Where is "there"?

YOUR TURN

Read a paragraph from the essay you answered prereading questions about. Be sure to annotate the paragraph by completing the following:

- Predict what will happen next.
- Look for key words or phrases that hint at the author's tone about the subject.
- Highlight the main idea of the paragraph.
- Place an X by sentences or ideas that are confusing.
- Circle unfamiliar words. Then write the definition next to the word.
- Write comments or questions in the margin.

"*Crazy Rich Asians* Has Survived Impossible Representation Standards," by Steven Nguyen Scaife

The Verge, August 28, 2018

I felt relief of a different kind while sitting in the theater watching *Crazy Rich Asians*. The leads have great chemistry. The jokes are funny. The film is profoundly normalizing and pleasant to watch. When a group is given such a small space in the media landscape, it leaves no room for error. Creators can't blow their handful of chances on financially unsuccessful or creatively unfulfilling projects: they need to make the most of their space by being powerful, enriching, and unique. When your voice is so rarely heard, you have little choice but to use every opportunity to prove that everyone should have been paying attention all along. A project like *Crazy Rich Asians* is a rare chance to change minds, and if it flops, it might be another 25 years before a similar chance comes along. That's why there's been so much backlash around *Crazy Rich Asians*. Detractors say the film fails to represent the true diversity of Singapore, while headlines ask whether it's "Asian enough." With so much pressure to get things right the first time, "right" has come to mean reflecting the sheer breadth of the Asian experience in a single film. The film has been heralded as a victory for diversity, so members of a widely diverse group are all hoping to see themselves represented.

Rereading [PECC = Connect]

Don't know the different parts of the essay? See Chapter 4.

In the first instance, reading is all about understanding the content of the essay (What is it about? What is the writer's opinion?). **Rereading** is sometimes also driven by the need to understand; if you are unclear as to the meaning of a piece of writing, reading it a second time can often help. But rereading can also deepen the connection you make with the essay. Rereading may happen more than once, particularly if you are reading a difficult and/or long essay. You will want to reread the essay until you understand and make connections with it. When you reread, you should read for a deeper meaning—asking questions and looking at each individual part of the essay, as well as the structure of the essay.

What Should I Do When I Reread?

- **Focus on Confusing Areas**—During your initial reading, you may have marked confusing sections, sentences, or areas with a "?" or an "X." Go back to those areas specifically and read them again. Look up words that might be stumping you and look up any phrases or terminology that you don't understand.

- **Talk Back to the Essay**—Imagine that you are having a conversation with the essay. When there is something in the essay that reminds you of a personal experience or makes you feel any emotion, such as sadness, happiness, and so on, mark that in the margin. You can mark it with a ☺ or ☹, but be sure to write a comment like, "I love this description!" or "This argument seems unclear" or "Compare this account with that of Smith" to remind you later about what you were thinking. Making comments will help you remember the essay content better, and it also will help you learn to take better notes.

- **Ask Questions to the Writer**—As you read, write down questions you'd like to ask the writer in the essay. Why did the writer pick that specific example? Why did the writer choose that particular word? Interrogate the writer about why he or she feels a particular way. Even though you may not get answers from the writer directly, such questions can help you think further about the essay and can help you understand the essay from the writer's point of view.

- **Ask Questions about Content**—While you read, ask questions in the margin about the subject matter of the essay. Write down any questions you might want to research later, particularly if you need or want background information that isn't present in the essay.

- **Ask Questions to Yourself**—Questions to the writer and questions about the content help you understand the initial information in the essay; however, questions to yourself are equally important. During your initial read, you should be writing down your emotions about and reactions to each section/paragraph. Now is the time to go back and ask yourself why you felt the way you did or why you had that thought.

- **Always Try to Answer "So What?"**—As you read, stop once in a while and ask yourself "So what? Why does this matter?" This may give you clues as to why the writer included that information in the essay, and how the information fits in with the rest of the essay.

MEDIA EXAMPLE OF REREADING

Rereading isn't found only in essays. It can also be found in the media. Check out online once again the music video for the song "We Are Young" by fun., featuring Janelle Monáe.

During your second viewing of the video, what personal connections can you make with the song? What were some of the questions you wanted to ask yourself while listening to the song again?

Dalton now begins to reread the paragraph he just annotated. While he rereads, he does the following. He makes sure to use a different colored pen to show the difference between his first set of annotations and those he makes when rereading.

As Dalton is rereading, he

- Focuses on the area(s) he marked with an X and asks himself why that area was confusing, and what he thinks the section means now that he's reread it.
- Talks to the essay by placing a ☺, a ☹, or a comment next to a part of the essay that includes an idea he wants to explore.
- Asks questions to the author. (Dalton writes these in the margin or on a Post-it Note.)
- Asks himself questions. (Again, he writes these in the margin or on a Post-it Note.)

"Our Zombies, Ourselves: Why We Can't Get the Undead Off Our Brains," by James Parker

The Atlantic Monthly, April 2011

I've seen this show. It's great!

The author's tone is excited. He uses the word "gladness" and says the zombies "never looked better."
I wonder why we're so drawn to zombies. They're just death and destruction.

I think the next paragraph of the essay will discuss specific examples about The Walking Dead.

Sometimes a zombie is just a zombie. Strike that: a zombie is always just a zombie. The blow-'em-all-away success of *The Walking Dead* is no mystery: the show, and the comic-book series by Robert Kirkman on which it's based, mark a triumphant return to zombie orthodoxy, to the non-galloping zombie and his icons. Once again, and with great gladness, we see shotguns, frantically tuned radios, smoke pillars of apocalypse on the horizon—the full zombie opera. The zombie himself has never looked better, dripping with wounds, full of conviction. With his dangling stethoscope, or his policeman's uniform, or his skateboard, he exhibits the (pathos) *"feeling of pity or sadness"* of his ex-personhood. He flaps and sighs.

He crookedly advances. He's taking his time. X But he'll get there.

Yuck! ☹

X Where is "there"?
I'm still not sure where there is, but I guess it's to the people he wants to eat.

Reread the paragraph from the essay you previously annotated. Complete the following tasks. Be sure to use a different colored pen from the one you used when you first annotated the paragraph.

- Focus on the area(s) you marked with an X. Why was that area confusing? What do you think the section means now that you've reread it?
- Talk to the essay. Place a ☺, a ☹, or a comment next to an area that you want to explore.
- Ask questions to the author. (Write these in the margin or on a Post-it Note.)
- Ask yourself questions. (Again, write these in the margin or on a Post-it Note.)

"*Crazy Rich Asians* Has Survived Impossible Representation Standards," by Steven Nguyen Scaife

The Verge, August 28, 2018

I felt relief of a different kind while sitting in the theater watching *Crazy Rich Asians*. The leads have great chemistry. The jokes are funny. The film is profoundly normalizing and pleasant to watch. When a group is given such a small space in the media landscape, it leaves no room for error. Creators can't blow their handful of chances on financially unsuccessful or creatively unfulfilling projects: they need to make the most of their space by being powerful, enriching, and unique. When your voice is so rarely heard, you have little choice but to use every opportunity to prove that everyone should have been paying attention all along. A project like *Crazy Rich Asians* is a rare chance to change minds, and if it flops, it might be another 25 years before a similar chance comes along. That's why there's been so much backlash around *Crazy Rich Asians*. Detractors say the film fails to represent the true diversity of Singapore, while headlines ask whether it's "Asian enough." With so much pressure to get things right the first time, "right" has come to mean reflecting the sheer breadth of the Asian experience in a single film. The film has been heralded as a victory for diversity, so members of a widely diverse group are all hoping to see themselves represented.

Postreading [PECC = Confirm & Critique]

After you have read an essay multiple times, you need to look back at the essay as a whole and reflect upon it. This is called **postreading**. During postreading, you tie up any loose ends, answer any remaining questions you have, and begin confirming your earlier inferences to see if you were correct. This is also the time where you can begin to critique the essay overall, giving your evaluation of the essay.

What Should I Do When I Postread?

- **Answer Questions You've Asked**—Look through the questions you asked throughout the reading stages. Try to answer each one directly by trying to answer them yourself, by looking at the essay, or by researching the subject online or in a book.
- **Check Earlier Inferences**—Look to see what you inferred during the prereading, reading, and rereading stages. Where were you wrong? Where were you right? Why do you think you made those inferences?
- **Repair Gaps in Comprehension**—Go back to make sure you have fully understood all of the concepts, ideas, and examples presented in the essay. If you still don't understand something, be sure to reread the section for clues; research it online or in a book; discuss it with a friend, family member, and/or classmate; or ask your instructor.
- **Evaluate the Essay**—After you've read the essay multiple times and have your notes, begin critiquing the essay. This is your chance to decide if the writer was successful in presenting his or her topic and/or argument. Also be sure to note whether the essay changed or reinforced your own opinions on the subject. Ask yourself if you liked the essay, if it was confusing, if you understood it fully, and if the writer was able to convince you of his or her argument (if applicable).

> **ⓘ**
> When evaluating an essay, looking at the writer's rhetoric is also important. For more information, see Chapter 8.

STUDENT EXAMPLE

After Dalton has read the paragraph from "Our Zombies, Ourselves" twice and annotated it in two different colors, he begins the postreading process. He answers the two questions below:

1. Look back at the questions you answered in prereading. Were your inferences correct? Why/Why not?
   Yes. The paragraph was about zombies and how popular they are in comic books and television shows.

2. Overall, do you think the author was successful at writing this paragraph? Why/Why not?
   Yes. The paragraph is really descriptive. The author makes me "see" the zombie, even without a picture.

YOUR TURN

Now that you've read the paragraph from "*Crazy Rich Asians* Has Survived" and annotated it twice, answer the following postreading questions:

1. Look back at the questions you answered in prereading. Were your inferences correct? Why/Why not?

2. Overall, do you think the author was successful at writing this paragraph? Why/Why not?

What If I Don't Understand the Essay? What If It's Too Hard?

If you don't understand the essay or you find it too difficult, do not fear! There are a few things you can do in order to better grasp a difficult essay. Remember that even the best readers often don't understand an essay the first (or second) time through.

First, take it slowly. When you read, don't try to go quickly or skim the essay. Remember the analogy of a meal and PECC from earlier in this chapter? This is especially true with the first reading. You want to make sure that you take your time and really focus on each section and paragraph.

Second, try talking about the essay with classmates, family, or friends. Just verbalizing your thoughts or confusion about an essay may help you get through your confusion or problems.

Third, take a break. Sometimes, you just need to put the essay away and sleep on it or move on to something else to give your brain a rest from the essay. When you come back to the essay later, you will be more refreshed and more likely to retain the information and remain focused.

Fourth, reread the essay. All good readers reread multiple times. Don't assume that you'll fully understand an essay the first time through. You may see details that you didn't notice during the first read. Rereading also allows you to focus on something different in the essay each time you read through. For example, the first time you read through the essay, you can look for vocabulary you aren't familiar with and just get an overall understanding of the main point. The second time you read through, you can look for places where you can make a connection with the text.

Lastly, annotate the essay each time you read. When you annotate, you write down your notes, thoughts, questions, and more in the essay itself. Each time you annotate, write in different colors so you can keep track of your notes.

For a student example and an essay where you can practice annotation, see the practice reading that follows.

Practicing Reading

Now that you've learned all about PECC, you can try each step with a full essay. Below is a student example, followed by an opportunity for you to practice using your new skills.

STUDENT EXAMPLE

Katelyn has been asked to go through the reading process and annotate the essay "Hey, Kids! We've Got Sugar and Toys," by Amanda Spake, published in *US News & World Report* on November 17, 2003. While she goes through the reading and rereading stages, she decides to annotate the essay and place Post-it Notes in the margin of her paper to mark her notes while she reads. She even decides to use a black pen during her first reading, a red pen during her rereading process, and a green pen during her postreading process to make her notes from each stage clearer. Before she reads though, she will answer a few "Before You

Read" questions, asking her to make some inferences about the essay based on the information presented earlier in the chapter. After she reads the essay, she'll also be prompted to answer a couple of "After You Read" questions to double check her prereading predictions.

BEFORE YOU READ

1. Just based on the title, what do you think this essay will be about? Why do you think this?

   I think this essay will be about children and candy and toys. My guess is it will be about the connection between toys and candy. The words "toys" and "children" are in the title, so that's why I know they'll be discussed in this essay. I think of candy because the title says "sugar," and candy is full of sugar.

2. Do you know anything about the writer? If so, what?

   I know that she is a woman, because very few men are named Amanda.

3. Where was the essay published? What does that tell you about the essay or the audience of the essay?

   The essay is published in what looks like a newspaper. I think it's a newspaper because it was published with a month and a day. Magazines are usually published every month. I know that newspapers are written to everyday readers in the newspaper's area. However, because this newspaper doesn't have a city name in it, I think it's more general, like for the entire nation.

4. When was it published? Is it current (within two years)? What effect do you think this will have on your interpretation/understanding of the essay? In other words, how might this change your understanding of the content?

   It is not current. This tells me that the candy and toys she's going to be referring to are probably outdated. They may not even exist anymore!

"Hey, Kids! We've Got Sugar and Toys," by Amanda Spake

US News & World Report, November 17, 2003

☺ *I used to eat ChocoDonuts as a kid!! What a great cereal.*
After reading this again, I realized that as a child, I was marketed a lot of sugary and fatty foods. The commercials work on kids.

"Mommy, Mommy, look!" Morgan Foster, 5, pulls a box of Quaker Oats' Cap'n Crunch's Oops! ChocoDonuts cereal off a low grocery shelf. The cereal is displayed so he can easily see the picture of the *Rugrats*, Nickelodeon's popular cartoon characters, on the box. "Mommy, I want this," Morgan says.

"Why do you like that?" Pam Foster, 36, of Shady Side, Md., asks her son.

"It's good," Morgan explains. "I saw it on Cartoon Network!"

Harvard psychologist Susan Linn calls it "running the gantlet"—negotiating supermarket aisles filled with products heavily marketed to children. Today, in the face of a huge increase in childhood obesity, kids are bombarded by an unprecedented avalanche of food advertising. Indeed, food marketing aimed at children increased from $6.9 billion in 1992 to $15 billion in 2002.

I highlighted that sentence because it seems like it's the first important point, and it summarizes the example at the beginning. It's probably the main idea.

This week, the Center for Science in the Public Interest is releasing the first comprehensive report detailing the (plethora) "excess" of ads, toys, Web sites, movie and television tie-ins, school programs, and other marketing practices designed to make children want—and eat—food, most of it unhealthful. "Food marketing has become so pervasive that it's everywhere children are throughout their day," says Margo Wootan, the center's director of nutrition policy and the author of the report.

Wow. That's a lot of money! Especially since kids don't have money.
But their parents do, and that's what matters.

A trip to any grocery store or fast-food restaurant or an hour of watching children's television proves her point. Disney's Princess Fruit Snacks—little more than fruit candy—are formed into glass slippers and other characters familiar to little fans of the Disney Princess movies. There are cheese crackers, pasta, cereal, fruit snacks,

I wonder.... does the author have any children?
I Googled the author and couldn't find any information either way, but I bet she is a parent because she is so interested in this topic.

and more shaped like Cartoon Network's popular detective dog, Scooby-Doo. The Hulk sells Oreo cookies and Oscar Mayer "Lunchables" (some with 38 grams of fat per lunch). For preteens, there's American Idol Hot Fudge Sundae Pop-Tarts. McDonald's, a pioneer of "advertoys," had 14 different toy sets to promote its "Happy Meals" in 2001.

That's so true! As a kid, I had to have all four of the Bratz toys from the Happy Meals! I didn't know that was marketing!
I think they're taking advantage of kids with these advertoys because kids are naïve and want to have fun.

Here's the marketing genius, though: Each set was available only for three or four weeks, pressuring parents to be regular patrons to collect all the toys for their kids. "What the marketers want to do is get kids to nag their parents for the food, for the toys," says Linn, associate director of the media center at Judge Baker Children's Center in Boston. A 1998 study on the "Nag Factor" showed that 1 in every 3 visits to a fast-food outlet was attributable to children's begging.

Television advertising—especially on kid-oriented channels like Nickelodeon and Disney—remains marketers' prime tool for selling food to kids. Harvard's Linn says that before age 8, children "don't understand persuasive intent, that an ad is designed to manipulate them to buy something." Linn taped six hours of weekend television on Nickelodeon, the network with 41 of the top 50 children's programs, and counted 40 food ads. "Most ads don't mention taste,"

I think this is another main idea because it goes along with the first sentence I highlighted about food advertising. This just explains the type of ad is on kids' television channels.

she says. "The message is eating will make you happy, cool; eating will give you friends. These are exactly the messages we don't want kids to have about food."

More than 90 percent of the products advertised on children's television are high in fat, sugar, or salt. A nutritional analysis of ads on afternoon and Saturday television for kids found that 50 percent were for foods in the "fats, oils, and sweets" categories. Nearly 26 percent of the ads were for high-sugar cereals. None promoted fruits or vegetables.

Yale psychologist Kelly Brownell, author of the recent book *Food Fight*, says most parents want their children to develop healthful eating habits but find it hard to compete with the ad blitz. Moreover, he believes marketing fuels kids' desires not only for food but for large portions. In McDonald's current Monopoly game promotion, for example, kids can win video games and DVD players by collecting Monopoly pieces—but they're available only with medium, large, and supersize french fries, and large and supersize drinks.

Food makers argue that "all foods have a place in a balanced diet. The key is balance," says Michael Diegel, communications director at the Grocery Manufacturers of America. But the CSPI report shows how out of balance kids' diets have become. Only <u>2 percent of children</u> currently eat a diet consistent with the U.S. Department of Agriculture recommendations: 98 percent eat too much fat, sugar and salt; 84 percent (combined) eat too much artery-clogging saturated fat. Overall, children's caloric intake increased by about 80 to 230 calories a day (depending upon age) between 1989 and 1996, says CSPI.

Children are also eating more fast food. In 1977, 1 in 10 meals kids ate was from fast-food restaurants; by 1996, 1 in 3 meals was fast food. Fast-food kids' meals contain nearly twice the calories of meals prepared at home. Fast food is also encroaching on the National School Lunch Program. In 1990, only 2 percent of schools offered Pizza Hut, Taco Bell, and other brand-name foods as part of this federal nutrition program. In 2000, 20 percent served fast foods.

Before he ever saw children's commercial television, says Foster, Morgan ate multigrain cereal for breakfast with fruit juice to drink. "Now, I've had to buy Scooby-Doo Cinnamon Marshmallow Cereal with Scooby-shaped pieces," says Foster, "and when I ask if he wants milk or juice with dinner, he slips in, 'I'll have a soda.' He was so excited when he found this new world of products. <u>But for me,</u>" she sighs, "<u>I feel like I've given in.</u>"

AFTER YOU'VE READ

1. Were your inferences from the **Before You Read** section right? Why/Why not?
   Kind of. If I had to give myself a score, I'd say I was 65 percent right. I thought it was about toys, and it was, but not the toys I thought. This was more about

toys with happy meals and toys associated with food. I also thought it was about candy, and it was more about fast food and snacks.

2. Overall, do you think the author was successful at writing this essay? Why/Why not? What are your feelings toward the essay? Did you enjoy reading it?
I think she was very successful at arguing. She provided facts that convinced me that what she was saying was true. She also told stories of other parents and their children. Both the facts and stories helped me believe her argument more.

YOUR TURN

Below is an essay published in the February 13, 2006, edition of *The San Francisco Chronicle* titled "Out of the Retail Rat Race: Consumer Group Doesn't Buy Notion that New Is Better" by Carolyn Jones. As you preread, read, reread, and postread, remember to apply all of the annotation skills you've learned.

BEFORE YOU READ

1. Just based on the title, what do you think this essay will be about? Why do you think this?

2. Do you know anything about the writer? If so, what?

3. Where was the essay published? What does that tell you about the essay or the audience of the essay?

4. When was it published? Is it current (within two years)? What effect do you think this will have on your interpretation or understanding of the essay? In other words, how might this change your understanding of the content?

"Out of the Retail Rat Race: Consumer Group Doesn't Buy Notion that New Is Better," by Carolyn Jones

The San Francisco Chronicle, February 13, 2006

While many people will spend countless hours this year lining up at Wal-Mart and maxing out their credit cards at Nordstrom, a small Bay Area group has declared it will do just the opposite.

About 50 teachers, engineers, executives and other professionals in the Bay Area have made a vow to not buy anything new in 2006—except food, health and safety items and underwear. "We're people for whom recycling is no longer enough," said one of the members of the fledgling movement, John Perry, who works in marketing at a high-tech company. "We're trying to get off the first-market consumerism grid, because consumer culture is destroying the world."

They call themselves the Compact. They have a blog, a Yahoo group and monthly meetings to reaffirm their commitment to the rule, which is to never buy anything new. "I didn't buy a pair of shoes today," said Compacter Shawn Rosenmoss, an engineer and a San Francisco resident of the Bernal Heights neighborhood. "They were basically a $300 pair of clodhoppers. But they were really nice and really comfortable, and I haven't bought new shoes for a while. But I didn't buy them. That's a big part of the Compact—we show that we're not powerless over our purchasing."

Compacters can get as much as they want from thrift shops, Craigslist, freecycle.org, eBay and flea markets, as long as the items are secondhand. And when they're in doubt, they turn to their fellow Compacters for guidance. "We had a little crisis when Matt and Sarah had to replace their shower curtain liner and we said no," said Perry, who lives in Bernal Heights. "But we put the word out and someone found one for them. It's like the Amish—we help each other out. We raise a barn every week."

The Compact started two years ago when Perry and a group of his friends, who were tired of devoting so much of their time and money on items they don't need, vowed to go six months without buying anything new. American consumerism, they say, has led to global environmental and socioeconomic crises, and the only way to reverse it is to stop buying into it.

The Compact—named after the revolutionary credo of the Mayflower pilgrims—proved immensely popular and quickly increased its membership. Then one couple remodeled their house and couldn't find used drywall. After that, "it all started to unravel," Perry said. But after a breather, the group decided to recommit and try to expand its membership. Kate Boyd, a drama teacher at Lick-Wilmerding High School in San Francisco, said she enjoys the extra time, money and perspective that a consumer-free life brings. "It's just a relief to get away from the pressure to always have new clothes, gadgets and other things we don't need," she said. "And I find that I have more money to spend on the dried cherries for my Manhattans."

The Compact is part of the larger trend of consumers beginning to "tread gently on our planet," said Peter Sealey, adjunct professor of marketing at the Haas School of Business at UC Berkeley. "It sounds marvelous. It's a wonderful example for all of us," said Sealey, a former chief of marketing at Coca-Cola and Columbia Pictures. "It's a crystal-clear statement about what can be done to get us away from being a disposable society." The boom in green building, Oakland's recent crackdown on fast-food litter and the surge in biofuel-powered cars are all part of the movement toward more responsible consumerism, he said.

Northern California is often at the forefront of environmental and social trends, and the Compact is likely to garner a devoted following, he said. "Will the Compact ever become mainstream? I don't think so, but it's an excellent way to bring attention to the reality that we need to be more gentle with our resources." One especially appealing aspect of the

Compact is its social component, members say. Fellow Compacters offer advice, moral support, help locating needed items and partners for thrift-store runs.

One couple, Matt Eddy and Sarah Pelmas, met through the Compact and got married six months ago. But the main advantage of being in a group is "you can brag to someone," said Boyd. Perry agreed. "After a while you get this bravado. You want to brag more and more," he said. "I found a Razor scooter for $15 at Thrift Town. That was great, but it doesn't top the free sewing machine I got on Craigslist. The stakes just keep getting higher."

Perry, who said he loves to shop, went into withdrawal the first few weeks of entering the Compact. For many people, shopping is a recreational and social activity that almost transcends consumerism. Boyd described it as an urge to "line the nest." "But after a few weeks the buzzing in your head subsides," Perry said. "Although if I continue to shop crazily at thrift stores, is that any better?" He thought about it for a moment. "I think it is."

AFTER YOU'VE READ

1. Were your inferences from the **Before You Read** section right? Why/Why not?

2. Overall, do you think the writer was successful at writing this essay? Why/Why not? What are your feelings toward the essay? Did you enjoy reading it?

Assessing Your Knowledge

KEY POINTS	REMINDER	HOW WELL DID YOU UNDERSTAND THIS MATERIAL?	PAGE(S)
Learn about and understand the reading process	There are four stages to **the reading process**: ▪ **Prereading** ▪ **Reading** ▪ **Rereading** ▪ **Postreading** The process can also be remembered with the acronym **PECC**: P—Predict E—Envision C—Connect C—Confirm & Critique	☐ I've Got It! ☐ Almost There ☐ Need More Practice	pp. 21–33

Understand and practice prereading strategies	**Prereading** involves thinking about the essay before you read. During prereading, you focus on making inferences, or guesses, about the essay.	☐ I've Got It! ☐ Almost There ☐ Need More Practice	pp. 21–23
Understand and practice annotating and reading strategies	The act of **annotation** is where you place notes, comments, and explanations within the text, in the margin, or on Post-it Notes on the essay itself. This act allows you to understand the essay better, remember the information, and make connections. At the end of this chapter, you found a student annotation example, as well as a blank essay where you could practice annotating. When you **read** for the first time, you need to read for the "plot" of the essay. This is when you try to understand what the essay is about, including looking up any concepts or words you are unfamiliar with.	☐ I've Got It! ☐ Almost There ☐ Need More Practice	pp. 24–28
Understand and practice rereading strategies	When you go back to the essay to read again, this is called **rereading**. During rereading, you are making a connection with the essay and trying to interact with it on a deeper level.	☐ I've Got It! ☐ Almost There ☐ Need More Practice	pp. 28–31
Understand and practice postreading strategies	**Postreading** occurs after you read and reread. Postreading allows you to go back to the inferences you made during your prereading and decide whether you were right and why you made those predictions. You can also evaluate the essay overall and give your opinion of it during postreading.	☐ I've Got It! ☐ Almost There ☐ Need More Practice	pp. 31–33

Deepening Your Understanding

If you would like to go beyond the material in this chapter, explore additional connections, and get more practice, check out these related topics:

- **The Writing Process**: The reading process closely mirrors the writing process. When you understand the reading process fully, you can apply that knowledge to the writing process and ultimately become a better reader and writer.

- **Vocabulary**: You can't understand what you read if you don't know what the words mean. The more advanced essays you read, the more developed vocabulary you will need.

- **Parts of the Essay**: No matter what type of essay you read or where you found the essay, understanding what an essay looks like and recognizing the parts is important to the reading process. Identifying these parts of the essay allows you to better understand where to find an essay's main point and how the essay is organized.

- **Essay Introductions, Conclusions, and Titles**: You can find prereading clues just by looking at the title of each essay. The introduction and conclusion can provide clues about the main idea and the writer's tone.

Writing

THE WRITING PROCESS

"Writing isn't a skill that some people are born with and others aren't, like a gift for art or music. Writing is talking to someone else on paper. Anybody who can think clearly can write clearly, about any subject at all."
—William Zinsser

FACT OR FICTION?
Prewriting can be done at any time. It is okay to stop while I am writing my essay and use a prewriting strategy.

FACT.
The word prewriting may seem to imply that it can be helpful only at the beginning of the writing process; however, prewriting can help you improve and develop your argument at any stage.

Discovering Key Points

- Identify the stages of the writing process
- Write to demonstrate knowledge of the prewriting strategies
- Describe the writing stage
- Identify revising as part of the rewriting stage and why it is important
- Identify editing as part of the rewriting stage and why it is important

The series of activities that writers go through from the very beginning of the assignment to the finalized product is called **the writing process**. While this process may differ somewhat for everyone, all writers plan, write, and review their work. These basic stages are called **prewriting**, **writing**, and **rewriting**.

The parts of the writing process do not occur just once. They tend to recur many times before a paper is finished. Most successful writers revisit parts of the writing process several times before they consider their work completed. If a writer uses only one part of the writing process—that is, if the writer does not use prewriting or rewriting—the paper will not be as interesting and sophisticated as it could be. Using all three parts of the writing process helps to create a more interesting and developed final product. For example, you may start with prewriting and then move onto writing, but if you find you need more ideas, don't be afraid to prewrite again to further explore your topic. Similarly, you may discover during rewriting that you have not directly addressed the whole assignment. In this case, you would return to prewrite and write about the "missing parts" of the topic in order to make your paper more complete.

Prewriting

Prewriting strategies are used to help writers generate, explore, and develop ideas for use on an assignment or paper. Once a writer has ideas he or she wishes to use, prewriting can even assist in constructing an organization and evaluating how to effectively fulfill the assignment. These prewriting strategies are sometimes called invention strategies because of their ability to help writers create new arguments and develop new points at any stage of the writing process. There are many prewriting strategies; **reading**, **freewriting**, **brainstorming**, **questioning**, **discussing**, **clustering**, and **planning** are some of the most common.

Reading

For more information about reading, see Chapter 2.

One way to discover ideas is to read about your topic. Investigating a topic that you are unfamiliar with will help you formulate an informed opinion and provide you with strong examples. In some of your classes, you may be asked to write a paper so you can research and learn about a topic in depth; reading is the beginning of this process. You may find general information about your topic online or in a newspaper or magazine article. More specific and in-depth information may be found in a journal article or a book. Write down what you have discovered through your reading. Include interesting and important facts, notable experts, and any questions you might have. To keep your information organized, a useful strategy is to put any factual information you find in one column and your thoughts and questions in another.

Howie needs to give a description of a local charity and has been assigned Opportunity Village. He has decided to read about the charity and record the information he finds as well as his thoughts.

Opportunity Village

Facts and Information	Thoughts and Questions
Opportunity Village is a non-profit charity in Nevada for people with intellectual disabilities.	The charity tries to help people with disabilities become part of the community and even find jobs.
Opportunity Village was founded in 1954. They help 3,000 people a year and estimate they have saved taxpayers 22 million dollars in education and services.	They seem to help a lot of people. If I had someone in my family with a disability, I would want them to be a part of an organization like this. Are there more charities like this in other states? What makes this one so successful?

YOUR TURN

Imagine you were asked to write a description of the American Cancer Society. To learn more about the subject and get ideas for the assignment, read about the American Cancer Society and record the information you find as well as your thoughts.

American Cancer Society

Facts and Information	Thoughts and Questions

Freewriting

The act of writing engages our brain and stimulates our creativity. Freewriting can help you generate ideas through the process of writing. When you freewrite, the goal is to record all of your ideas on a topic in a casual and free-form way for a set period of time. During that time, record all of your ideas without evaluating them. In order to get the most out of your freewrite, don't worry about grammar, spelling, punctuation, or organization. Worrying about these issues may slow your flow of ideas and draw your concentration away from your goal.

To freewrite, start with a blank page. You may find it helpful to write a word or phrase at the top to help you keep focused. Then set a time limit for yourself. Many writers free-write for ten minutes; this will give you enough time to think and explore your topic, but not enough to censor your ideas. If you think you have run out of ideas, keep writing. You can repeat a word or phrase, but you should keep writing until the time is up.

STUDENT EXAMPLE

Marie has been asked to freewrite about how technology can be a distraction.

Technology is a distraction. I see technology everywhere, and I often find myself pulled away from what I am doing to check my email, post to Pinterest, or update my Facebook page. While I watch television and have a phone, I spend the most time on my computer. Even if I get online to do one simple task, such as pay a bill, I find that I always end up following an ad to a new page. I spend hours on Facebook. I chat with my friends, play games, and look at pictures. It is so easy to forget why I got on the computer in the first place. When I try to clean out my email, I end up opening an email that leads to an hour of reading about breaking news or investigating a sale. Inevitably, I miss something while I am online. I should probably spend more time on my homework.

YOUR TURN

Your sociology professor has assigned a short paper on rude behavior and lapses in common courtesy. You are going to write about people who use their cell phones, to talk or text, while watching a movie in the theater. Freewrite about whether you think this is rude behavior.

Brainstorming

Brainstorming, like freewriting, is a casual and free-form style of prewriting. A brainstorm, as the name implies, is often disorganized and chaotic, like a storm. Unlike a freewrite, which is timed and may contain sentences, a brainstorm often takes the form of words and phrases. When you are brainstorming, record ideas and examples as you think of them.

The purpose is to think of as many ideas as possible without worrying about organization, spelling, grammar, or punctuation. Your brainstorm might be scattered over a whole page, or it might resemble a list.

STUDENT EXAMPLE

Nate is going to write a paper discussing how businesses change and adapt to new consumer habits. He has decided to brainstorm in the form of a list to develop a few ideas.

- Businesses have to change to keep up with the consumer
- Creative new products and inventions
- Things that make our lives easier
- Sometimes services change too
- Physical stores not needed; Redbox stands are the closest
- Customers want to access their purchases instantly, e.g., InstaWatch from Walmart
- Can stream movies and television shows from Amazon, Vudu, and Netflix
- Can watch on phone, gaming system, Apple TV, computer

YOUR TURN

Choose your favorite holiday, such as Valentine's Day, Thanksgiving, or New Year's Eve, and create a brainstorm that will help you to describe this holiday and explain why it is your favorite. Remember that your brainstorm can be created in a number of formats and styles, including unorganized notes or a list, and may express your ideas as words and phrases.

Questioning

As the author of your paper, you will need to supply your readers with the information they need to know and answers to the questions they might have. Questioning is a prewriting strategy that helps you anticipate your reader's questions. Answering who, what, when, where, why, and how (also known as journalistic questions or the 5 Ws and 1 H) will support your essay's development.

Who?	Who is involved? Who does the issue affect?
What?	What has happened? What are you writing about?
When?	When did the event occur? When did the situation change?
Where?	Where did the event or topic take place?
Why?	Why are the above questions important? Why should your reader pay attention?
How?	How did the event or topic happen? How can the problem be solved?

These questions are also helpful when discussing supporting details. For more information, see Chapters 4 and 5.

Eva writes for the school paper, and her assignment this week is to cover the student response to the drastic reduction in the university's library hours. Before she begins her article, she uses questioning to make sure she has every angle covered.

Who?	*Students, library staff, and administration are involved.*
What?	*The effect of shortened library hours on students and how they feel about the issue.*
When?	*A week ago.*
Where?	*Our campus library.*
Why?	*This is important because the library provides resources for students, such as group study rooms, individual study tables, computer labs, and research materials. Shortened hours means we will have limited access to these resources.*
How?	*Budget cuts were given as the reason for shortening the library's hours. They might keep the library open longer if more money were raised; the students could organize a fundraiser or get a donation. Students might also petition to keep it open longer and cut something else instead.*

YOUR TURN

Imagine there has been a food poisoning incident in your school cafeteria. Now, pretend you are a journalist for your school's newspaper, and your editor has asked you to investigate and write an article about this incident. To prepare, use questioning to explore the issue. Make sure to record your answers for all six questions: who, what, when, where, why, and how.

Who? _____

What? _____

When? _____

Where? _____

Why? _____

_____

How? _____

_____

Discussing

Discussing your paper topic with others can create positive momentum in your writing process. The person you talk to doesn't need to be in your class. Friends, family members, and roommates can offer insight and personal perspectives and even ask questions that you wouldn't be able to form on your own. In addition, verbalizing your thoughts, arguments, organization, and questions can help you solidify your position and overcome the challenges you are facing. Talking about your paper topic with a friend or family member at any point may be helpful to you. Once you have a draft, you can discuss the strength of your argument, the evidence you want to incorporate, or the solution you plan to offer. It is important that you write down the content of your discussion so that you can remember what was said.

STUDENT EXAMPLE

Hamond is writing an email to his boss requesting a raise, but he has decided to discuss the issue with his older brother before starting. He takes notes during the conversation to record any helpful ideas.

Discussing why I should get a raise with my brother

He said that businesses usually want to reward good employees because they want them to stay and be happy in their jobs. Sometimes companies can't give a raise just because someone asks, but it doesn't hurt to try. He said I should give reasons why I am a valuable member of the staff and remind my boss of how long I have worked there. I am reliable and trustworthy. I have never been late to work. He even reminded me of the time when I went out of my way to help a customer to her car.

YOUR TURN

You must make a PowerPoint presentation in your economics class about whether students employed by your university should be able to work more than 20 hours a week. Discuss the matter with a friend or classmate and record notes about your conversation.

_____

_____

_____

_____

_____

Clustering

Clustering not only helps you think of ideas; it also helps organize them by identifying the relationships between your ideas. This strategy is often used to further develop a topic after reading, freewriting, brainstorming, questioning, and discussing because it helps organize the ideas discovered in these strategies. Clustering is sometimes called bubble clustering, webbing, web mapping, or spider webbing.

First, put a keyword or phrase in the center of a blank sheet of paper. Circle the key word or phrase. Then think about how this topic can be broken down into different categories or examples. Write these related ideas near the first circle. Circle the newly added words and phrases, and draw a line to show the relationships with other circles. Continue this process until you have recorded all of your ideas.

STUDENT EXAMPLE

Franklin has been asked to write about his favorite type of movie. He uses clustering to map his thoughts.

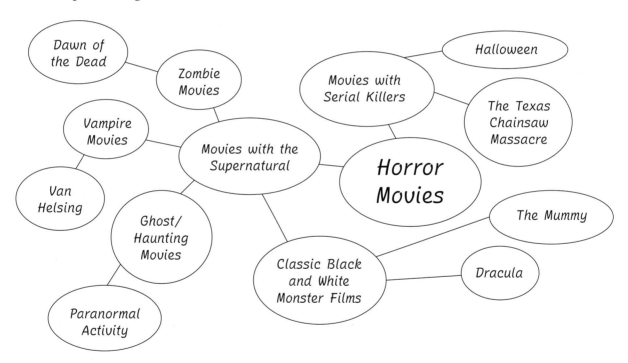

YOUR TURN

Imagine you have been given an assignment to write about action movies. Collect your thoughts by creating a cluster for action movies. Make sure to connect with a line any ideas that are related.

Planning

Before you begin to write your paper, you will need to formulate a plan. Planning consists of selecting a **subject**, an **audience**, and a **purpose**.

The subject of your paper should be appropriate for the assignment you have been given. In many cases, you will be given a paper topic. Make sure you are fully addressing the topic assigned. If you were not given a specific topic, use various prewriting strategies to decide on a topic that is narrow enough to fit the other requirements given, such as page length.

Consider the audience of your paper. Your paper should be written with the right level of formality, jargon (vocabulary specific to a group or profession), and background information to satisfy your audience. Also, consider the age, profession, and special interests your audience might share. For example, a doctor at a medical conference could assume certain things about the audience. The audience would have a medical background and would understand medical terminology. They would also expect a formal presentation from a well-educated and professional speaker.

Consider the purpose of your paper. The purpose of a paper may be to inform, entertain, and/or persuade your audience. Some papers may have more than one purpose; many academic and scholarly articles are meant to both inform and persuade readers.

For more information about audience and purpose, see Chapter 5.

- **To inform**—Informative papers are meant to educate your audience. Think about what your readers will already know about the subject and what you will need to tell them.
- **To entertain**—Entertaining papers often tell a story and engage the readers' attention. Think about what your audience might find interesting, funny, or touching.
- **To persuade**—Persuasive papers use information, examples, and reasons to convince the reader that the argument being presented is valid. Think about what your readers might already believe about the subject.

You may have an assignment that requires you to explore only one of these purposes. However, strong arguments will often be informative, entertaining, and persuasive. Arguments can be presented to us in many forms. We normally think of finding arguments in essays or newspaper columns, but arguments can be found in advertisements, songs, news broadcasts, and many other places. Some arguments, such as commercials, try to entertain viewers to keep their attention long enough to inform them about a product. In your own arguments, your instructors will expect you to show that you understand the content you are presenting and to persuade others to accept your position.

STUDENT EXAMPLE

Farah is creating a commercial for a local non-profit organization to educate others on the struggles of women in the criminal justice system. She uses planning to make sure her commercial will be effective.

Subject	What is your subject? Is it narrow enough? How do you know?
	My general topic is women in the criminal justice system, but because I am making a two-minute commercial, I am only going to focus on mothers who are incarcerated or on parole.
Audience	Who is your audience? What do they know about the subject? What are their expectations?
	The audience is my local community. If they have not been affected directly by this issue, then they may not know much about the topic. The people in my community may not know how the prison system is different for men and women, especially mothers.
Purpose	What is your purpose? How do you know? What do you need to do to fulfill this purpose?
	The purpose of my commercial is to inform and persuade. I need to provide as much information as I can in two minutes. This means that my message needs to be very clear. Because it is a commercial, I plan on using photos and video to help make my point.

YOUR TURN

Imagine you are the student body president on your campus and you are preparing for a podcast in which you will encourage your fellow students to donate to the local homeless shelter. To ensure your plea is successful, use planning to define the subject, audience, and purpose.

Subject	What is your subject? Is it narrow enough? How do you know?
Audience	Who is your audience? What do they know about the subject? What are their expectations?
Purpose	What is your purpose? How do you know? What do you need to do to fulfill this purpose?

Writing

Once you have ideas, you can start the writing stage of the writing process. In the writing stage, you will develop your thoughts more thoroughly. Start with reviewing your prewriting—and then begin to write in a more considered way. As you are working on your first draft, you may find you run out of ideas and can't think of anything else to write about. In that case, look at your prewriting again. You can always complete another prewriting strategy to create more ideas and examples. The first draft is usually rough, and once you complete it, you may immediately see where you want to make changes.

To finish your assignment or essay, you may find that you need several drafts. The work that is done between drafts is called rewriting.

Part of writing a paper is deciding on and following a pattern of organization. If your paper lacks clear organization, your reader is likely to become lost and may even lose interest in your argument. Following common patterns of organization will help readers to recognize the structure of your essay. **Specific to general**, **general to specific**, **chronological**, **spatial**, and by **importance** are all common forms of organization that can be applied to a paragraph, a part of an essay, or a whole essay.

ⓘ Want to know how to develop a body paragraph? See Chapter 4.

Specific to General

Imagine you are watching Monday night football at a friend's house. Your favorite player has just run in for a touchdown. You boast that he is also on your fantasy football team and will help you win this week's game. Your friend scoffs and argues that the league that you both belong to is rigged because you always win.

The conversation you had with your friend is organized from specific to general: from a single player, to a team, and then to a league. An essay or piece of writing that uses a specific-to-general organization gives a detail or example and then shows the reader the importance of this information by generalizing and showing how it belongs to a larger category. This organization is useful when you want to lead your readers step by step from an example to a particular conclusion.

You may find specific-to-general organization in the following types of writing:

Description—Because description essays favor details and examples, a specific-to-general organization allows an author to highlight a specific event, example, fact, or detail first, catching the reader's attention before showing its connection to other important ideas.

Scientific Report—Scientific reports often require that the writer define, describe, and test a specific problem before providing a discussion of how the results might help and apply to a variety of situations.

> **MEDIA EXAMPLE OF SPECIFIC-TO-GENERAL ORGANIZATION**

Specific-to-general organization isn't found only in essays. It can also be found in songs. Search online for the song "Footloose" by Kenny Loggins.

What specific information does the song mention? How is the information in the song generalized?

Howard is going to organize his essay about dyslexia using a specific-to-general organization. He decides to start with a specific example. Then he knows his information needs to become more and more general.

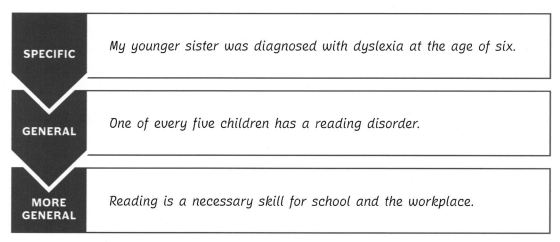

SPECIFIC	My younger sister was diagnosed with dyslexia at the age of six.
GENERAL	One of every five children has a reading disorder.
MORE GENERAL	Reading is a necessary skill for school and the workplace.

YOUR TURN

You have been asked to write about superheroes. Practice using a specific-to-general organization. Start with a specific fact or detail about a superhero you are familiar with. Then generalize, creating two statements that become more and more general.

SPECIFIC	
GENERAL	
MORE GENERAL	

General to Specific

Imagine you must buy a dress for a relative's wedding. You decide to try your luck at the mall, where you enter a store you like. Since the store carries a variety of clothing, you must also find the women's formal section. Your shopping trip is organized from general to specific. An essay or piece of writing that uses a general-to-specific organization starts with a broad category and then narrows to the subject being discussed. This organization is helpful when you want to use examples to support a larger argument.

You may find general-to-specific organization in the following types of writing:

Research Papers—A research paper requires you to support your argument with numerous facts and examples. The main argument is given toward the beginning of the paper in the thesis statement. Then more specific points and detailed examples are given.

Illustration Essays—An illustration essay might start with a general concept, provide examples, and then describe specific details.

MEDIA EXAMPLE OF GENERAL-TO-SPECIFIC ORGANIZATION

General-to-specific organization isn't found only in essays. It can also be found in commercials. Search online for a commercial that uses this organization style. Consider looking at longer commercials, sometimes called infomercials, for skin care products or vacuum cleaners.

What general information is provided at the beginning of the commercial? What specific information is given as the commercial progresses?

STUDENT EXAMPLE

Char is going to organize her essay about drunk driving using a general-to-specific organization. She decides to start with a general statement. Then she knows her information needs to become more specific.

GENERAL	*Car accidents kill thousands of people each year.*
MORE SPECIFIC	*Many of these accidents are caused by those driving under the influence.*
MOST SPECIFIC	*The legal blood alcohol limit for people over 21 is .08.*

YOUR TURN

Imagine you have been asked to prepare a speech for your communications course about how to stay safe on your campus at night. Practice using a general-to-specific organization. Start with a general statement. Then create two statements that provide specifics.

Chronological

Imagine you are applying for graduation from your college. When you look at your transcript, you notice that the courses you took in your very first semester are at the top. Each semester's courses are listed in order, and the most recent one is at the very bottom. Your transcript is organized chronologically. An essay or piece of writing that uses a chronological organization works much like a timeline, explaining events in order, usually from the past to the present. You might find this pattern of organization helpful when you are giving background information or when you show your reader how something has changed over time.

You may find chronological organization in the following types of writing:

Biographical Essays—Biographical essays tell the story of a person's life. Most of these start with the individual's childhood and then cover his or her teen years before discussing his or her adult life.

Process Analysis Essays—Essays that explain how something was created or how a process can be copied have a chronological organization. Starting at the beginning stage, they go step by step until the finished product is completed.

MEDIA EXAMPLE OF CHRONOLOGICAL ORGANIZATION

Chronological organization isn't found only in essays. It can also be found in social media. Examples of chronological organization can be found on Twitter, Instagram, and Facebook.

Why would a social media site like Twitter or Facebook be organized chronologically? What advantage would this have over other forms of organization?

Adan is going to organize his essay about reality television using a chronological organization. He starts by explaining his topic, beginning with the events that happened first and continuing with events that happen closer to the present.

FIRST	NEXT	LAST
The first reality television show was aired in 1971.	*The writers' strike in 2007 caused a huge increase in reality television because no writers were needed.*	*Now, people are addicted to reality television. Some would rather watch it than anything else.*

Imagine you have been asked to act out your favorite fairy tale in your theater course. To get ready for your performance, practice using chronological organization to tell the story. Start by explaining the events that happened first. Then continue with events in the order in which they happen until the tale is over.

FIRST	NEXT	LAST

Spatial

Imagine you are walking to your car after class. A woman passing by asks for directions to the administration building. You tell her that she needs to head south past the sculpture, and then take a right when she comes to the library. The administration building is just west of the library. When you give directions, you organize your ideas spatially. An essay or piece of writing that uses spatial organization shows how items are related based on where they are located. Spatial essays may discuss items in a variety of different spatial orders (e.g., from left to right, from north to south, from here to there).

You may find spatial organization in the following types of writing:

Travel Essays—A travel essay is organized spatially to highlight specific locations as well as the distance and travel required to get from one place to the next. For example, an essay about a road trip on Route 66 would describe each town and sightseeing opportunity from the starting point to the destination.

Description Essays—A description essay of a room could be based on spatial organization. The author might start on one side of the room and work clockwise until he or she has come full circle. The author might even describe a room from top to bottom.

MEDIA EXAMPLE OF SPATIAL ORGANIZATION

Spatial organization isn't found only in essays. It can also be found in music. Search online for the song "California Girls" by the Beach Boys.

How can you tell that this song is organized spatially? What directions or phrases guide the organization of the song?

STUDENT EXAMPLE

Belen is going to organize her essay about her city's crime rate using a spatial organization. She starts by discussing the issue in a specific part of town before discussing the other nearby areas.

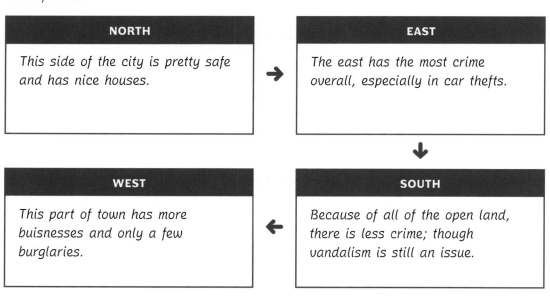

NORTH

This side of the city is pretty safe and has nice houses.

EAST

The east has the most crime overall, especially in car thefts.

WEST

This part of town has more buisnesses and only a few burglaries.

SOUTH

Because of all of the open land, there is less crime; though vandalism is still an issue.

Practice using spatial organization by describing how to get to your favorite restaurant in town from campus. Start with a specific place or location on campus. Describe how to get to the restaurant, highlighting specific locations you would see along the way.

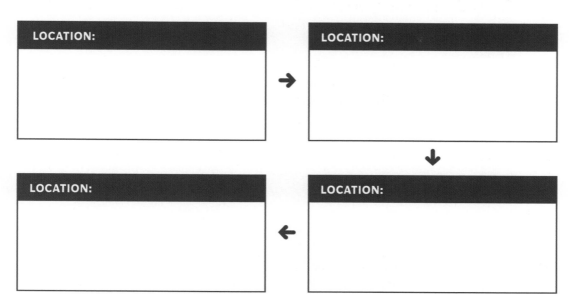

Importance

Imagine you are making a list of homework you must complete in the next few days. At the top of your list, you put the assignments that are worth the most points or percentage of your grade. Because you want to maximize your time and effort, you prioritize your list. You decide to work on the most important assignments first. After these assignments are completed, you will work on the smaller assignments. Your list is organized by importance. An essay or piece of writing that uses an order-of-importance organization may contain points that increase or decrease in importance. If a paper uses increasing importance, it offers less impressive or important points first. Then increasingly stronger points are provided. If an essay uses decreasing importance, it will provide the most important point first and share points that are less and less important as the essay continues.

You may find importance is used to organize the following types of writing:

Argument Essays—Argument essays typically start with points that are less important and build toward those that are more important.

Newspaper Articles—Newspaper articles tend to begin with the most important information, in order to catch the reader's attention. Journalists start (or "lead," as they call it) with the most important information and follow with explanations and details, which increase the reader's understanding but are less important.

MEDIA EXAMPLE OF ORGANIZATION BY ORDER OF IMPORTANCE

Organizing by importance isn't found only in essays. It can also be found in the media. Movie box-office ratings are also an example of this organization style. Search online for recent box-office ratings.

List the order of the movies from least to most popular. What else do we rate based on popularity or votes?

STUDENT EXAMPLE

Monroe is going to organize his essay about the homeless shelter using order-of-importance organization. He starts by discussing the least important idea. Each idea increases in importance, and his most important idea is given last.

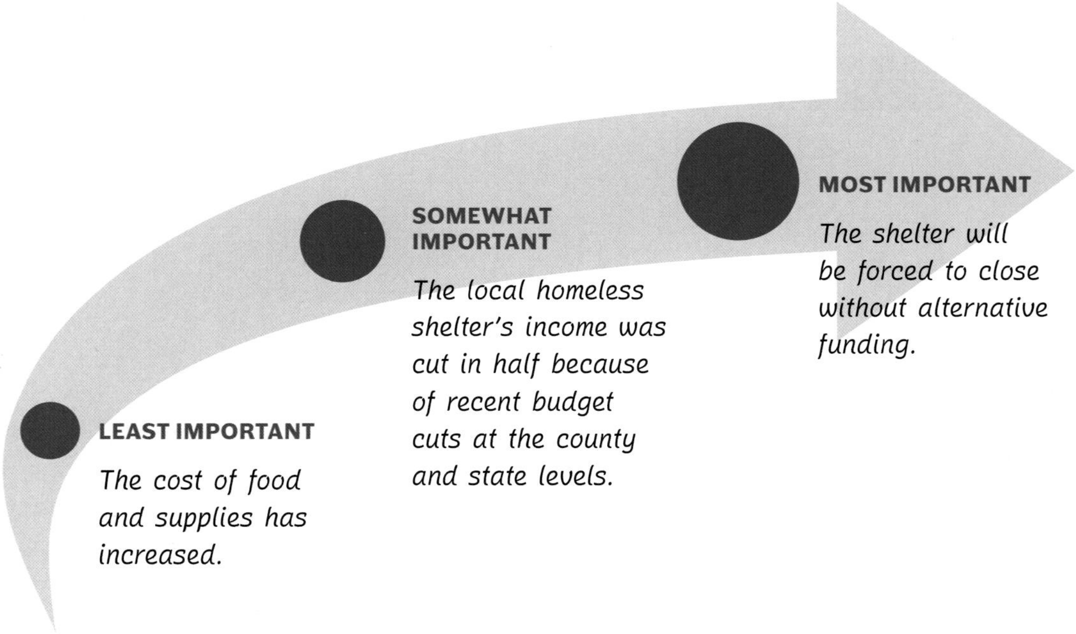

LEAST IMPORTANT
The cost of food and supplies has increased.
SOMEWHAT IMPORTANT
The local homeless shelter's income was cut in half because of recent budget cuts at the county and state levels.
MOST IMPORTANT
The shelter will be forced to close without alternative funding.

YOUR TURN

Imagine you have been asked to write a letter to seniors in high school explaining how to pass a class in college. Practice using importance to organize your thoughts. Start by discussing the least important idea. Each idea should increase in importance, and your most important idea should be given last.

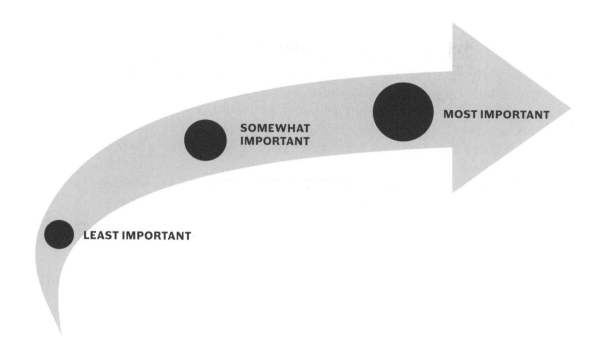

SOMEWHAT
IMPORTANT

MOST IMPORTANT

LEAST IMPORTANT

Rewriting

Rewriting is an essential step in writing a paper. If this step is skipped, a piece of writing will almost always be insufficiently developed and lacking in clarity or detail. Rewriting an assignment provides you with a chance to correct mistakes and add to your ideas. Rewriting can be divided into two main categories: revising and editing. Revising and editing both improve your writing, but each focuses on different issues in an assignment.

Revising

Revising is the process of looking at larger issues that affect how well the reader understands the piece of writing. Your professors will be interested in the content, the information provided, and the form—the presentation or organization—of your writing. In a revision, you should look to see what can be improved in your draft. Taking a short break between revisions of your draft can help you to see any mistakes or gaps in your paper more clearly.

For more information about essay organization, see Chapter 5.

COMMON REVISING QUESTIONS

Are you answering the assignment completely? Take another look at the assignment you were given. Some assignments have specific requirements for the topics that need to be covered. They may involve requirements for page length, for example, or for number of sources. Following the directions and covering all the required topics is very important. If you omit information, it may lead your instructor to believe that you didn't do your best or didn't think the assignment was important. Does your writing meet all the assignment requirements? If something is missing, revision is the perfect time to add it in.

Did you write with your audience and your purpose in mind? During the revising stage, you should confirm that your paper still addresses the audience's expectations. Your writing should use the appropriate level of formality and the terminology or jargon your audience expects—and it should provide the background information your audience needs. You should also check that your paper fulfills its purpose. If you have chosen to be informative, look to see that you have included enough information and examples. If you are writing to entertain, you can strengthen the appeal of a story with interesting details. If your goal is to persuade, you can test your argument to verify that it is convincing.

Did you cover your subject completely? Go through your prewriting again. Highlight any unused ideas and decide if they should be incorporated into your paper. Not all of your original ideas may be helpful, but you don't want to accidently forget any points or examples that will strengthen your argument. Before you add new ideas into your paper, carefully consider where they should be incorporated.

STUDENT EXAMPLE

Cameron has written an essay giving his position on whether music with a political message should be encouraged. He has marked his ideas for how to revise in the margin on yellow Post-it Notes and made changes in the draft (note that this draft hasn't been edited yet).

Political Music

In my prewriting, I had notes about freedom and creativity that I would like to use in the intro.

Not all things are how people see them. Some people suffer disorders where they see letters on a page differently from others and some see colors in a different light than most. But for artists of all forms, there is a completely different light shed on so many different views of life that they as people are sometimes seen as backwards to the rest of the world. We love music because it is an art form. The creativity that produces this art should not be shackled by a request or a political agenda. When a artist creates music it should grow organically out of the artist emotion. Artist should express what they are feeling, not just what they are asked to. Encouraging any kind of music, especially political music, would ruin the freedom and creativity that musician now have, and ruin music as we know it.

Well-loved, popular music is not created by an order or request. Much of the music people love is a genuine expression of a simple, pure emotion. The Beatles, one of the most popular groups, didn't have fanatical fans because someone told them what to say in their music. They captured the feeling of love in there music because that is what they felt. Some of there songs were written in response to political ~~actions~~ unrest, but at the core of those songs, they still attempted to express there desire to see love. It is a simple ~~idea~~ concept expressed in their music in response to the wars occurring at the time, but the love the Beatles sang about was not a political agenda as much as it was an answer all the violence.

While the Beatles sang about love in response to politics because it was at the core of their beliefs, and would have been expressed regardless of world events. Through music the Beatles expressed many ideas and did not push any political agenda, but displayed their emotions whether it was a result of world events or personal events. John Lennon once said that "song writing is about getting the demon out of me. It's like being possessed. You try to go to sleep, but the song won't let you. So you have to get up and make it into something, and then you're allowed to sleep." The Beatles would have never sung about anything they did not believe in, thus they did not convey feeling about welfare or health care in there ~~tunes~~ lyrics.

Music is a beautiful form of art with a lot of power. The main purpose of music is for an artist to communicate there feelings about ~~anything~~ their beliefs in a tasteful way; the idea cannot be forced. Music is a way voice feelings. If an artist attempts to communicate anything they have no emotional connection with all beauty that could be in the art, rendering it purposeless.

My purpose is to persuade—make an argument and defend it.
-show how examples prove my argument

Who is my audience?
-my instructor
-expects a formal essay
-use formal language

The assignment requires one quote. Add one in here.

Editing

Editing is the process of looking for sentence-level errors, such as grammar, punctuation, and spelling. Because so much of your paper can change during revision, you should wait to edit your paper until after you are finished revising. Many writers find it is hard to see mistakes in their own writing; evaluating your paper with a strategy or plan for finding errors can help. Most successful writers find they need to go through their papers more than once, so they use several different strategies.

COMMON EDITING STRATEGIES

Read your draft out loud. Reading your draft out loud will help you catch mistakes that you might miss when reading it silently. Because writers are so familiar with their own work, they often overlook distracting errors, such as missing letters and words. Reading out loud makes writers pay attention to each word and allows them to catch more errors.

Read your draft sentence by sentence from the end to the beginning. During editing, it is easy to get carried away by a stirring argument or an emotional story and fail to notice grammatical errors. By reading the draft sentence by sentence, starting from the end, you can focus on the sentence structure, grammar, and spelling.

Look for frequently made errors. Writers tend to make the same mistakes frequently. Even experienced writers have weaknesses; they are just better at finding and correcting them. Knowing the kind of mistakes you make most often will give you the opportunity to fix them before you turn in your assignment. Examine your draft for mistakes you commonly make while writing. If you don't know what your weaknesses are, you can look at your instructor's comments from previous papers or drafts. You can also visit a tutoring center.

REVISED STUDENT EXAMPLE

Cameron has revised his draft but still needs to edit it. His ideas for editing are marked on blue Post-it Notes, and changes are marked in the draft.

Political Music

Reading out loud, I found missing words and letters.

We love music because it is an art form. The creativity that produces this art should not be shackled by a request or a political agenda. When an artist creates music, it should grow organically out of the artist's emotions. Artists should express what they are feeling, not just what they are asked to. Encouraging any kind of music, especially political music, would ruin the freedom and creativity that musicians now have, and ruin music as we know it.

Well-loved, popular music is not created by an order or request. Much of the music people love is a genuine expression of a simple, pure emotion. The

I often confuse there and their. Look for more in the draft.

Beatles, one of the most popular groups, didn't have fanatical fans because someone told them what to say in their music. They captured the feeling of love in ~~there~~ their music because that is what they felt. Some of ~~there~~ their songs were written in response to political unrest, but at the core of those songs, they still attempted to express ~~there~~ their desire to see love. It is a simple concept expressed in their music in response to the wars occurring at the time, but the love the Beatles sang about was not a political agenda as much as it was an answer to all the violence.

~~While~~The Beatles sang about love in response to politics because it was at the core of their beliefs, and would have been expressed regardless of world events. Through music, the Beatles expressed many ideas and did not push any political agenda, but displayed their emotions whether it was a result of world events or personal events. John Lennon once said that "song writing is about getting the demon out of me. It's like being possessed. You try to go to sleep, but the song won't let you. So you have to get up and make it into something, *and then you're allowed to sleep." The Beatles would have never sung about anything they did not believe in, thus they did not convey feelings about welfare or health care in ~~there~~ their lyrics.*

> *Music is a beautiful form of art with a lot of power. The main purpose of music is for an artist to communicate ~~there~~ their feelings about their beliefs in a tasteful way; the idea cannot be forced. Music is a way to voice feelings. If an artist attempts to communicate anything, they will have no emotional connection with all beauty that could be in the art, rendering it purposeless.*

Reading the essay backward, I found missing commas.

Peer Revision and Peer Editing

Revising and editing with the help of your classmates can be extremely helpful and productive. Your peers can help you spot errors you didn't see in your own writing and make suggestions that help you improve your draft. When you play the part of the peer reviewer, remember that your job is to be a good audience member and provide helpful feedback. Helping others improve their work is part of being a good writer and is good practice for revising your own writing.

Be empathetic. Respond to the draft just as you would want someone to respond to yours: with helpful tips and suggestions for improvement. Providing some praise along with constructive criticism will let your peer know if there are any changes to be made without hurting his or her feelings.

Focus on the draft. You may find yourself tempted to start a conversation during the revision. However, getting distracted by asking questions not related to the draft or sharing a story of your own won't help your partner improve his or her writing. Use the time you have wisely, and try to offer as much help as you can.

Be a mirror. Let your peer know what you see. Retelling a true story is harder than it seems. Beginning writers often forget to fully explain all the necessary background or fill in all the details their readers need. Point out where you were confused or wanted more information. If you enjoyed a story or found an example helpful, let your partner know. Telling your peer review partner how it felt to read the draft will help them write more effectively.

Avoid judgmental reactions. You don't need to agree with everything in your peer's paper. For example, the information in some personal essays might bother you, or you may not agree with the argument given. Keep in mind that it is your job to help your classmate improve his or her paper. Your responses should be focused on the draft and how it can better address the assignment.

Plagiarism and Academic Integrity

The process of writing is not always easy; writing is hard work, but difficulty is never an excuse for **plagiarism**. Plagiarism is presenting someone else's work as your own or using another author's words or ideas without the proper citation. Students must understand that this includes turning in someone else's paper as their own or taking parts of a book, article, or website without credit.

Academic integrity goes beyond the issue of plagiarism. Turning in the exact same paper twice without getting permission from your instructors, for example, is considered dishonest behavior on many campuses. Learning institutions value education and want all students to practice honesty in their pursuit of knowledge. While every university has a different process for dealing with plagiarism and academic dishonesty, all of them consider it a grave offence. The punishment for plagiarism or academic dishonesty can include attending classes on plagiarism, counseling, failing an assignment or course, and even expulsion.

Sometimes students can unintentionally plagiarize information due to inexperience or confusion. Such offences are still very serious; if you are unsure how to use documentation or what kind of information should be cited, you can consult your instructor, tutoring center, or writing center.

ⓘ

Want to learn more about using sources and documentation? See Chapters 15 and 16.

Assessing Your Knowledge

KEY POINTS	REMINDER	HOW WELL DID YOU UNDERSTAND THIS MATERIAL?	PAGE(S)
Identify the stages of the writing process	**The writing process** consists of three parts: **prewriting**, **writing**, and **rewriting**.	☐ I've Got It! ☐ Almost There ☐ Need More Practice	p. 43
Write to demonstrate knowledge of the prewriting strategies	There are seven prewriting strategies covered in this chapter: ▪ **Reading** ▪ **Freewriting** ▪ **Brainstorming** ▪ **Questioning** ▪ **Discussing** ▪ **Clustering** ▪ **Planning** Practice these to make sure you can use them successfully.	☐ I've Got It! ☐ Almost There ☐ Need More Practice	pp. 44–52

Describe the writing stage	The **writing** stage can be started after prewriting. The first draft is usually rough and needs several revisions.	☐ I've Got It! ☐ Almost There ☐ Need More Practice	pp. 53–61
Identify revising as part of the rewriting stage and why it is important	The first step in rewriting a draft is **revising**. Revision focuses on content and formatting.	☐ I've Got It! ☐ Almost There ☐ Need More Practice	pp. 61–64
Identify editing as part of the rewriting stage and why it is important	The second step in rewriting is **editing**. Editing focuses on grammar, punctuation, and spelling. You should wait to edit until your revision is compete.	☐ I've Got It! ☐ Almost There ☐ Need More Practice	pp. 63–64

Deepening Your Understanding

If you would like to go beyond the material in this chapter, explore additional connections, and get more practice, check out these related topics:

- **Getting Started**: Good writing takes time and planning. Before you sit down to write a draft, consider how you can prepare your workspace so you are successful. Having a strategy to stay focused will be helpful as you write.

- **Parts of the Essay**: Formatting is important in any assignment, and the most common form of writing in college is the essay. Check to see if you know all the parts of a complete essay.

- **Developing and Organizing a Paragraph**: Adding details to develop a paragraph is one way to revise. Readers appreciate paragraphs with clearly explained and organized ideas.

- **Spelling**: Check for misspelled words when you are editing a paper. Correctly spelled words allow the reader to better understand your argument, and this increases the chances that they can be persuaded by the information you present.

Writing

PARTS OF THE ESSAY

"Almost all good writing begins with terrible first efforts. You need to start somewhere."

—Anne Lamott

FACT OR FICTION?
Writing the introduction is the hardest part of the essay.

FACT (FOR SOME AT LEAST).
For many, getting started is incredibly hard. Often, sitting at a blank screen is a scary experience. Nonetheless, this chapter discusses many ways to start your essays.

Discovering Key Points

- Learn about and identify the parts of the essay
- Understand, identify, and practice writing introductions, conclusions, and titles
- Understand, identify, and practice writing thesis statements and topic sentences
- Understand, identify, and practice writing body paragraphs and supporting details
- Understand, identify, and practice writing transitions

There are multiple parts of the essay, each of which is just as important as the next. You can think of these parts as the pieces in a puzzle. If one piece is missing, your puzzle is incomplete. The essay "puzzle" can be divided into seven parts:

- Thesis Statements
- Introductions
- Topic Sentences
- Body Paragraphs
- Transitions
- Conclusions
- Titles

What Is an Essay?

The essay is a piece of non-fiction. In its simplest form, it consists of an introduction with a thesis statement at the beginning, body paragraphs in the middle, and a conclusion at the end.

The introduction begins your paper. It's the place for you to grab your reader's attention. The introduction often ends with a thesis statement specific to your essay.

The body paragraphs support your thesis statement. They form the bulk of your paper; this is where you provide specific, detailed examples.

The conclusion is the ending of your essay. The conclusion begins more specifically than does the introduction, and ends more broadly. In the conclusion, you will restate your thesis and restate your main points. You may also make a "call to action" here.

What Does an Essay Look Like?

For MLA and APA formatting rules and example papers, see Chapter 16.

For a typed essay, the beginning of each paragraph should be indented one tab. You will want to talk to your instructor to see if he or she has specific rules about page numbering, headings, cover pages, font, margins, spacing, and so on.

Thesis Statements

A **thesis statement** expresses the **main idea** of your entire essay in concise form. The thesis statement can be anywhere from one to three sentences in length, depending on how detailed and difficult your topic is. Your thesis statement announces your topic to your readers and presents your main idea about that topic. When you write a thesis statement, you want to be specific; only cover the topic you will be discussing in your essay. Make sure you narrow this topic down to what you can specifically cover in your page length.

Importantly, your main idea can't be obvious or trivial. For example, if social media use were your topic, which of the following would be a good thesis settlement?

"Use of social media sites has become very widespread."
"Those who use social media heavily need to be aware of the risks."

You may also be asked to write a **listing thesis statement**. A listing thesis statement allows you to create an even more detailed blueprint for yourself and your readers. The listing thesis statement states the reasons for your opinion or main idea in the thesis. This then becomes the outline for the body paragraphs' content. A listing thesis statement looks like this:

Though New York City is no longer the world's largest city, it can still claim to be the world's most important city—because of its importance as a center of the financial world, the intellectual world, and the world of entertainment.

Tips for Writing a Thesis Statement

- **Decide on your topic**. This may require you to pick a new topic, or this may be a topic that is given to you by your instructor. Either way, be sure that the topic is specific. This means you may need to narrow down your topic enough so that it meets your page requirement for the assignment. For example, if your topic was "problems with drunk driving," and you had only three pages to write your essay, you'd want to narrow down your topic to something manageable, like "teenage drunk drivers."
- **Consider wording**. Think about what type of wording you want to use for the thesis statement. Try to avoid words that aren't specific and can have multiple meanings, like *good*, *bad*, *interesting*, and *unique*.
- **Write a statement**. Thesis statements should not be questions. They are always statements.
- **Make sure it's in the right spot**. The thesis statement most often will appear at the end of your introduction; however, your instructor may expect the thesis in a different spot.
- **Be ready and willing to revise**. You may find that after you write your essay, you need to go back and revise your thesis to match your finished draft. This is a normal part of the writing process.

Two Types of Thesis Statements

Argumentative—This type of essay makes a claim and tries to prove that claim through examples and evidence from research.

"In college, too many students value grades more than learning."

Analytical—This type of essay breaks a topic into multiple parts and then evaluates the topic as a whole. These essays answer *how* something does what it does or *why* it is the way it is.

"An analysis of college life reveals two kinds of students: those who want to have a social life and those who want to do well in their courses."

Examples of Thesis Statements

"BAD" THESIS	REASONING	REVISED THESIS
Is it right to kill animals?	A thesis statement should not be a question. Also, this thesis statement does not have a main idea or opinion.	We should not kill animals because they, like humans, have the right to live.
My paper is about P90X, which is my favorite type of exercise.	A thesis statement does not announce what the paper is doing.	P90X is my favorite exercise because it is difficult, but effective.
Twilight is an interesting movie.	A thesis statement should be more specific.	*Twilight* is an example of a classic film because it portrays a perfect romance and eternal love.
Sex education.	A thesis statement needs to be a full sentence, not just a topic.	Sex education in public schools will lead to healthier sexual behavior among students in their later lives.
The NBA draft causes many problems.	This thesis statement is too broad. Readers of this paper might be disappointed when the paper doesn't discuss all the problems caused by the NBA draft that they were expecting to read about. Thesis statements should be specific to the essay length.	The NBA draft is an unfair practice that makes the sport a popularity contest and makes other players have low self-esteem.
New York is the most populous US city.	Very rarely are thesis statements factual statements. They almost always reflect a judgment or present a main idea to the readers.	New York is the best city in the US for tourists, and everyone should visit.

A thesis statement expresses the main idea in an essay. The main idea can be expressed in different ways in different media. Search online for the music video for "Fight for Your Right (to Party)" by the Beastie Boys.

After watching the music video, identify the main idea for the song. How do you know? What examples or reasons are given?

STUDENT EXAMPLE

Maxx is asked to write a paper about a crime and why it is wrong. He chooses to write about gnome-napping, the act of stealing garden gnomes. He decides to write a listing thesis statement to help him focus on the main points of his paper.

The law should be taking the gnome-napping more seriously because people are committing a crime. Gnome-napping is stealing personal property, and it is illegal, morally wrong, and disrespectful.

YOUR TURN

Choose a specific city that you think is the best city. This can be a city you currently live in, visited once, or even one that you've never been to. After you've chosen the city, write a thesis statement. You may choose to write a listing thesis statement or not. Just be sure that you have a topic (the city) and a main idea or opinion (why it is the best city).

Introductions

The **introduction** is the first piece of your essay. In the introduction, you want to grab your reader's attention and make them want to read your essay further. The introduction also provides your reader with an idea of what your essay will be about. The introduction often is made up of three parts; however, that does not mean that you will have only three sentences in it.

1. **Start with an attention getter**. The beginning of your essay needs a way to get your reader's attention and "hook" them into reading more of your essay.

2. **Create a bridge with transition sentences**. These sentences support your attention getter and link it to your thesis statement. The most common bridge to make is to explain the importance of the topic. Why is this topic important to your audience? Who would this topic be important to? How might your topic affect your audience?

3. **End with your thesis statement**. The thesis statement states the purpose and main idea of the whole essay.

Ways to Start Your Introduction

- Provide some **interesting background** about the topic in the form of a general statement.
- Use a thought-provoking **quotation**.
- Ask a **question** about your topic.
- State a **surprising fact** or make a **puzzling statement**.
- Start with a **short story**.
- State a **common misconception**.
- Describe a **problem**.
- Give an **analogy** (saying something is like something else).
- Show how the topic is related to the **reader's experience**.

MEDIA EXAMPLE OF INTRODUCTION

Introductions aren't just a part of the essay. They can also be found in the media. Search online to find the theme song/introduction for the television show, *The Brady Bunch*.

What does this theme song tell you about the plot of the show and the characters?

STUDENT EXAMPLE

Maxx has been asked to write an essay about a specific crime. He has chosen the topic of gnome-napping, the act of stealing garden gnomes. He reviews each strategy and decides to write an example of each, just to give himself options for his paper.

STRATEGY	EXAMPLE
Provide some **interesting background** about the topic in the form of a general statement.	*Today's gnome owners become tomorrow's leaders.*
Use a thought-provoking **quotation**.	*"Gnomes are creatures to be loved, not feared!" —Dr. S. Rosner*
Ask a **question** about your topic.	*Why don't many people like gnomes?*
State a **surprising fact**.	*In 2004, Travelocity introduced "The Roaming Gnome," voiced by Harry Enfield.*
Start with a **short story**.	*Little Susie looked out her window, only to see her precious gnome, Willard, was being stolen....*
State a **common misconception**.	*People believe they learn bad habits from gnomes.*
Describe a **problem**.	*Everyone knows what a problem gnome-napping has become in our society.*
Give an **analogy** (saying something is like something else).	*Gnomes are just like children.*
Show how the topic is related to the **reader's experience**.	*Most people know how difficult it is to take care of garden gnomes.*

Now that Maxx has practiced attention getters, he decides to start writing his introduction. He has color coded the parts of the introduction. He writes the attention getter (or "hook") in orange, the bridge of transition sentences in blue. He adds his thesis statement from earlier at the end in black.

In 2004, the Gnome Liberation Front (GLF) was created. **This group of people believes that gnomes should be free, not prisoners of their owner's garden. That same year the GLF began gnome-napping—stealing gnomes and "freeing them" in the wilderness. The law is often unwilling to do anything about such crimes. In many cities the police state that stealing gnomes is not a serious enough offense and that they have larger crimes to deal with.** The law should be taking gnome-napping more seriously; people are committing a crime. Gnome-napping is stealing personal property, and it is illegal, morally wrong, and disrespectful.

YOUR TURN

Go back to the thesis statement you wrote about the best city. Now write an introduction for the city. Be sure to include an attention getter and the transition sentences. Finally, add your thesis statement at the end.

Topic Sentences

Topic sentences state the main idea of your body paragraphs. They typically occur at the beginning of each body paragraph. You may also think of them as mini thesis statements for each body paragraph. They tell the reader what the paragraph is about. A good topic sentence serves two purposes:

1. Naming the topic of the paragraph

2. Giving the focus or controlling idea of the paragraph

Tips for Writing Topic Sentences

- **Be clear and specific.** You want to make sure that your readers fully understand you, so you'll need to be as clear as you can. As with thesis statements, use specific language, avoiding vague words (such as *good, bad, unique,* and *interesting*).
- **Write an outline.** Look at your thesis statement. From there, write down what you'd like each body paragraph to be about. Polish each topic statement before writing the

body paragraphs. Make sure each of your topic sentences reflects your main idea or thesis statement.

- **Write a statement.** Your thesis statement shouldn't be a question, and neither should your topic sentences.
- **State your objective clearly.** As with your thesis statement, you want your topic sentence to have a specific purpose but not to announce it explicitly.
- **Revise if necessary.** After you write your paragraph, go back and make sure that your topic sentence really does encompass what you actually wrote in the paragraph.

MEDIA EXAMPLE OF TOPIC SENTENCES

Topic sentences organize thoughts within paragraphs by making a point and giving several reasons for it. Sometimes there can be parallel structures in the media. Search online for the music video called "Mmm Mmm Mmm Mmm" by the Crash Test Dummies.

In this music video, there are multiple stories provided as examples for the main idea. For each story, what is the topic sentence?

STUDENT EXAMPLE

Maxx needs to write his topic sentences. He starts by looking at his thesis statement again. He marks three items he wants to talk about based on what he wrote in his listing thesis. Then he uses those topics later when he writes topic sentences for each paragraph.

> Thesis: The law should be taking the gnome-napping more seriously because people are committing a crime. Gnome-napping is stealing personal property, and it is illegal, morally wrong, and disrespectful.
>
> Gnome-napping is stealing someone's personal property, and stealing is illegal.
>
> Even if a person disregards the law, there is still a moral issue involved.
>
> Because they are taking items that do not belong to them, the GLF is being highly disrespectful as well.

YOUR TURN

Reread the thesis statement you just wrote about the best city. Now write at least two topic sentences to support your thesis. Remember to use specific, descriptive words.

Body Paragraphs

The body or **body paragraphs** make up the majority of your essay. They support and develop the idea expressed in your thesis statement. They also provide examples and points of comparison that help to prove your main thesis or support your opinion. Each paragraph should be around five to seven sentences long. The number of body paragraphs you have in your essay depends on the topic's complexity, the length specified for the assignment, and your purpose for writing. Like the introduction, body paragraphs are typically made up of three parts; however, that does not mean that you will have only three sentences in each paragraph.

1. **Begin with a topic sentence**. When you're learning to write essays, it's best to begin each body paragraph with a topic sentence that states the main idea of each paragraph. You can think of these as mini thesis statements.

2. **Provide supporting details**. Supporting details are specific examples that allow your readers to understand the topic or argument better.

3. **End with a closing statement**. The closing statement sums up the idea of the paragraph, reminds readers of the topic, and connects each paragraph with the thesis statement.

Tips for Developing Body Paragraphs

Supporting details are used to prove or support the main argument, to illustrate, to give evidence, and to help your reader understand your main idea.

- **Play the reporter**. Supporting details often answer questions that a reporter would ask: Who, What, When, Why, Where, and How. These are known as the 5 Ws and 1 H (see also Chapter 3).
- **Plan the paragraphs out**. Before you start, make a list of the items and examples you'd like each paragraph to contain. Is there anything that you've forgotten to put in the paragraph? Are there any examples to prove your main ideas that you haven't used yet?
- **Arrange your items**. Ensure that your paragraphs are in a logical order. For instance, if you're writing an essay about a historical event, like the Battle of Waterloo, you probably want to arrange your paragraphs chronologically.
- **Double (and triple) check**. Read through your paragraphs again (or better yet, have a friend or family member read through them). See if you forgot anything that your readers might need to know. Be sure you fully described all of your examples.

Need a reminder about essay organization? See Chapter 3.

STUDENT EXAMPLE

Maxx now needs to write the body paragraphs for his essay about gnome-napping. First, he reviews the topic sentences he wrote for each paragraph. Then he writes the body paragraphs to give supporting details for each topic.

Thesis: The law should be taking the gnome-napping more seriously because people are committing a crime. Gnome-napping is stealing personal property, and it is illegal, morally wrong, and disrespectful.

Stealing is illegal. If a person were to go into the mall and steal a shirt, an alarm would be set off, and the cops would come and arrest the person. While gnomes are not in a store, they are still personal property. Stealing is stealing, no matter where it happens. Any act of theft should be treated as such, and the thief or thieves should be prosecuted.

It is morally wrong to take anyone's property, whether it is a gnome or a car. When you steal, you are taking something away from a person without his or her permission. We are all taught as children to follow "The Golden Rule"— "Treat others how you want to be treated." They would not want their items taken. We should all be kind to one another and not take things that are not our own.

The GLF is being incredibly disrespectful as well. They don't have respect for anyone's personal property or boundaries. If they did, they wouldn't be stealing. They also do not understand the legal and moral repercussions of stealing. They are also being disrespectful to the law.

YOUR TURN

Reread the topic sentences you just wrote. Develop your topic sentences into at least two body paragraphs, being sure to support your thesis. Remember to use specific examples and supporting details.

Transitions

When you write an essay, you always need to keep your audience in mind. They, unfortunately, cannot read your mind and connect your ideas; therefore, it is your job as the writer to join your ideas, sentences, and paragraphs together for your readers. We do this by providing **transitions**—individual words, groups of words, or even sentences that help tie your ideas together. To write the best essay you can, your paragraphs and sentences must flow smoothly and you must bridge any gaps readers might experience while they read your essay.

Examples of Transition Words and Phrases

These are not all of the possible transitions you could use; however, these may give you ideas when you are writing your essay and need help connecting the topics in your essay.

Words used to show **location**	above, outside, throughout, under, between, beyond, among, around
Words used to show **time**	while, first, after, during, yesterday, finally, next, then, afterward
Words used to show a **comparison**	likewise, also, while, similarly, in the same way
Words used to show a **contrast**	but, however, yet, still, although, otherwise, on the other hand
Words used to **emphasize a point**	again, in fact, especially, to emphasize, for this reason
Words used to **summarize/conclude**	finally, therefore, as a result, to sum up, all in all, because
Words used to **add information**	again, another, in addition, for example, additionally, as well

Tips for Writing Transitions

- **Get help from a friend**. Have a friend or family member read your paragraph to see if there are any gaps between ideas, sentences, or paragraphs.

- **Cut apart the sentences**. Print out your paper, then physically cut your paragraphs apart sentence by sentence. Then, as if the sentences were a puzzle, try to see what the relationships are between the sentences. Note that not every sentence will require a specific transition word or phrase, but check to see if any connection isn't as clear as it could be.

- **Be clear**. In your mind, the connections between your body paragraphs are clear. However, for a reader who is new to the information, the essay may read as choppy, and the connections might be less obvious. You want the transitions that you choose to be as clear and concise as possible to help your readers better understand the information.

- **Go with your gut**. Your transitions shouldn't feel forced. If you can think of only one transition word, it is probably the right one to use; don't worry about finding a fancier alternative.

STUDENT EXAMPLE

Maxx now needs to look at the body paragraphs he's written and figure out how to better link together his thoughts. He looks at how his paragraphs and ideas can be tied together and then writes down transition words, phrases, and sentences to help connect them. He marks each of these transitions in orange.

In 2004, the Gnome Liberation Front (GLF) was created. This group of people believes that gnomes should be free, not prisoners of their owner's garden. The GLF began gnome-napping—the act of stealing gnomes and "freeing them" in the wilderness; *however*, the law was often unwilling to do anything. The police stated that stealing gnomes was not a serious enough offense to stop them. In many cities they have larger crimes to deal with. This is not acceptable. The law should be taking the gnome-napping more seriously because people are committing a crime. Gnome-napping is stealing personal property, and it is illegal, morally wrong, and disrespectful.

First, gnome-napping is stealing someone's personal property, and stealing is illegal. *For example,* if a person were to go into the mall and steal a shirt, an alarm would be set off, and the police would come and arrest the person. While gnomes are not in a store, they are still personal property. Stealing is stealing, no matter where it

happens. *Consequently,* any act of theft should be treated as such, and the thief or thieves should be prosecuted.

Even if a person disregards the law and doesn't care about what is legal or illegal, there is still a moral issue involved. It is morally wrong to take anyone's property, whether it is a gnome or a car. When you steal, you are taking something away from a person without his/her permission. *Furthermore,* we are all taught as children to follow "The Golden Rule"—"Treat others how you want to be treated." They would not want their items taken. We should all be kind to one another and not take things that are not our own.

Because they are taking items that do not belong to them, the GLF is being incredibly disrespectful as well. They don't have respect for anyone's personal property or boundaries. If they did, they wouldn't be stealing. *Additionally,* they also do not understand the legal and moral repercussions of stealing. *Therefore,* they are also being disrespectful to the law.

YOUR TURN

Read the body paragraphs you've just written about the best city. Where can you add in transitions between ideas, sentences, and paragraphs? Revise your essay, specifically adding transitions to help your reader fully understand the connections between your ideas.

Conclusions

The end of your essay will be a paragraph called the **conclusion**. In your conclusion, you can recap your ideas and remind readers of your thesis. Generally, conclusions do not offer any new information; however, they may include a **call to action**. A call to action asks your readers to do something after reading your essay. For example, a political ad might urge viewers to contact their senator about a certain problem. In your conclusion, you want to leave a positive impression on your reader and keep them thinking about your topic and ideas or argument after they've finished reading your essay.

Tips for Writing a Conclusion

- **Bring it home**. Remember, these are the last words your reader will see. Make sure you are focused and strong.
- **Avoid being a copycat**. Don't merely copy and paste your thesis into the conclusion. While you'll want to remind readers of your thesis, try wording it differently for the conclusion.
- **Steer clear of new information**. This is not the place to add a new source, example, or idea. Be sure any new information you think of while writing the conclusion gets added to an appropriate place in the body paragraphs instead.
- **Focus on the big picture**. Don't just restate one example that you presented in your essay. You want to convey the main argument you have made throughout the essay.
- **Convince your readers to do something**. You can add a call to action in the conclusion if you want to persuade your readers to do something after they read your main points. Remember that this is your "sales pitch" to your readers.

MEDIA EXAMPLE OF CONCLUSIONS

Just as in essays, a conclusion drawn in the media can recap the information presented earlier, sum up information, or even ask the reader or viewer to do something. Search online for a political campaign television advertisement. Based on the commercial you just viewed, what is the conclusion asking the viewers to do?

STUDENT EXAMPLE

Maxx now has to end his essay with a conclusion that recaps his main points.

The GLF believes that they are justified in stealing because they are "liberating" the gnomes. They are not. They are simply glorifying what they are really doing: stealing. Stealing is always wrong. Stealing is illegal, immoral, and disrespectful. The police should take a more active role in gnome-napping and hold these individuals like members of the GLF accountable for their actions.

YOUR TURN

Go back and reread the essay that you've written thus far. Now write your conclusion, focusing on recapping the main ideas.

Titles

A **title** is what you choose to name your essay. When writing a title, you want to grab your reader's attention. The title is the first impression your reader has of your paper, so you want to make sure that it is memorable. Your title should always be something specific to your paper, and it should be unique. For example, if you were writing a paper about exercise, you would not simply title the essay "Exercise." You want to have a specific, catchy title that tells your readers a little more about your topic.

When you write your title, the general rule for capitalization is to capitalize every word, except articles (*a*, *an*, *the*), coordinating conjunctions (*for*, *and*, *nor*, *but*, *or*, *yet*, *so*), and prepositions fewer than five letters (*on*, *at*, *to*, *from*, *by*, etc.).

INCORRECT	CORRECT
Cultural Ideology Across The Nation	Cultural Ideology Across the Nation
Technology Is Important For Everyone And So Is Learning About It	Technology Is Important for Everyone and so Is Learning about It
EXCHANGING YOUR BAD HABITS FOR BETTER ONES	Exchanging Your Bad Habits for Better Ones

Tips for Writing a Catchy Title

- **Write your essay first**. Writing a title for a paper you haven't written yet is difficult. Coming up with a title first may help shape the tone of your paper, but it may also limit your writing. You may want to wait until you are finished writing your paper to come up with a title.
- **Think about what your essay is about**. Your thesis should be stated (or at least hinted at) in the title. You also need a title that mirrors your purpose and tone in the essay. For example, if you are writing a serious essay, you would not have a humorous title.
- **Put yourself in your audience's shoes**. If you were the audience, what would you want out of a title? Humor? Seriousness? Simplicity?
- **Look through your essay for key phrases or quotes**. Perhaps there is a key phrase that you like or that is crucial to the main point of the essay that you could use. If you are using sources, you may also want to look at the quotes you use to see if there are any words or phrases that you could use in your title.

- **Keep it short and simple**. Try to avoid long titles and scientific language.
- **Be creative**. Can you use any puns, metaphors, or similes in your title? Are there any pieces of media (songs, television shows, and so on) that you can imitate to create a title?

STUDENT EXAMPLE

Maxx has now finished his essay draft, and he starts brainstorming ideas for titles. Here are the titles he came up with.

Title Idea #1: Gnome Stealing in America: Why It's Bad and What Should Be Done
Title Idea #2: Just Say "GNO" to Liberating Gnomes
Title Idea #3: Stealing Gnomes Is Bad
Title Idea #4: Gnomes Have Rights Too!

Which title do you think he should use? Why?

YOUR TURN

Brainstorm four possible titles for the essay you've been writing in this chapter. Then, choose one title and explain why you've chosen that particular title. Be sure to pay attention to the capitalization rules of titles.

Title Idea #1: _____

Title Idea #2: _____

Title Idea #3: _____

Title Idea #4: _____

Which title will you choose? Why?

_____

_____

_____

Assessing Your Knowledge

CHAPTER TARGETS	REMINDER	HOW WELL DID YOU UNDERSTAND THIS MATERIAL?	PAGE(S)
Learn about and identify the parts of the essay	An essay is made up of an introduction, body, and conclusion. Specifically, however, there are seven main parts of the essay: ▪ Thesis Statements ▪ Introductions ▪ Topic Sentences ▪ Body Paragraphs ▪ Transitions ▪ Conclusions ▪ Titles	☐ I've Got It! ☐ Almost There ☐ Need More Practice	pp. 69–70
Understand, identify, and practice writing introductions, conclusions, and titles	**Introductions** come at the beginning of the essay and include an attention getter, transition sentences, and a thesis statement. **Conclusions** appear at the end of essays and recap the main ideas of the essay. **Titles** are the names that writers choose to give their essays.	☐ I've Got It! ☐ Almost There ☐ Need More Practice	pp. 73–75, 81–83
Understand, identify, and practice writing thesis statements and topic sentences	A **thesis statement** is the main idea of the essay. There are two types of thesis statements: ▪ Argumentative ▪ Analytical A **topic sentence** is a mini thesis statement that occurs at the beginning of each body paragraph. These topic sentences tell the reader what the paragraph is about.	☐ I've Got It! ☐ Almost There ☐ Need More Practice	pp. 70–73, 75–76
Understand, identify, practice writing, and develop body paragraphs and supporting details	**Body paragraphs** support the main idea or thesis statement. They contain **supporting details** to provide specific examples for the reader to fully understand the topic at hand.	☐ I've Got It! ☐ Almost There ☐ Need More Practice	pp. 76–78

| Understand, identify, and practice writing transitions | **Transitions** are the glue that holds your ideas and paragraphs together. Transitions can be words, phrases, or sentences that connect your sentences and/or paragraphs. | ☐ I've Got It!
 ☐ Almost There
 ☐ Need More Practice | pp. 78–80 |

Deepening Your Understanding

If you would like to go beyond the material in this chapter, explore additional connections, and get more practice, check out these related topics:

- **Adjectives and Adverbs**: Having strong descriptive words is important when you write your thesis statement, as well as your topic sentences. These descriptive words help your readers fully understand your concepts and ideas.

- **Parallelism**: If you write a listing thesis statement, be sure that the sentence is parallel. If it is not, your sentence might be unclear to your readers.

- **Sentence Structure**: When you write your thesis statements and topic sentences, understand the overall structure of the sentence. This can help you write more interesting, clearer sentences.

- **Vocabulary**: In order to explain your main ideas and develop them with specific examples, make sure you choose the best words. Developing your vocabulary can help you choose the best words for what you want to write.

Parallels Between Reading and Writing Skills

"Writers have monumental responsibilities in the execution of their art, but readers also have great responsibilities. They have to make something valuable from their reading."

—Ben Okri

FACT OR FICTION?
As a reader and a writer, I have a lot of duties and things to pay attention to.

FACT.
As a reader and a writer, just as with any job, there are skills that you need to polish and practice. These skills will help you become better at both reading and writing.

Discovering Key Points

- Understand why reading and writing skills are important, as well as the links between them
- Identify the different reading and writing skills
- Identify the types of questions to ask yourself to use the different reading and writing skills
- Demonstrate an understanding of all reading and writing skills and apply them to a text

Thus far, you have learned about various reading skills and writing skills separately; however, many of these skills are intertwined. Once you understand the links between them, they can help you become a stronger writer and reader.

You learned in Chapter 2 that reading is an activity in thinking. Reading helps you increase prior knowledge, vocabulary development, the organization and structure of an essay, precise word choice, and descriptions. Frequent readers also know how to make inferences and can recognize clear, detailed descriptions. You can take the skills you learn while reading and then apply them to writing. Good writers can anticipate the reader's needs.

Here are six reading and writing skills:

- Identifying Main Ideas
- Finding Supporting Details
- Recognizing Essay Organization
- Detecting Audience and Purpose
- Recognizing Tone
- Making Inferences

You should recognize all of these skills, as they were covered briefly in previous chapters. This chapter will help you begin to put these skills together and connect the pieces of the essay you're reading. As a reader, these skills allow you to learn to "read between the lines."

Reading and writing skills allow you to become a closer reader, as well as a more skilled writer. As you read, you begin to learn the most effective ways to build sentences, build your vocabulary, develop an argument, and move or persuade an audience.

Identifying Main Ideas

Need a refresher about thesis statements? See Chapter 4.

In Chapters 2 and 4, you learned about main ideas (also known as the argument or thesis statement). Main ideas occur in our daily lives as well. Imagine you went to see a midnight showing of *Avengers: Infinity War*, an action/superhero film based on a Marvel comic book. The next day, your friend asks you how it was and what it was about. You say something about what the movie was about and give a short summary of the story.

What you've just done is provide the **main idea** of the film for your friend. The main idea of an essay is the topic and the point or argument the writer is trying to make. The main idea is the most important part of the essay.

A main idea may be either **stated** directly or **implied**. If the main idea is stated directly, that means you can easily point to a statement or idea in the essay that sums up the writer's main idea. An implied main idea is not directly stated in the essay; it is merely hinted at. With an implied main idea, you will need to do some detective work as a reader to identify what the main idea is and put it into your own words.

How to Find the Main Idea in an Essay or Your Own Writing

1. Find the topic.
    - Look for ideas or key words or phrases that are repeated.
    - Discover the common thread or bond that the details share.

2. Locate the argument.
    - What is the overall message or point the writer is trying to make?

3. In a sentence or two, summarize the essay in your own words.

4. Decide whether the main idea is stated or implied.

5. If the main idea is stated, highlight or write it down word for word, just as it is stated in the essay.

6. If the main idea is implied, look at the summary you've written in Step 3.
    - Is there anything you want to rephrase or revise?

Main Idea: Comparing Reading to Writing

READING	WRITING
To find the main idea, look for repeating key words or an overall topic.	Make sure all your body paragraphs and examples support your argument or are instances of your main idea.
Often, you will find the main idea in the introduction.	You may consider putting a key word in your title to hint toward your main idea.

Main Idea: Moving from Reading to Writing

MEDIA EXAMPLE OF MAIN IDEA

Finding the main idea isn't just a reading and writing skill. It's also an important skill to have when you are watching television, listening to the radio, or watching video clips on the Internet. Find a video clip on any topic relating to the news or public affairs. Write a short paragraph expressing in your own words the main idea.

STUDENT EXAMPLE

Patricia has been given an article excerpt from her instructor. After reading the excerpt, she has to answer two questions about the main idea.

"When Social Media Is Really Problematic for Adolescents," by Perri Klass, MD

The New York Times, June 3, 2019

A study, just published in JAMA Psychiatry, showed a suicide bump among 10- to 19-year-olds (both boys and girls, but a larger increase in girls) at the time of the release of the Netflix series "13 Reasons Why"; the study shows association, not causation, but raises the question of "media contagion"—that is, the possibility that the show and the intense discussion of it on social media may have led to some imitative behavior, and cites "the need for safer and more thoughtful portrayal of suicide in the media." Dr. Michael Rich, an associate professor of pediatrics at Harvard Medical School and the director of the Center on Media and Child Health at Boston Children's Hospital, cautioned against the impulse to look for binary answers to complex problems by drawing too-simple connections between social media and suicide, or video games and violence. "What we need to do is look at the whole picture around these young people; we need to look at how kids and how we all are using social media," he said.

> **QUESTIONS**

1. Just from reading this paragraph, what is the main idea the author is trying to convey?
   The main point is that social media and television shows may have an impact on teenagers and suicide rates; therefore, we need to examine how teens use social media accounts.

2. Is the main idea stated or implied? How do you know?
   The main idea is stated. The title of the essay is the main point. The entire paragraph is stating facts and interviews regarding the theme of teens, suicide, and social media.

> **YOUR TURN**

"Commercializing Childhood: The Corporate Takeover of Kids' Lives," by Susan Linn

Multinational Monitor, July/August 2008

Marketing in schools is terribly troubling. It carries more weight than other kinds of marketing because even if kids don't like school they know that it's supposed to be good for them. Everything marketed in a school implicitly carries that school's endorsement. That's one reason why companies love to market in schools. Another reason is that they get what's known in the advertising industry as "a captive audience." Kids in school can't escape the marketing they're subjected to in class or in the halls. I wish we could be sure that Channel One [a television channel aired in schools that shows two minutes of ads for every 10 minutes of content] was on the decline, but it actually seems to be reviving. Last year, it was bought ... by a tween/teen marketing company called Alloy and it recently received an infusion from NBC, which is going to be producing content for it. These days marketing in schools takes lots of other forms as well, from Coke and Pepsi's vending machines, to companies sponsoring athletic teams, to incentive programs like the Pizza Hut Bookit Program, fundraising schemes like the General Mills Boxtops for Education Program, to naming rights for gymnasiums, to corporate-sponsored teaching materials from companies like McDonald's, Revlon and Exxon, to name just a few. Ronald McDonald goes into schools to teach reading, health and values.

QUESTIONS

1. What is the main idea the author is trying to convey in this paragraph?

2. Is the main idea stated or implied? How do you know?

WRITING TOPIC

1. Look at the picture below. Write a paragraph about what seems to you to be the main idea of the picture.

Finding Supporting Details

You first learned about supporting details and body paragraphs back in Chapter 4. Supporting details don't occur only in essays; they are in our everyday lives too. Imagine you have gone to a concert. The next day, your friend asks you how it was. You recount the previous night to your friend—the appearance of the performer(s), the music that was played, the atmosphere, how the crowd responded at various times, and so on.

Want to practice finding supporting details some more? See Chapter 4.

What you've done here is explain to your friend the **supporting details** of the evening. Supporting details are the specific examples that back up and strengthen the main idea, also known as the thesis. When speaking to your friend, your thesis might be that the concert was mind-blowing—the best concert you had ever attended. The supporting details would be the specifics of the evening. Supporting details are used to provide examples, to prove or support the main argument, to give evidence, to illustrate, and to make sure that all the ideas are understood. Supporting details are important because they help the reader better understand the main idea. When you write your supporting details, you will have to think about your reader's needs. The amount of supporting detail given will depend on how difficult the main idea is to explain and how familiar the audience is with the subject. The writer should answer any questions the reader has about the subject area, such as Who, What, When, Where, Why, or How. Not all of these questions will be applicable, but be sure to fully answer each one when you write supporting details for your own essays.

How to Find Supporting Details in an Essay or Your Own Writing: Ask Yourself the 5 W and 1 H Questions

1. **Who**—Ask what person/which people were involved
   - Who is involved/Who is it about?

2. **What**—Ask for information about the subject
   - What happened?

3. **When**—Ask about time
   - When did it take place?

4. **Where**—Ask about a place or position
   - Where did it take place?

5. **Why**—Ask for the reason something occurred
   - Why did it happen?

6. **How**—Ask about the manner or the degree to which something occurred
   - How did it happen?

Supporting Details: Comparing Reading to Writing

READING	WRITING
Supporting details support the author's main idea or argument and are specific, clear, and detailed.	Be sure to revise your essay multiple times to make sure you are on topic and all your supporting details are clear and specific.
In order to find supporting details while reading, try summarizing, outlining, or annotating the essay.	Before you write, you may want to write an outline to help plan what your supporting details will be.

Supporting Details: Moving from Reading to Writing

MEDIA EXAMPLE OF SUPPORTING DETAILS

Supporting details aren't important only in texts. They can also be found in the media. As an example, find online the music video for the song "Red Solo Cup" by Toby Keith.

What are some of the supporting details that Toby Keith provides in talking about why the red Solo cup is so great? Remember to refer back to the 5 W and 1 H questions.

STUDENT EXAMPLE

Patricia rereads the article excerpt from her instructor. After reading the excerpt, she has to answer two questions about supporting details. She goes back to review and reread "When Social Media Is Really Problematic for Adolescents" on page 90.

QUESTIONS

1. Answer the 5 W and 1 H questions. Be sure to support your answers with specific evidence from the paragraph.

   a. Who is involved/Who is the piece about?
   This essay is about 10–19-year-olds.

   b. What has been happening?
   There has been an increase in suicide rates.

   c. When did it take place? Is the same sort of thing still happening?
   This is pretty recent since the article was written in 2019.

   d. Where has it been happening?
   I assume it's happening in the United States since the article was written in the New York Times, and I know that JAMA stands for the Journal of the American Medical Association.

   e. Why has it been happening?
   The media are showing suicide more regularly.

   f. How did it happen?
   Audience members viewed shows and other pieces of media that showed suicide or even glorified it.

YOUR TURN

Review and reread the practice essay "Commercializing Childhood" on pages 90–91.

1. Answer the 5 *W* and 1 *H* questions. Be sure to support your answers with specific evidence from the paragraph.
   a. Who is involved/Who is the piece about?
   b. What has been happening?
   c. When did it take place? Is the same sort of thing still happening?
   d. Where has it been happening?
   e. Why has it been happening?
   f. How did it happen?

WRITING TOPIC

1. Write an essay reviewing your favorite restaurant. Remember to provide lots of clear, specific supporting details.

Recognizing Essay Organization

Organizing your essay is a very important skill—one you first read about in Chapter 3. In that chapter we touched on five types of essay organization: **specific to general**, **general to specific**, **chronological**, **spatial**, and by **importance**.

Types of Essay Organization

TYPE	DEFINITION	USE WITH ESSAYS THAT
Specific to General	Begins with details and ends more broadly	• build anticipation • present an argument slowly
General to Specific	Begins with general statement, then each paragraph gives specific details and examples	• build readers' attention • explain a topic unfamiliar to readers
Chronological	Organizes by time	• explain historical or biographical events • narrate a story • describe and analyze a process
Spatial	Organizes by order of appearance	• are about traveling • describe a place
Importance	Organizes by order of importance	• present arguments • are concerned with division/classification • are concerned with comparison/contrast • are definitions • are illustrations

How to Find the Essay Organization in an Essay or Your Own Writing

1. Look for key words being used.

- If words like "in 1988," "later," or any references to time are being used, the essay may be (but is not necessarily) organized chronologically.
- If words referring to physical position, such as "left" or "north," are used, then the essay may be organized spatially.
- If words like "most importantly," "second," or any references to importance are being used, the essay may be organized by importance.

2. Look at the topic sentences of each body paragraph.
   - Are the topic sentences broader at the beginning and more detailed at the end? If so, the essay may be organized from general to specific.
   - Are the topic sentences more detailed at the beginning and broader at the end? If so, the essay may be organized from specific to general.

Essay Organization: Comparing Reading to Writing

READING	WRITING
The way in which the essay is organized can tell you which ideas are the most important to the writer.	You should choose your essay organization before you start writing your paper. No matter which way you choose, a solid organization structure helps shape your ideas.
Essay organization includes transitions as cues to help guide the reader through the essay smoothly.	Transitions help your readers understand and connect your ideas.

Essay Organization: Moving from Reading to Writing

MEDIA EXAMPLE OF ESSAY ORGANIZATION

Essay organization isn't just a reading and writing skill used in texts. It can also be found in the media. Find online the music video for the song "Pimpin' All Over the World" by Ludacris.

Based on the five types of essay organization, how do you think this song is organized? Why did you choose that type?

STUDENT EXAMPLE

Patricia rereads the article excerpt from her instructor, found on page 90. After reading the excerpt, she has to answer two questions about essay organization.

QUESTIONS

1. How is the paragraph organized?
   The paragraph is organized by importance.

2. How do you know? Give specific examples from the paragraph.

I know this because the author is presenting arguments. The author begins by explaining one of the problems at hand regarding social media and teens, and then follows up with examples via interviewing an expert.

YOUR TURN

Review and reread "Commercializing Childhood" on pages 90–91.

QUESTIONS

1. How is the paragraph organized?

2. How do you know? Give specific examples from the paragraph to prove your answer for question #1.

WRITING TOPIC

1. In an essay, practice one of the types of essay organization listed on page 94, using a topic of your choice.

Detecting Audience and Purpose

Want more information and examples of audience and purpose in your own writing? See Chapter 3.

Imagine you are watching *African Cats*. Your friend asks if this film would be appropriate for his children to watch. In order to answer this, you need to think about the film's plot, violence level, etc. After you consider all of these factors, you can answer your friend. What you've just told your friend was an assessment of the **audience** and **purpose** of the documentary. For written work, the audience is the group of readers the piece is written for. As a writer, you should identify your audience—and understand that a piece of writing may appeal to more than one audience. Your audience may be your classmates, your instructor, or another group of people, as decided by you or by the instructions you are given. You might use a different tone or provide more or less background information, depending on the audience.

Want to know more about tone? See Chapter 2.

The purpose is the reason you are writing the essay. Recall that there are three main purposes a writer can have: to entertain, to inform, and to persuade. When you write your essays, focus on your purpose before you begin writing; your purpose can help you determine what mode of writing to use, how to organize your writing, how to incorporate your sources, and how formal or informal your style should be.

How to Find the Audience and Purpose in an Essay

1. In what publication has the essay appeared?
   - What does that tell you about the audience? (For example, the average audience for *Forbes* is very different from the audience for *Parents*.)

2. In what part of the world has the essay been published? (An essay published in *The Times* of London will be aimed at a different audience than an essay published in *The New York Times*.)

3. What is the subject area?
   - Is the subject area very specific?
   - Does the writer give a lot of background information (as if for an audience that was not already "experts" in the subject)?

4. What type of language, vocabulary, and style does the writer use?
   - Is the language used formal or informal?
   - Does the writer use slang or profanity?
   - Does the writer use jargon, vocabulary specific to an occupation or collection of people?

5. Does the essay include a great many facts?
   - If yes, you might ask yourself whether the primary purpose is to inform or to persuade.

6. Does the essay tell a story or include humorous elements?
   - If yes, the purpose of the essay might be to entertain.

7. Does the essay try to get you to do something?
   - If yes, the purpose of the essay might be to persuade.

Audience and Purpose: Comparing Reading to Writing

READING	WRITING
Look at where the source was published for a hint about the audience.	You must know who your audience is before you begin to write. What do they already know about the subject? What do they not know?
Look to see what mode(s) the essay is using. For example, is the essay arguing? If so, the essay's purpose is to persuade.	Know your purpose before you sit down to write. That way, you can write the best first draft.

Audience and Purpose: Moving from Reading to Writing

MEDIA EXAMPLE OF AUDIENCE AND PURPOSE

Audience and purpose aren't just reading and writing skills used in texts. They can also be found in the media. Find a clip online from the television show *So You Think You Can Dance?*

Based on the short clip you just watched, who do you think is the audience for this show? What is the purpose of the show? How do you know?

Patricia rereads the article excerpt from her instructor, found on page 90. After reading the excerpt, she has to answer five questions about audience and purpose.

1. Where was the essay published?
   The New York Times

2. What does that tell you about the audience?
   I know the name of this newspaper. It is very famous. I know that many people read this newspaper as well, so the audience is varied. They include adults who care about the news from a well-known, trusted source.

3. What is the subject area?
   Social media, suicide, and teens

4. What type of language, vocabulary, and style does the writer use?
   She uses very formal language. She and her interviewee don't use any jargon.

5. Is the paragraph's purpose to inform, to entertain, or to persuade?
   I believe it's to inform the audience, but also to persuade them of the dangers of social media regarding teens.

To review and reread "Commercializing Childhood" again, see pages 90–91.

1. Where was the essay published?

2. What does that tell you about the audience?

3. What is the subject area?

4. What type of language, vocabulary, and style does the writer use?

5. Is the paragraph's purpose to inform, to entertain, or to persuade?

1. Think about the last movie you saw. Now write an essay, answering the following questions. Be sure to give specific details:
   a. Who is the intended audience of the film? How do you know?
   b. What is /are the intended purpose(s) of the film? How do you know?

Recognizing Tone

While reading Chapter 2, you were introduced to the topic of tone. Questions of tone arise continually in our daily lives just as much as they do in our writing. Imagine you want to end your long-distance relationship with your boyfriend or girlfriend by email. You must decide on the way you want to "break it" to him or her. Do you want to let him or her down easy and still be friends? Do you want to tell him or her how angry you are?

How you choose to write your email to your soon-to-be ex-boyfriend or -girlfriend will impact your **tone**. Tone is the writer's attitude or feelings toward a subject. In writing, the specific language you choose will change your tone in writing. You don't write the same way in an academic essay as you do in a text to your friend. Likewise, you wouldn't speak the same way to your friends as you do to your grandparents. Word choice, subject matter, and use of slang or profanities all can help you figure out the tone of the essay.

ⓘ Hungry for more examples of tone in the media? See Chapter 2.

Examples of Words That Can Be Used to Describe a Writer's Tone

Note: These are not the only words to describe a writer's tone. Feel free to look in the thesaurus for similar words as well. Also note that a writer can have more than one tone in his or her essay.

angry	confused	fearful	nostalgic	skeptical
anxious	demanding	happy	panicked	sympathetic
approving	depressed	harsh	questioning	uncertain
arrogant	detached	humorous	sarcastic	upset
boring	direct	impartial	serious	urgent
concerned	dramatic	indifferent	shocking	
confident	excited	joking	silly	

EXAMPLES

TONE	SENTENCE
Questioning	Were you at the party?
Excited, Dramatic	You were at the party!
Shocked, Upset	Why were *you* at the party?
Approving	This party was really great.
Arrogant	Once I arrived, the party could finally start.

How to Find the Tone in an Essay or Your Own Writing

1. Look at the word choice.
   - Many times, words have positive or negative associations. Pay attention to these associations, as they will hint at the writer's true feelings toward the subject.

2. Look at the descriptions and examples the writer provides.
   - Is the writer being humorous? Serious? Sarcastic?
   - Is the writer trying to persuade the reader?

3. Look beyond the words on the page.
   - What information isn't included in the essay? Was there anything that the writer chose not to include?

4. Think about how the reader(s) might feel.
   - How do you, as a reader of the essay, feel? How you feel may point to the writer's tone. For example, if, as a reader, you feel angry or sad, chances are good that the author is using a similar tone.

Tone: Comparing Reading to Writing

READING	WRITING
Tone is determined by keywords and phrases.	Tone is determined by your word choice and what type of essay you are writing.
Often, the reader must infer (or make an educated guess) what the author's feelings are toward the subject.	As a writer, your job is to make it clear to your readers your feelings about the topic.

Tone: Moving from Reading to Writing

MEDIA EXAMPLE OF TONE

Tone is just as important in the media as anywhere else. Search online for the ASPCA commercial in which Sarah McLachlan appears and watch the commercial.

What is the tone of the commercial? How do you know? Is it an effective tone?

STUDENT EXAMPLE

Patricia rereads the article excerpt from her instructor, found on page 90. After reading the excerpt, she has to answer two questions about tone.

QUESTIONS

1. What tone is the author using in this paragraph?
   She is serious and concerned about social media, teens, and suicide rates. She seems to view social media usage by teens as negative.

2. What are some specific examples from the paragraph that support your answer for question #1? *She uses the word "contagion," which reminds me of a horrible illness. She also interviews someone to prove her argument that social media usage by teens is problematic.*

YOUR TURN

To review and reread "Commercializing Childhood" again, see pages 90–91.

QUESTIONS

1. What tone is the author using in this paragraph?

2. What are some specific examples from the paragraph that support your answer for question #1?

WRITING TOPIC

1. Write a paragraph using a formal tone. Now rewrite the same paragraph using an informal tone.

Making Inferences

When you read Chapter 2, you received an introduction to inferences and why they are important when you read essays. We make inferences every day, often without realizing it. Imagine your sister visits you. She is normally quite loud and happy; however, today, she is unnaturally quiet, keeping to herself. She won't even make eye contact. She is just sitting on the couch, staring at the floor. "Is everything okay?" you ask.

When you ask that question, you are making **inferences** about your sister and how she is feeling. An inference is a hypothesis or a realistic guess. An inference from a reading is a guess about something that the essay doesn't tell you. These presumptions must be based on the information you're given in the reading, however, and they must be well reasoned and logical. Inferences are based on your own personal knowledge and experiences, as well as on clues given to us in the text. For example, a woman is walking with an umbrella in her hand. You know from personal experience that umbrellas are used to shield one from the rain and sun. Therefore, you can infer that she is bringing the umbrella because she is preparing for the weather to be rainy or sunny today.

> Inferences go hand in hand with errors in thought or reasoning. Want more info? See Chapter 2.

How to Find Inferences in an Essay or Your Own Writing

1. Look for the author's tone.
   - Just as you need to look for word choice and key words in tone, you'll need to do the same here.

– Overall, is the author positive or negative toward the subject?

– Does the author seem to have taken a serious or humorous tone with the subject?

2. Read sections of the essay at a time.
   - Take groups of three to five paragraphs.
   - Ask yourself after each group if it reminds you of any scenario you've encountered.
   - Predict what will happen next.

3. As you read further, check your predictions, and keep making new predictions.
   - If your predictions are right, that means you are making connections.
   - If your predictions are not right, go back to figure out why you were wrong.

Inferences: Comparing Reading to Writing

READING	WRITING
We make inferences because the essay doesn't always tell us all of the information.	We write logical conclusions about the information we've provided.
We create meaning when we infer within the text. When we make these guesses, we are connecting with the essay, and we are drawing conclusions—both important skills to exercise.	When you are writing a research paper, you will want to fully explain the sources you use. This helps your readers make better (and clearer) inferences.

Inferences: Moving from Reading to Writing

MEDIA EXAMPLE OF INFERENCES

Inferences aren't just reading and writing skills used in texts. Find online the music video for "Bad Blood," a song performed by Taylor Swift, featuring Kendrick Lamar.

Based on the music video you just viewed, what inferences can you make about how Taylor Swift feels about her subject area?

STUDENT EXAMPLE

Patricia rereads the article excerpt from her instructor, found on page 90. After reading the excerpt, she has to answer two questions about inferences.

QUESTIONS

1. What do you predict will come next in this essay?
   I think the author will give more statistics and facts about why the suicide rates have increased and include examples from 13 Reasons Why as well.

2. Why do you believe this? Provide specific examples from the paragraph to support your point.
   I believe this because the author is writing about a published study and has

already included one interview in the essay. Because studies often include data and other forms of evidence to prove the argument being made, I think she'll start discussing other facts. I also think she will discuss the TV show more because she brings up the Netflix show only by name. I think that the author will need to explain why this show in particular is causing this issue.

YOUR TURN

To review and reread "Commercializing Childhood" again, see pages 90–91.

QUESTIONS

1. What do you predict will come next in this essay?
2. Why do you believe this? Provide specific examples from the paragraph to support your point.

WRITING TOPIC

1. Look at the picture below. In an essay, make inferences as to who the man is and what you "know" about him, based solely on the picture. Think about age, occupation, religious beliefs, hobbies, likes, dislikes, and so on. Be sure to back up any inferences with proof from the picture.

Assessing Your Knowledge

KEY POINTS	REMINDER	HOW WELL DID YOU UNDERSTAND THIS MATERIAL?	PAGE(S)
Understand why reading and writing skills are important, as well as the links between them	Reading and writing skills allow you to become a closer reader, as well as a more skilled writer. Developing your reading skills allows you to improve your writing skills.	☐ I've Got It! ☐ Almost There ☐ Need More Practice	pp. 87–103

Identify the different reading and writing skills	Here are six reading and writing skills, which you can find both in readings and media: • **Main Ideas** • **Supporting Details** • **Essay Organization** • **Audience & Purpose** • **Tone** • **Inferences**	☐ I've Got It! ☐ Almost There ☐ Need More Practice	pp. 88–103
Identify the types of questions to ask yourself to use the different reading and writing skills	Each reading and writing skill has specific questions to ask yourself when you are reading a text. These questions will help you figure out how to apply this skill.	☐ I've Got It! ☐ Almost There ☐ Need More Practice	pp. 88–103
Demonstrate an understanding of all reading and writing skills and apply them to a text	When you train to run a marathon, you must exercise your muscles and your body. When you learn to become a better writer and reader, you must exercise the six skills from this chapter and learn to apply them to the essays you read, as well as the essays you write. In this chapter, each skill provided media examples for you to apply the skills.	☐ I've Got It! ☐ Almost There ☐ Need More Practice	pp. 88–103

Deepening Your Understanding

If you would like to go beyond the material in this chapter, explore additional connections, and get more practice, check out these related topics:

⊙ **Using Exact Language**: Looking at the language and word choice in an essay can give you a hint about both the purpose and tone of the essay. It also allows you to make inferences.

⊙ **Parts of the Essay**: When you understand what an essay looks like and what the parts of the essay are, it makes it easier to spot the main idea, organization, and purpose of the essay.

⊙ **Topic Sentences**: The topic sentences in an essay will give you clues as to what the supporting details will be in that particular paragraph. Knowing where topic sentences are and what their function is will help you even further.

⊙ **The Research Process**: The function of a research paper is to make use of facts and opinions to further help the writer's main argument. Being able to distinguish facts from opinion is crucial in the interweaving of sources and opinion.

6

What Are Modes of Writing?

"You can take for granted that people know more or less what a street, a shop, a beach, a sky, an oak tree look like. Tell them what makes this one different."

—Neil Gaiman

FACT OR FICTION?
I will write papers with only one mode of writing in them.

FICTION.
The modes of writing work together. Research papers, for example, make use of illustration, argumentation, and description, and also often use definition, cause/effect, and comparison/contrast. These modes of writing work together to make your writing stronger and more effective.

Discovering Key Points

- ➡ Identify the elements and purpose of each mode of writing
- ➡ Practice prewriting for each mode of writing in a visual organizer
- ➡ Write examples of each mode of writing

You can do many things in writing—among them, use your words to describe, to define, to compare or contrast, to illustrate, and to construct an argument. These are often referred to as *modes of writing*. These modes are used to your advantage in two ways. First, as a writer, modes of writing make your essay stronger. Second, for your readers, modes of writing help them connect with your essay.

As you may remember from Chapter 3, choosing your paper's purpose is just as essential as choosing your organization. The purpose of your paper could be to inform, to entertain, or to persuade. Modes of writing go hand in hand with choosing the purpose of your writing. Each mode offers a different way to present information to your readers. For example, if you wanted to write an informative paper about the differences and similarities between high school and college, you would want to first describe each one fully using specific examples; then compare the two, showing how similar they are; and finally contrast them, showing the differences. You might even include an argument about which is better in your opinion and why. Presenting information by utilizing different modes allows your readers to more easily follow the transitions you make in your paper, and also to better understand your objective for writing.

The Modes of Writing

In this chapter we will look at nine modes of writing:

- Illustration
- Definition
- Description
- Narration
- Comparison and Contrast
- Cause and Effect
- Division and Classification
- Argumentation
- Process Analysis

These modes are frequently found with one another. Rarely will you find a paper that does nothing but describe, without also doing some defining, narrating, and classifying. You'll want to make sure that you choose your modes wisely for each paper—you wouldn't want too much narration, for example, in a typical research paper. In this chapter, some of the modes of writing will be presented together to show you how these modes work together.

Illustration and Definition

Passages of illustrative writing explain a concept by means of specific *examples*. Examples can be specific cases, points, or stories. These examples support your main point and make it more believable. Illustration is one of the most common modes of writing, because all writing, whether informative or argumentative, will require specific examples.

When you define something in writing, you explain what a word, idea, or topic means. With this sort of writing, it is important to be very clear when defining something for readers. Definition may make a term or idea understandable by telling what it IS, and sometimes what it is NOT. It may also be helpful to compare it to something similar and then explain the distinguishing features.

ⓘ
To provide examples, the illustration mode requires strong words that describe. For more information, see Chapter 17 on adjectives.

ⓘ
The definition mode requires strong word choices. For help with easily confused words, see Chapter 26.

STUDENT EXAMPLE

Bart has been asked to write a paragraph, using the illustration and definition modes, on the word "love." He is not sure where to start, so he fills out the organizer below. Then he gathers his prewriting and writes his paragraph.

GRAPHIC ORGANIZER

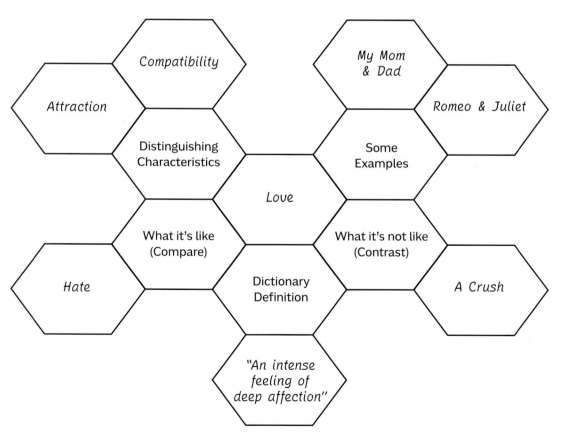

Love is defined by the dictionary as "an intense feeling of deep affection." Love can be seen as a physical or emotional attraction towards someone. It can also be seen as compatibility among two people. Love is like hate because they are both strong emotions that you feel towards someone or something. Love is not like a crush because a crush is just a temporary reaction to someone. My mom and dad are an example of love because they have been married for many years, have several children, and share many of the same interests. Romeo and Juliet are also an example of love because they were willing to defy their families and friends because they wanted to be together and ultimately die for each other.

YOUR TURN

How would you define "war"? Fill out the graphic organizer below, providing definitions for the word, as well as specific examples. Then, when you are finished, take your prewriting and write a paragraph defining and providing examples of "war."

GRAPHIC ORGANIZER

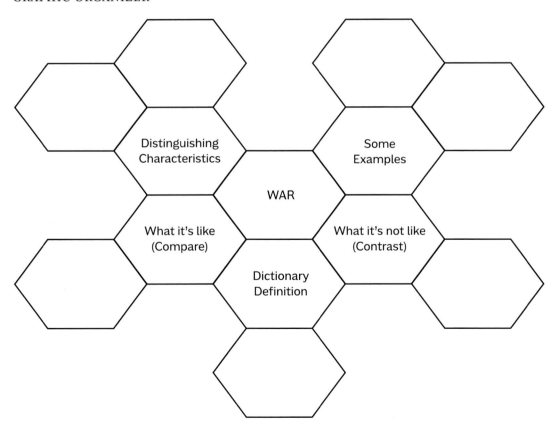

Description and Narration

Passages of description describe something—a person, a place, an object, even a feeling. Description captures the topic in words so that others can imagine it. Using descriptive words, such as adjectives or adverbs, is important in writing descriptions, as you want to make sure your examples use the senses (sight, smell, hearing, taste, and touch) to convey an image or represent an idea.

You use narration in your writing to tell the story of what happened, the specific events that happened, and the people who were involved. Narration typically organizes facts and details in a clear chronological order. Such writing may use first, second, or third person.

Adverbs are essential to description essays because they help describe your topic to the readers. See Chapter 17 for more help.

Remember to be consistent in your use of personal pronouns. For help with personal pronouns, see Chapter 17. For help with pronoun-antecedent agreement, see Chapter 19.

STUDENT EXAMPLE

Carmen has been asked to write a paragraph using description and narration. She decides she wants to tell the story of a life-changing experience she had, but she also wants to make sure she uses lots of specific sensory details, describing the event fully for her readers. To gather her thoughts and make sure she remembers all of the parts of the story, she fills out the organizer below.

GRAPHIC ORGANIZER

Who was involved in the story?	My dog, Sadie, and me.
What happened?	I was walking Sadie, and the leash got loose from my hand. Sadie ran and I started to run after her. Just as I was about to catch her, a car hit me and broke my leg. The pain was intense. I could taste blood in my mouth from hitting my head on the pavement.
When did it occur?	It happened October 5, 2009. It was a cool, windy evening. The air was crisp and clean. Many of my neighbors had out their Halloween decorations.
Why did it happen?	I was being irresponsible. I accidentally let the leash loose, and I ran out into the street after her without looking to see if any cars were coming.
Where did it occur?	This happened in my own neighborhood in North Carolina. We were actually two blocks away from my home.

I will never forget October 5, 2009. It was the day I broke my right leg. It was a cool and windy evening. The air smelled crisp and clean. I decided to take my dog Sadie out for her evening walk. Many of the Halloween decorations were out *in my neighborhood in North Carolina. On both sides of the road, I could see huge inflatable cats, witches, and ghosts. All of a sudden, Sadie jolted forward, and I lost control of her leash. As I ran out after her, I forgot to look both ways before crossing the street. I had caught up to Sadie, and I was just about to pick up her leash when BAM! A dark blue SUV hit me. My body went flying over the car and onto the pavement. Pain traveled through my body, but settled mostly on my right leg. I could taste the metallic flavor of blood in my mouth. With all the adrenaline pumping through my body, most of that evening became a blur after that.*

YOUR TURN

What was your most life-changing experience? Be sure to use examples that describe the event using your senses (sight, smell, hearing, taste, and touch). When you are finished with the graphic organizer, write your story into a paragraph.

Who was involved in the story?
What happened?
When did it occur?
Why did it happen?
Where did it occur?

Comparison and Contrast

> **ⓘ**
> Even though you are comparing and contrasting two different items, you need to make sure that your verb tense is the same for both. For help with consistent verb tense, see Chapter 18.

Comparison examines the ways in which two persons, places, or things are similar. Contrast examines the ways in which they are different. These modes help the reader understand one person, place, or thing in relation to another. Many times, the goal of a comparison is evaluation. For example, if you are comparing various fast-food restaurants, you will want to reach some conclusion about which restaurant is the best. Therefore, you need to use some specific criteria (e.g., price, healthiness) on which to base your comparison.

Ty is writing a comparison and contrast paragraph about texting friends and writing formal essays for school. He starts his prewriting by filling out the organizer below. After he is finished, he takes his prewriting and writes his comparison and contrast paragraph.

GRAPHIC ORGANIZER

Texting Friends	Writing Essays
What is it?	What is it?
Using my phone to talk to friends casually	*An assignment for a class*

Similarities:

both use language; modes of writing used in both; you get your points across; use feeling and tone; way to interact with people

Differences:

essays are graded; texts are casual and essays are formal; profanity, abbreviations, and slang accepted in texts; essays sometimes need documentation and research

Texting friends and writing essays have similarities and differences. Texting and writing essays are similar because in both an essay and when texting, you are responding to your topic. You have to interact with both. When I text, I have to interact with the person I'm texting. In an essay, I must interact with the readers and the topic. Also, they are similar because you are expressing how you feel about what you're writing as well as texting, and sometimes, you can misinterpret and take things out of context when doing either. When I write a text that is sarcastic, sometimes my friends don't get it. There are also differences between writing an essay and texting. When texting, abbreviations and slang are acceptable, but when writing an essay, that kind of informal writing makes it harder to take the writer seriously. When texting, you can also get away with using symbols, such as smiley faces and hearts, but putting those in an essay is inappropriate. Lastly, when writing an essay, a lot of thought and effort has to be put into the writing, whereas texting doesn't require much thought or effort.

YOUR TURN

Compare and contrast writing essays to writing paragraphs, giving at least three examples for each. After you are finished, write a paragraph comparing and contrasting the two types of media.

Writing Essays	Writing Paragraphs
What is it?	What is it?
Similarities:	
Differences:	

Cause and Effect

When you write a cause and effect essay, you must be careful that your predictions are logical and do not contain any errors. For help, see Chapter 9: Errors in Thought.

Passages of cause and effect writing refer to direct relationships between events and often answer the question, "why did something happen, and/or what results did it have?" With a cause and effect essay, sometimes you will choose a topic where there are numerous causes and effects. In that case, it is best to focus on a few and give specific examples, rather than list numerous causes and effects without providing detail.

STUDENT EXAMPLE

Bella is assigned a cause and effect paragraph to write on the results of being absent from class, but first, she wants to start brainstorming, using the organizer below. After she is finished, she takes her notes and writes her paragraph.

GRAPHIC ORGANIZER

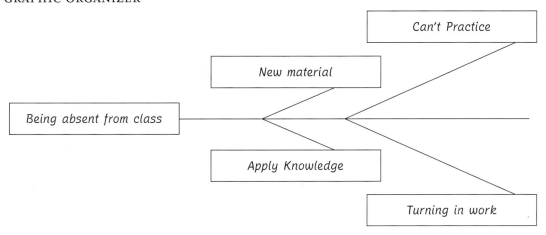

When you don't come to class, many things happen. First, you don't get the information you need in class. This means when there is a lecture or a new topic presented in class, like thesis statements, you won't know about the topic. Even if you get notes later, they're not as good as being in class because the notes always leave something out. Also, if you miss class, you miss out on practicing the skills you learn. For example, if we have a peer edit in class or a day where we get to practice writing transitions and you miss that day, you miss out on what we've done in class. You can't apply what you learned to previous lessons either, which means you are even more behind for the next class period. Lastly, when you miss class, you miss out on turning in your work on time. This means that you're automatically behind for the next class, and that's never good.

YOUR TURN

What are the effects of a natural disaster, like a hurricane? When you are finished filling out the graphic organizer, take your notes and write a cause and effect paragraph.

GRAPHIC ORGANIZER

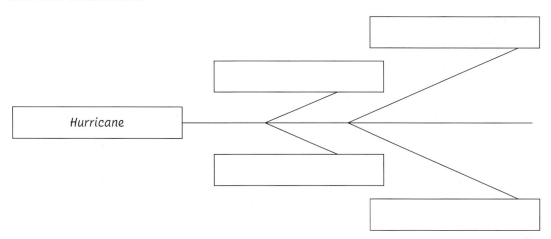

Division and Classification

Division means to take one item and break it (or divide it) into its component parts. Classification means to take several items and put them together (or classify them) into various groups according to what they have in common. For example, in a grocery store, the aisles are divided by what is in that aisle (for example, "dairy"). Then, in each aisle, the items are classified by product and brand (for example, all of the milk is together, then the different brands of milk are separated within that group).

Sometimes, you will be asked to provide an evaluation when you write a division and classification essay. If you were asked to compose a passage of classification writing on

In division and classification essays, transitions help put the puzzle of your paper together and help readers see how the parts of your paper are directly related. For help with transitions, see Chapter 4.

baseball, football, and hockey, you could discuss two things the sports have in common: rules and uniforms. If you were to compose a passage of division writing on basketball, you could separate the sport into two categories to focus on: positions and teams.

STUDENT EXAMPLE

Ariel has been asked to write a division and classification paragraph about cereal. First, he decided to divide the cereal into three categories. Then he classified each group by giving four examples of each category. When he is finished, he looks at the notes from his graphic organizer and writes his paragraph.

GRAPHIC ORGANIZER

Cereal with Marshmallows	Cereal with Chocolate Flavor	Cereal with Flakes
• Lucky Charms • Boo Berry • Marshmallow • Alpha-Bits • Marshmallow Pebbles	• Cocoa Pebbles • Count Chocula • Special K Chocolatey Delight • Cocoa Puffs	• Frosted Flakes • Wheaties • Raisin Bran

There are three main types of cereal I eat: cereal with marshmallows, cereal made with chocolate flavors, and cereal with flakes. The most delicious marshmallow cereal is Lucky Charms because it has the most variety with marshmallows, and it is colorful. The least delicious marshmallow cereal is Marshmallow Pebbles because while it does have a high marshmallow-to-cereal ratio, the crisp airy texture of the pebbles is missing here. Also, the flavor of the pebbles is pretty gross—it tastes like old birthday cake. The best chocolate flavored cereal is Cocoa Pebbles (which is funny since the Marshmallow Pebbles are so gross). They are crispy, delicious, and full of real chocolaty flavor. Cocoa Puffs is the worst chocolate-flavored cereal because the chocolate tastes fake, and the cereal gets soggy really quickly. The best flake-filled cereal is Frosted Flakes. They are sweet and keep their crunch really well, which is something important in a flake cereal. The worst flake cereal is Raisin Bran because the flakes get mushy, and who really wants to eat raisins in their cereal? Gross!

YOUR TURN

Choose any television show that you watch. First, divide the characters into three categories. Then classify by giving at least two characters for each category. When you are finished, look at your notes from the graphic organizer and write your division and classification paragraph.

GRAPHIC ORGANIZER

Name of television show: _____

Argumentation

Argumentation aims to convince your readers of your main point. This mode of writing is also known as persuasion writing. A well-written piece of argumentative writing should convey the issue clearly, provide sufficient information for readers to follow easily, and state not only your viewpoint but also reasons and evidence to back up that claim. Often, argumentative writing also discusses the opposing argument, or counterclaim. Arguments also sometimes involve using outside sources and references to other writers.

> Often, argumentative essays will require you to use sources. For help with how to use quotation marks properly with sources, see Chapter 25. For help finding and integrating sources into your paper, see Chapters 14 to 16.

STUDENT EXAMPLE

Yana is writing an argumentative paragraph on the importance of academics. She has decided to write about how many students are concerned with their grades, rather than the education they receive. When she is finished providing specific details in her graphic organizer, she begins to write her paragraph.

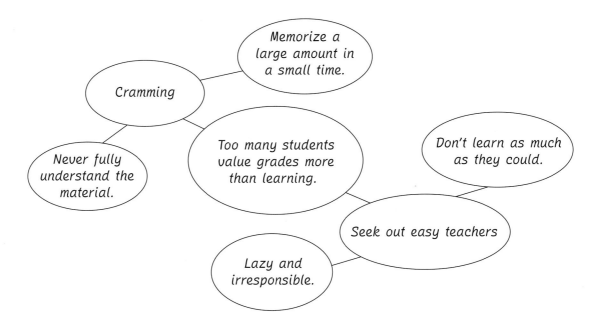

Students are often more concerned with receiving good grades than actually learning in school. Often, students seek out easy teachers, rather than taking a good, but more difficult, teacher. This means the students don't learn as much in the class. This type of behavior is lazy and irresponsible. The students are paying for an education; however, they are not receiving one when they just take easy teachers and courses. Students must challenge themselves in their courses. Students also fall into the pit of cramming before tests, rather than regularly reviewing the material. Memorizing such a large chunk of material in a short time doesn't allow the student to retain any of the information. Therefore, the students never fully understand the course material either. They simply take a course one semester, and they forget all the material by the next test.

YOUR TURN

Do you think that advertising encourages people to buy things that they do not want/need? Why or why not? Give specific details. When you are finished, take your notes from the graphic organizer and write an argumentative paragraph.

Process Analysis

Process analysis writing describes how to do something, how a particular event occurs, or how something works. The instructions for writing a process analysis essay are very similar to those for writing a narration essay.

STUDENT EXAMPLE

Harjeet is trying to get started on writing a paragraph about how to procrastinate doing an assignment. To start her prewriting, she decides to write down how to avoid doing work. When she is finished, she looks at her graphic organizer and writes her paragraph.

> ℹ Process analysis essays are organized chronologically. For more information on this essay organization technique, see Chapter 3.

1st	Receive assignment.
2nd	Ignore assignment.
3rd	Think of other activities to do, rather than complete assignment.
4th	Complete any other activities, rather than assignment.
5th	Reassure yourself that you will do the assignment when you can.
6th	When you begin to feel anxious about the assignment (generally the day or two before it's due), begin working on it.
7th	Stay up all night to work on assignment.
8th	Repeat for all future assignments.

To be a procrastinator, first you have to get an assignment, such as an essay, and completely ignore its existence until at least the day or two before it's due. This day for procrastination should be closer to the actual due time if the assignment is short. Most importantly, think of everything you would rather do and do these activities instead of starting your assignment. Next, keep repeating in your mind that you will start the assignment as soon as you can, but don't start it until you feel anxious enough to begin. After you finally begin your assignment, accept that you probably won't do your best, but tell yourself that on a positive note at least you did it. Finally, stay up all night if you need to, and if you procrastinated closer to the due time, be late to class. Repeat these steps with every assignment to do badly in school.

YOUR TURN

In exactly eight steps, how do you make your favorite sandwich? Be sure to not miss any steps, and be specific in your directions. When you are finished, write your steps into a process analysis paragraph.

GRAPHIC ORGANIZER

Name of My Sandwich: ______________________________

1st	
2nd	
3rd	
4th	
5th	
6th	
7th	
8th	

Practicing the Modes of Writing

Sara has been asked to write an essay using at least three modes of writing, responding to the following question: Is Facebook damaging human interaction and communication?

After Sara wrote her draft, she decided to place Post-it Notes in the margin of her paper where the three modes of writing were used, just so she was sure that she had followed the assignment.

The Facebook Revolution

Here, I'm using narration. I'm telling a story to begin my essay.

Once upon a time, long, long ago in a place called "Before Internet," or "B.I." for short, people would socialize and network in public and at social gatherings, but with the invention of the Internet and cyber social networking, those days have gone. Facebook has taken over social interaction as it was once known. It has taken away the face-to-face human aspect and engagement of another human being. Physical touch has been replaced with a keyboard, sight has been replaced with a monitor, and sound has been replaced with speakers. As technology evolves, so must the human race, which means that while face-to-face conversations are diminishing and social networking sites are on the rise, society must accept this evolution.

I'm showing by examples (that's illustration) the way that communication evolved.

Every year, society is bombarded with many facets of communication technology. This evolution begins from the transition from snail mail to email to social networking, from phone calls to text messaging, from personal visits to web chat sessions such as Skype. There are many different opinions as to how these changes have impacted society as a whole. While some people are afraid that this will damage human interactions, it is more important to focus on the benefits of this technology. Facebook is reconnecting people who have lost contact one way or another throughout the years. It keeps people millions of miles apart in close contact.

Families divided by time and distance may reconnect and also become participants in each other's lives. It is now possible to watch people live from a distance through photos and status updates. Also, there is the benefit of finding old colleagues or high school friends. In addition, Facebook can be used as a platform to advertise for a business or to promote a political campaign. Not every user is going to rely on the site as their only means of communication. The site is not going to erase the empathy humans feel for each other or take away a personal touch. Facebook can be used in an advantageous manner because a user may be able to console or congratulate someone they otherwise may not get to see face to face. It does not have to be used as a weapon. Facebook can certainly be used to maintain friendships and relationships if used properly.

The theme of Facebook is to "stay connected." This is because users in every country can meet new people, read live news updates from companies across the board, participate in surveys, keep up with friends' daily lives, or even follow their favorite music artists. The site even has profiles of authors and cooks who offer information on their books or recipes. It also has pages dedicated to fan clubs, television shows or series, and movies. A person can use this site as a method of entertainment, as well as a connection tool.

> In this paragraph, I'm using description. I'm describing all of the ways we "stay connected" with Facebook.

Overall, while Facebook may be used inappropriately, as is the case with any other social networking site, it does have many more options and opportunities than any of the other current or previous sites. It is not tarnishing relationships. Facebook is providing both a connection between people of all types and ages, while giving society an opportunity to share their personal lives and experiences, while also opening them up to other people's opinions and insights. It allows for people who might otherwise lose connection to share a bond. This bond may not be as personal as a face to face relationship, but that's America these days. In our society, almost everyone is busy working, going to school, raising families, being an activist, volunteering or participating in community events. Facebook is a tool to be used to provide communication in this busy generation.

> I just realized that throughout this whole essay, I'm arguing my opinion. That's my fourth mode!

QUESTIONS

1. Sara used multiple modes of writing in her essay. Which do you think was the most effective in this essay? Why?

2. Sara's instructor has asked her to revise this essay, adding in one more mode of writing she didn't previously use. Which mode should Sara choose? What are some ideas for how Sara can incorporate the mode?

YOUR TURN

Below is an essay published in the *Financial Post*. As you read, try to figure out which modes are being used.

"Social News Site Reddit the 'Groundskeepers' of the Internet," by Matt Hartley

Financial Post, March 21, 2012

When visitors arrive at the tiny Bay Area office that plays home to the "front page" of the Internet, they are greeted by a friendly dog named Mog.

Mog spends many of his days closely following his owner, Erik Martin, around the understated office of Reddit.com, one of the most popular community-driven social news sites on the Internet.

As Mr. Martin, Reddit's general manager, sits down for an interview in one corner of the loft-style office, under a shelf laden with coffee mugs and knick knacks shaped like Reddit's smiling alien mascot, Mog jumps up on the leather couch beside the reporter and promptly falls asleep.

Mog's friendly and gentle nature is emblematic of Reddit's downtown San Francisco office, an airy, relaxed and welcoming space that plays home to about a dozen employees. Still, the playful feel of the Reddit workspace belies the power of the site, an online destination that ranks in the Top 50 websites in the United States and draws more Canadians each month than Amazon.ca.

Founded in 2005 by University of Virginia graduates Steve Huffman and Alexis Ohanian, Reddit was designed as a social sharing and aggregation site to which users submit links to interesting stories and content from around the Web, which are then "upvoted" or "downvoted" by the site's community of users. The more upvotes a story gets, the higher it ranks on the site, and the more likely it is to be seen by other users.

Reddit was acquired by publishing giant Conde Nast—the same company that owns *Wired*, *GQ* and other magazines—in October of 2006, but last year the site was spun off as a wholly owned subsidiary of Conde Nast's parent company, Advance Publications.

Now, it's up to Mr. Martin—and newly appointed chief executive Yishan Wong, a former director of engineering at Facebook Inc.—to help Reddit evolve its business model and generate new advertising revenue, while at the same time applying a deft touch to the site's dedicated user base.

"In general, the vast majority of really good ideas or things that happen on Reddit happen without our involvement," Mr. Martin said.

"We definitely see ourselves as groundskeepers or plumbers or janitors—take your pick of someone working behind the scenes … We try to be agnostic with the content and say, here's an area where you can go."

Links are generally submitted to categories known as "subreddits," which tend to focus on specific areas of interest, such as "gaming," "politics" or "science." But in actuality there are nearly 70,000 subreddits, including one for almost every city in the world, every professional sports team and every U.S. college.

Mr. Martin said there are somewhere between 8,000 and 10,000 highly active subreddits with vibrant communities of users. If there's a video game you're passionate about that was produced in the past 20 years, chances are there's a subreddit devoted to it. There are subreddits centered around such topics as "Knitting" or "Frugal Male Fashion"; or "Grilled Cheese" in which sandwich aficionados trade secrets about how to create the greatest gooey treat possible.

Advertising on the site comes through two streams. The first tends to be from smaller businesses—many owned by Redditors themselves—who post ads targeted against specific subreddits or users. However, the site also offers more traditional direct sales for larger advertising campaigns promoting new video games and movies. Advertisers can also purchase sponsored headlines, which users can vote up and down just like any other story posted to the site.

In addition to the thousands of cat pictures and threads devoted to the latest Internet memes, Reddit has also become a place for community organizing. The recent boycott of the Web hosting service GoDaddy.com—due to the company's support of the unpopular SOPA bill in the U.S.—was fuelled by the Reddit community.

"We try to encourage some things, such as when a new subreddit is taking off, something like the SOPA subreddit," he said.

"We didn't promote any one initiative that came out of the community, but we promoted the SOPA subreddit saying, here's an important issue that could affect us as a business and the Internet at large, and we don't know what to do, but here's a place to talk about it."

QUESTIONS

1. Which modes of writing did you find in this essay?

2. Which, if any, of the modes of writing were used more than once?

3. Which mode of writing was the most effective in this essay?

Assessing Your Knowledge

KEY POINTS	REMINDER	HOW WELL DID YOU UNDERSTAND THIS MATERIAL?	PAGE(S)
Identify the elements and purpose of each mode of writing	There are nine modes of writing: ▪ **Illustration** (provides examples) ▪ **Definition** (defines a topic) ▪ **Description** (captures visually a person, place, event, etc.) ▪ **Narration** (tells a story) ▪ **Comparison and Contrast** (shows similarities and differences) ▪ **Cause and Effect** (explains reasons and consequences) ▪ **Division and Classification** (separates a single item into multiple components OR categorizes multiple items into groups) ▪ **Argumentation** (persuades readers to believe an idea) ▪ **Process Analysis** (describes steps or methods)	☐ I've Got It! ☐ Almost There ☐ Need More Practice	pp. 106–19
Practice prewriting for each mode of writing in a visual organizer	**Prewriting** is a crucial part of the writing and thinking process. For each mode of writing presented in this chapter, there was a visual organizer to better help understand the mode, as well as provide an example of how you could prewrite for that particular mode.	☐ I've Got It! ☐ Almost There ☐ Need More Practice	pp. 106–19
Write examples of each mode of writing	Practice really does make perfect. Each time you practice these modes of writing, you'll understand them better. In this chapter, each mode has writing prompts for you to practice writing those modes.	☐ I've Got It! ☐ Almost There ☐ Need More Practice	pp. 106–19

Deepening Your Understanding

If you would like to go beyond the material in this chapter, explore additional connections, and get more practice, check out these related topics:

- **Prewriting**: Prewriting is important, no matter what mode(s) of writing you are using. Prewriting allows you to come up with ideas for writing. It also serves to motivate you to begin writing.

- **Each Specific Mode of Writing**: Understanding what each mode is not only helps you practice the skill but also helps you see how all the modes work together when you write a paper.

- **Critical Thinking**: All around us, the media provide us with examples. Understanding how to "read" and analyze these visuals is key.

Timed Writing

"If you want to make good use of your time, you've got to know what's most important and then give it all you've got."

—Lee Iacocca

FACT OR FICTION?
Because it is timed writing, I don't need to bother with revising and editing. I should focus purely on getting out my thoughts in essay form.

FICTION.
Even though it is timed writing, you still need to incorporate the full writing process, including revising and editing. Timed writing is simply a matter of time management.

Discovering Key Points

- Understand timed writing and the causes of timed writing anxiety
- Recognize different types of timed writing prompts
- Apply important TWT (Timed Writing Tips) during timed writing
- Prepare to write effective timed essays

127

In your geology class, you may be asked to write a short essay for your midterm about rock formations. In religion, you may be asked to write an essay in class arguing how Hinduism differs from Buddhism. In English, you may be asked to respond in writing to a quotation from a literary text.

All these instances have one thing in common: they are all examples of **timed writing** (also known as in-class essays or essay exams). Timed writing is often stressful for students. It may help if you can understand why timed writing is important, recognize prompts you may encounter, and apply the important advice regarding timed writing that we will give you in this chapter.

Why Is Timed Writing Important?

Timed writing is important for various reasons:

- It lets you demonstrate knowledge of a topic.
- It tests your skills at thinking under pressure.
- It allows your instructor to assess the class's skill level in a timed setting.

Why Is Timed Writing So Difficult?

Reason #1: **General Anxiety**—Almost all students experience some sort of anxiety during timed writing.

Suggestions That Can Help—Get a good night's sleep before the timed writing. Remember to be calm and breathe deeply. If it helps (and if your instructor will allow it), bring headphones or ear plugs to help you feel more comfortable.

Reason #2: **Technology Anxiety**—Some students have forms of technology anxiety—whether a fear of things going wrong with the device they are typing on ("my computer may freeze, and I'll lose everything I've written!") or a fear of typing too slowly and running out of time.

Suggestions That Can Help—Practice typing on the computer. Bring a flash drive; save your essay frequently both on the flash drive and on the computer. There are many computer programs that teach faster typing skills; several, like typingclub.com, are free. Also look for computer classes at your university.

Reason #3: **Writing Anxiety**—Many students have anxiety regarding their ability to write under pressure. Unlike out-of-class essays, where students have "infinite" time, this type of writing relies heavily on quick thinking and writing abilities.

Suggestions That Can Help—Practice timed writing at home. When you go in to write the essay or take the test, be sure to prewrite before you write your essay; that should make it easier to present a coherent thesis supported by examples.

Reason #4: **Time Anxiety**—This is the most common of anxieties; many students fear running out of time.

Suggestions That Can Help—The ticking clock can be frightening. Create a timeline for yourself and try to stick to it. Practice timed writing at home to make sure that you are used to time limits.

Examples of Timed Writing Prompts

Below are examples of five types of prompts you may encounter in your classes. These are not the only types of prompts; you may be given a different type of timed writing prompt. Next to each type of prompt is a definition, as well as an example of that particular type.

The Mode-Based Prompt—These prompts ask you to use a mode you've learned about previously in class to write your essay.

Can't remember the modes of writing or need to see examples of them again? See Chapter 6.

Example: Compare and contrast Facebook and Twitter.

The Question-Based Prompt—These prompts ask you to reply to a direct question, often including a theme discussed in class.

Example: Should there be stronger regulations of alcohol ads? Why or why not?

The Role-Based Prompt—These prompts ask you to put yourself in a setting via role-playing and respond to a problem or situation.

Example: Imagine you are a television executive. You have been asked to write a letter to parents responding to their concern about too much sex on television.

The Quote-Based Prompt—These prompts ask you to respond to a quotation, often by asking you to agree or disagree, providing specific reasons why.

Example: Agree or disagree with the following comment. "Jon Stewart and Stephen Colbert speak the language of [youth]—sarcasm and curse words. Through mockingly analyzing news stories, the programs challenge viewers to think more critically about the information that is presented to them from news networks and the decisions made by the U.S. government."—Barry Falls Jr.

The Media-Based Prompt—These prompts provide you with a piece of media (a video, a picture, etc.), and then you are asked a question referring directly to the piece of media.

Example: Look at the picture below. Who owns this car? What do you know about this person based solely on the picture? Think about elements such as age, gender, etc.

Common Timed Writing Prompt Terms

Knowing the terms that you may encounter on your timed writing prompts can help you be better prepared and ultimately do better on your timed writing.

- **Agree/Disagree**: Take a position and stick with it. Don't switch sides or try to argue both sides.
- **Challenge**: Disagree with.
- **Compare**: Discuss both the similarities and the differences.
- **Contrast**: Discuss the differences.
- **Compare and contrast**: Some instructors use "compare and contrast" when they want to remind students to focus on differences as well as similarities.
- **Debate**: Discuss the arguments on both sides of an issue.
- **Define**: Explain a term in your own words.
- **Evaluate**: Give your opinion of and provide reasons for holding that opinion.

- **Illustrate**: Use specific examples to prove a point.
- **Justify**: Give reasons for.
- **List**: Examine points one by one.
- **Prove**: Show with specific examples how something is true.
- **Summarize**: Quickly review all important points.

Timed Writing Tips

Timed Writing Tips (TWT) are crucial to being successful during timed writing. Below are the timed writing tips you should keep in mind while you are writing timed essays.

Before the Essay/Test

- Practice outside of class. If you practice writing in a timed setting, you'll feel more comfortable with it later.
- See if your instructor will allow you to wear headphones or ear plugs, particularly if you work better with music or it calms you.
- Get a good night's sleep the night before.
- Come to class on time (or even early if possible).
- Be prepared to write.

The Day of the Essay/Test

- Take a deep breath and try to relax.
- Know that your instructor is not expecting perfection.
- Keep an eye on your time.
- Tackle formatting first. If your instructor requires double spacing, and/or specific margins and font, take care of the small items before you write.
- Read the prompt and be sure you understand it.
  - What is the prompt asking you to do?
  - Underline key terms and phrases. (See Common Timed Writing Prompt Terms, above, for some common terms you may see in the essay prompt.)
  - Highlight any terms you don't know.
    » Be sure to look them up in a dictionary if you are allowed to use one.
- After you read the prompt, try to summarize the issue or question in your own words. This way, you make sure that you understand what the assignment is asking.
- Begin planning out your essay by prewriting. You can try any of the following to pre-write before you begin writing:
  - **Outlining**—Try this if you like formal structure.
  - **Clustering**—Try this if you're a visual learner.

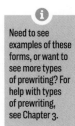
Need to see examples of these forms, or want to see more types of prewriting? For help with types of prewriting, see Chapter 3.

- **Listing**—Try this if you want to get all your ideas out but you don't need as much structure as an outline.
- **Making a Chart**—Try this if you're asked to compare and contrast or weigh the pros and cons of a topic.

▪ Be sure to have a clear thesis and strong, detailed, specific examples.

▪ Leave enough time (at least 10 minutes) to revise and edit your timed writing. Most people think this is the least important part of timed writing, but it is just as important as prewriting. If you are typing your essay on a computer, and you can't revise or edit on the screen, ask to print a draft.

STUDENT EXAMPLES

1. Kya has a timed essay in her class. She feels confident and has prepared herself for the time limit of one hour. Her eyes go immediately to the questions—one on global warming, and one on social media, both topics that the class has focused on this term. She glances up at the instructions, and says to herself, "I can do this!" Half an hour later, she's almost finished writing her essay on global warming, but she knows she must write about social media too. She frantically writes as much as she can on the second topic before the hour ends. There's no time to review what she's written, and neither topic has a full essay written, but she feels she's done everything she could.

   Later, she meets up with her friend Mal to compare notes and comment on how hard it was to complete both essays within a single hour. "Both essays?" Mal asks. "You were only supposed to write one!" She looks at the test instructions once more and a sickening feeling comes over her as she rereads the instructions:

   Read the following two questions carefully, choose one of the two, and write an argumentative essay on the topic.

2. Oren receives his timed writing prompt.

   Write an essay of between 400 and 600 words evaluating some of the key arguments on both sides of the issue of whether or not to use the term "freshmen."

   He writes the following essay.

   First-year college and university students have been called "freshmen" for centuries—and the longstanding use of the term has itself been advanced as a reason not to change. If it's served us perfectly well all these years, its defenders suggest, surely there's no good reason to change now. Moreover, those defenders argue, there's an inherent value in maintaining traditions; traditions honor the past and they connect the student of today to the student of yesterday.

A second argument made by supporters of the term "freshmen" is that they find alternatives such as "first-year students" to be cumbersome or awkward. Finally, those who want to retain the term "freshmen" argue that there's little point in making a fuss about such a small thing as a word; we should be focusing our attention on more important things. That's particularly the case when change would require some effort: in this case, a great many standard documents and web materials would need to be revised. Is it worth the effort? Defenders of keeping "freshman" argue that all that effort is definitely not worth it.

Those on the other side argue that the word "freshman" is an example of the sort of gendered usage that we should be abandoning in all areas of life. Just as we recognized decades ago that the term "police officer" was preferable to "policeman," and "flight attendant" was preferable to "stewardess," so too, according to those on this side of the argument, we should recognize that the term "first-year students" is far more appropriate than "freshmen" for a world in which we want to move away from gender bias. Opponents of "freshmen" also point out that when "freshmen" was first used, universities were male-only institutions, whereas women now make up more than half of the students on most campuses.

What of the argument that "first-year students" is more cumbersome to say than is "freshmen"? Opponents of "freshmen" point to the experience of other English-speaking nations. In Canada, for example, the term "first-year students" has been the norm at most campuses for generations.

Opponents of "freshmen" concede that the term takes longer to say than does the word "freshmen." But they note that "flight attendant" also takes longer to say than "stewardess," and "police officer" takes longer to say than "policeman." They suggest that these small differences are less important than the larger principle involved. What of that other argument made by the defenders of "freshmen"—that it's not worth making a fuss over a single word? Opponents of "freshmen" concede that one word may not make a huge difference. But it's a word that's often repeated—and opponents of "freshmen" cite various studies suggesting that the language we use affects the way we think.

Those are some of the key arguments on both sides of the issue.

He receives his essay back the following week, only to find he has failed. He feels that his essay was well written and that he touched on several arguments on both sides of the issue. He decides to go talk to his instructor to see why he received the failing grade.

His instructor responds that Oren missed or misunderstood a key word in the instructions: *evaluate*. He tells Oren that in order to evaluate an argument, a considered judgment must be reached as to how strong those arguments are. Unfortunately, Oren just listed points and summarized.

1. In the first student example, what should Kya have done differently?

2. In the second student example, what should Oren have done differently?

3. Have you ever taken a timed essay? If so, what was your experience? If not, how can you best prepare for your first timed essay?

4. What advice would you give to Kya and Oren about their next timed essay?

Sample Timelines

Having a sample timeline to follow can help keep you on task and manage your time better. Below, you'll find two timelines—one for a one-and-a-half-hour class and one for a two-hour class.

The One-and-a-Half-Hour Class Timeline

1 hour, 30 minutes left	read the prompt; look up words you're not familiar with; begin prewriting
1 hour, 15 minutes left	write introduction & thesis statement
55 minutes left	write body paragraphs
20 minutes left	write your conclusion
10 minutes left	revise & edit your draft
5 minutes left	turn in your final draft

The Two-Hour Class Timeline

2 hours left	read the prompt; look up words you're not familiar with; begin prewriting
1 hour, 40 minutes left	write introduction & thesis statement
1 hour, 25 minutes left	write body paragraphs
45 minutes left	write your conclusion
15 minutes left	revise & edit your draft
5 minutes left	turn in your final draft

Assessing Your Knowledge

KEY POINTS	REMINDER	HOW WELL DID YOU UNDERSTAND THIS MATERIAL?	PAGE(S)
Understand timed writing and the causes of timed writing anxiety	**Timed writing** is responding to a prompt or question in timed settings, and it is important for multiple reasons: ▪ Tests university and class standards ▪ Demonstrates your knowledge on a topic ▪ Tests your skills ▪ Allows the instructor to assess the class's skill/knowledge There are also four main kinds of timed writing anxiety: **general**, **technology**, **writing**, and **time**.	☐ I've Got It! ☐ Almost There ☐ Need More Practice	pp. 128–29
Recognize different types of timed writing prompts	There are many types of timed writing prompts. Five examples include **mode-based**, **question-based**, **role-based**, **quote-based**, and **media-based**.	☐ I've Got It! ☐ Almost There ☐ Need More Practice	pp. 129–31
Apply important TWT (Timed Writing Tips) during timed writing	There are many TWT to keep in mind when you write timed essays: ▪ Come prepared and be ready to write ▪ Breathe and try to stay calm ▪ Read the prompt carefully ▪ Prewrite ▪ Create a clear and strong thesis and examples ▪ Revise and edit your essay	☐ I've Got It! ☐ Almost There ☐ Need More Practice	pp. 131–34
Prepare to write effective timed essays	Time management is one of the most important keys to being successful at writing timed essays. Make sure that you follow a timeline or create your own.	☐ I've Got It! ☐ Almost There ☐ Need More Practice	p. 134

Deepening Your Understanding

If you would like to go beyond the material in this chapter, explore additional connections, and get more practice, check out these related topics:

- **The Writing Process**: Before you can practice timed writing, you must know the various parts of the writing process. Knowing these will help you when you must sit down and write in a timed setting.

- **Thesis Statements**: Thesis statements are very important in timed writing. Without a strong thesis, your essay will not be strong, and your reader will not have a blueprint for your essay.

- **Revising**: Revising is always an important part of the writing process, but it is essential during timed writing. This is because you get only a specific amount of time to put forward your best writing. You want to make sure that your essay makes sense and that it is organized in the most effective manner.

- **Editing**: This is one of the most overlooked items in timed writing. Like revising the essay, checking your grammar and mechanics is necessary during timed writing. Making sure you are clear in your word choice and free of errors can help you achieve a better grade.

What Is Rhetoric?

8

"Rhetoric then may be defined as the faculty of discovering the possible means of persuasion in reference to any subject whatever."

—Aristotle

Discovering Key Points

- Understand and identify ethos in an argument
- Understand and identify pathos in an argument
- Understand and identify logos in an argument
- Write to show understanding of each rhetorical appeal

Rhetoric is the study and art of persuasion, or effective argumentation. Classical rhetoricians were skilled orators and most arguments were given as speeches. For class, you will be asked to write persuasive arguments that take many forms. Some of these might include formal essays, proposals, speeches, and even discussion-board posts. Each time you write an argument, you will be charged with communicating your position, addressing opposing arguments, and convincing others to adopt your opinion as well.

Why Is Argument So Important?

Arguments constantly surround us. You make an argument when you try to get your friend to loan you her car or when you make a case to prove that your favorite baseball player really is the best in the league. We can also see arguments in advertisements, which encourage us to purchase one cleaning product over another or to vote for a specific candidate. We are challenged every day to make decisions based on the arguments we see and hear. Recognizing how we are being persuaded can help us make better choices. We can approach and understand these everyday arguments just as we do academic ones.

In an academic setting, you will be expected to evaluate and challenge the arguments of others as well as effectively formulate your own. Persuading others to accept your position is a valuable skill. Many of your courses will expect you to explain and defend your position either informally, in a class discussion, or formally, in a paper. Creating an argument with strong **rhetorical appeals** will increase its persuasiveness.

Aristotle's Rhetorical Appeals

According to Aristotle, a well-constructed argument can try to attract and persuade an audience in several ways. We call these strategies rhetorical appeals. Aristotle defined three sorts of appeal: **ethos**, **pathos**, and **logos.**

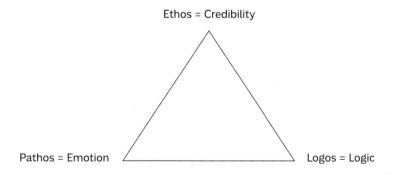

Ethos—An Appeal to Character

An appeal based on ethos attempts to show the audience that the writer is trustworthy and reliable. The audience must perceive the writer as a credible authority if they are to accept the argument. If the author seems misinformed or disorganized, the audience will suspect the entire communication.

To make an appeal based on ethos, the author must provide the audience with proof that he or she is reliable and knowledgeable on the subject being discussed. Sometimes, the reputation of the author lends credibility to his or her argument. If the author is well known or famous, the audience can rely on information that they already possess. Albert Einstein, for instance, is a well-known scientist. If you picked up one of his books for the first time, his positive reputation would encourage you to accept his argument and trust his judgment before you even started reading. A sense of trust can be created in other ways. Authors with experience and a record of sound research have stronger ethos than those with little to none.

In your writing, you can create an ethos appeal by providing support for your argument in the form of facts, expert opinions, statistics, and clear explanations. This will show that you have done the necessary research and understand your topic. Using information responsibly helps establish your credibility as an author. Correctly using documentation and proofing your work will also demonstrate that you are a careful and trustworthy author.

MEDIA EXAMPLE OF ETHOS

Ethos can also be found in the media. Below is an example of a website that contains an ethos appeal.

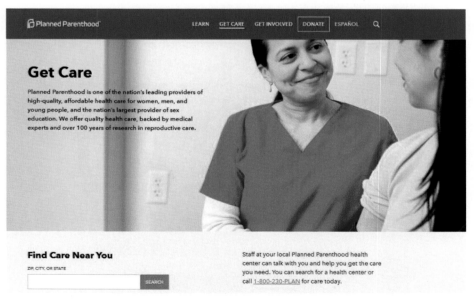

In what way(s) does ethos add to the persuasiveness of the website?

A coworker asks you if you know a good restaurant to go to on a first date. Write a paragraph recommending a restaurant. Include information that shows your recommendation is trustworthy.

Pathos—An Appeal to Emotion

A pathos appeal attempts to affect the emotions of the audience. Fear, anger, pity, desire, envy, greed, hope, joy, and pride are just a few of the emotions that a writer may attempt to make the audience feel. If successful, the force of an emotion can cause an audience to relate to the writer or even make a decision.

In a text, like one you might read for class, you may find that the author creates a pathos appeal through a vivid story or example. For instance, a story from the author's childhood may recount a time when he or she felt vulnerable and scared. The author hopes that the audience can relate to this experience and ultimately to the author's main point. An author might use language with strong connotations, or words with multiple meanings and feelings associated with them. A word like *manipulate*, meaning to influence or change, has negative connotations because of the thoughts and feelings we generally connect with that word. You might think of a time when you were tricked or felt forced to change your plans for someone else's benefit. Because people have different experiences and memories, they may have different emotional reactions to the same pathos appeal.

In your own writing, pathos is important because you will want the reader to become invested in your argument. Rather than read your work at an emotional distance, you want your reader to care about your opinion and your cause.

MEDIA EXAMPLE OF PATHOS

Pathos can also be found in the media. Below is an example of a website that contains a pathos appeal.

How does an appeal to pathos add to the persuasiveness of the website?

You desperately want to audition for the school play, but you miss your scheduled time. Write an email to the director asking for another opportunity to audition by appealing to his or her emotions.

Logos—An Appeal to Logic

An appeal based on logos attempts to persuade on the basis of logic, reason, and factual information. An author hopes that providing logical information and explanations will allow the audience to come to the same conclusion as the author has.

In a text, a logos appeal can take many forms. Such appeals often employ examples, make comparisons, describe how a process is completed, or explain why an action was taken. Definitions, statistical data, and expert opinions are among the tools that can be used in an appeal based on logos.

In academic writing, it is very important that you make a strong logos appeal. For many disciplines, a valid academic argument relies on evidence or research rather than on opinions and emotional appeals.

Logos can also be found in the media. Below is an example of a website that contains a logos appeal.

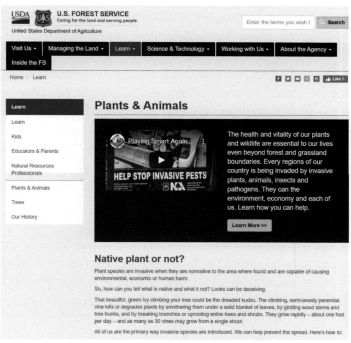

How does an appeal to logos add to the persuasiveness of the website?

You are applying to get a raise at your job. Write a letter or memo to your boss explaining, with facts, why you deserve a raise.

Using Ethos, Pathos, and Logos in Your Writing

Using ethos, pathos, and logos together can help you build a strong persuasive argument.

Walter is asked to write a persuasive letter to school administration concerning absolute free speech in the school's newspaper. In some schools, administrators edit out information that they consider too controversial or inappropriate. Because he wants his argument to be as successful as possible, he includes ethos, logos, and pathos appeals.

> Dear Administration,
> While completing my degree in Journalism, I have worked at the Chronicle for four years, beginning as a proofreader and now serving as Editor in Chief. In that time, we've published numerous controversial stories, including editorials that have criticized the school administration and articles representing unpopular opinions. Though these stories have at times annoyed our readers, they've also served an essential role: they've kept our student body knowledgeable about the issues that affect them, and aware of the diversity of opinions and beliefs on campus. Students need this information in order to make informed decisions and participate effectively as members of our college community. When we asked students about this as part of the Chronicle's opinion survey last year, the overwhelming majority said that they feel the paper is doing good work. It would be a terrible mistake to give in to pressure from those who think the Chronicle should be censored by the administration. We should aim to have an active and engaged student body, not one that is sheltered and ignorant; and for that reason, the Chronicle must remain free from interference.

Should there be absolute free speech on the Internet? Some blogs and message boards have started editing out information that they consider too controversial or inappropriate. Write an email to the moderator of a message board explaining your opinion. Because you want your argument to be a successful as possible, make sure to include ethos, logos, and pathos appeals.

Assessing Your Knowledge

KEY POINTS	REMINDER	HOW WELL DID YOU UNDERSTAND THIS MATERIAL?	PAGE(S)
Understand and identify ethos in an argument	An **ethos** appeal attempts to show the audience that the writer is credible and reliable. An author's reputation can help gain the trust of the audience.	☐ I've Got It! ☐ Almost There ☐ Need More Practice	pp. 139–40
Understand and identify pathos in an argument	A **pathos** appeal attempts to alter the emotions of the audience in a way that will more easily persuade them. Emotions like fear, anger, desire, and hope can be used to persuade an audience.	☐ I've Got It! ☐ Almost There ☐ Need More Practice	pp. 140–41
Understand and identify logos in an argument	A **logos** appeal attempts to use factual information and reason to persuade an audience. Providing proof and evidence for claims in academic writing is important.	☐ I've Got It! ☐ Almost There ☐ Need More Practice	pp. 141–42
Write to show understanding of each rhetorical appeal	It is helpful to understand how each **rhetorical appeal** works individually and how they work together to create a strong argument. This chapter provides writing practice for each appeal individually and in combination with one another.	☐ I've Got It! ☐ Almost There ☐ Need More Practice	pp. 140–42

Deepening Your Understanding

If you would like to go beyond the material in this chapter, explore additional connections, and get more practice, check out these related topics:

- **Prewriting**: There are many elements of an effective argument, and constructing a strong argument takes practice and planning. Prewriting is a way to prepare your thoughts before you start writing.

- **Critical Thinking**: Sometimes information takes the form of pictures or graphs. Understanding how to read and incorporate non-verbal information can help you create a successful logos appeal.

- **Description**: Getting others to understand your point of view is made easier when the right words are used. Description is a great way to help communicate clear examples and experiences to the audience.

- **Argumentation**: Ethos, pathos, and logos appeals are important in an argument. An argumentative paper has many important features that the author should be aware of. Understanding how to add rhetoric into a paper will help you become more persuasive.

Errors in Thought

"Logic is not everything. But it is something—something which can be taught, something which can be learned, something which can help us in some degree to think more sensibly about the dangerous world in which we live."
—David Fischer

FACT OR FICTION?
I can believe anything that I read in a source.

FICTION.
Unfortunately, it is not safe to believe everything you read. Even published articles can contain misinformation and logical errors. You should look for flawed logic in any article you read. You can avoid being misled if you are aware of logical errors.

Discovering Key Points

- Identify and understand the logical error bandwagon
- Identify and understand the logical error stereotyping
- Identify and understand the logical error hasty generalization
- Identify and understand the logical error false dichotomy
- Practice locating logical errors

A logical error is a flaw in the construction of an argument. While there are many mistakes and errors that can be made in an argument, a logical error specifically refers to a mistake made in reasoning.

Want to know more about argument? See Chapters 6 and 8.

Being aware of **errors in thought** is an important self-defense strategy. Despite being flawed by errors in thought, some arguments can still be powerful; they may manipulate our emotions, causing us to focus on our insecurities or accept unfair generalizations. Any argument, whether you read it or hear it, could have the potential for error. Errors in thought can be divided into categories based on the kind of error that is made. There are numerous types. Here are a few that you will frequently encounter: **bandwagon**, **stereotyping**, **hasty generalizations**, and **false dichotomy**.

Bandwagon

Want to know what the bandwagon error looks like in advertisements? See Chapter 11.

Imagine your friend asks you about your plans for the weekend. When you mention you might stay in town and pick up an extra shift at your job, your friend argues, "Everyone is going to Ben's house party at the lake. It's obviously the most fun thing you could do!"

A bandwagon error is found in arguments that claim that an idea is true because many people believe it to be, or that a person should do something because many others are doing it.

Idea **A** is very popular, so idea **A** must be correct (or the best).

My whole family is voting for this candidate; she must be the right choice.

World of Warcraft is a very popular game, so it must be the best.

The bandwagon error can be powerful because it causes a person to feel that if they don't conform, they will be left out or rejected. In general, be suspicious of any argument that mentions the popularity of an idea, and look at the information carefully.

ERROR IN THOUGHT	DEFINITION	QUESTIONS TO ASK TO DETECT AN ERROR
Bandwagon	Bandwagon errors are based on the reasoning that an idea is true because many people believe it to be true.	Are you being asked to join a larger group? Are you made to feel left out?

STUDENT EXAMPLE

Rene was asked to find the bandwagon error in McDonald's "America's Favorite" commercial and to answer the following questions.

What does the commercial argue the viewer should do or believe after watching? What is the consequence for not agreeing with the argument?

The commercial states that the eleven million people who eat at McDonald's each day have a wonderful experience, and the audience should, too. The song says that McDonald's makes people talk, laugh, and smile all while eating yummy and affordable food, implying that if you don't eat at McDonald's, you miss out on the food and fun. Additionally, by not eating there, you cannot be a part of the amazing partnership McDonald's has with its customers.

YOUR TURN

There are many examples of the bandwagon error in commercials. Search online for a commercial that contains a bandwagon error and answer the questions below. You might check out advertisements for different types of drinks, deodorant products, dental products, or phone providers.

What does the commercial argue the viewer should do or believe after watching? What is the consequence of not agreeing with the argument?

Stereotyping

Imagine a classmate has asked for a ride. When you get into the car, you put in your favorite Killswitch Engage CD and turn up the volume. Your classmate makes a face and blurts out, "You don't look like the kind of person who listens to heavy metal!"

Stereotypes are assumptions or generalizations about a whole group based on a trait or characteristic and are often used as a way to judge or evaluate an individual based on that assumption.

Everyone in group X has trait Y. Person A belongs to group X; therefore, person A also has trait Y.

College students are notorious procrastinators. Therefore Sammy, a freshman, will wait until the last minute to study for his test.

Kids hate vegetables. Tyrone, my nephew, is a toddler, so he will not eat the broccoli on his plate.

While many of the stereotypes we recognize are negative, stereotypes can also make assumptions that sound positive. Regardless of whether they are positive or negative stereotypes, they are still harmful; they can be incorrect and rob a person of his or her individuality or uniqueness.

ERROR IN THOUGHT	DEFINITION	QUESTIONS TO ASK TO DETECT AN ERROR
Stereotyping	Stereotyping errors are an assumption or generalization about a whole group based on a trait or characteristic.	What assumptions about an individual are being made based on his or her being part of a larger group?

STUDENT EXAMPLE

Rene was assigned the task of finding the stereotypes in a Taylor Swift Wonderstruck perfume commercial and answering the questions below.

What stereotypes are presented in the commercial? Are the stereotypes positive or negative?

There are several stereotypes in the commercial. The main one is that girls like frilly dresses, pink, and chandeliers. While this may be true for some girls, it isn't true for all of them. This stereotype is presented in a positive way, but it could be interpreted by viewers as offensive if they do not share these interests.

YOUR TURN

Search online for an example of stereotyping in a commercial. You might check out advertisements for perfume, hair care, or shaving products.

In the commercial you have found, identify traits or characteristics highlighted within the advertisement. Are these traits or characteristics shared by all members of the group? Which stereotypes are presented as positive in the advertisement you have selected? Which are presented as negative?

Hasty Generalizations

Imagine you are planning to see a new movie in the theater. You ask your aunt, who saw the movie last night with a friend, if she liked it. She says, "We both hated it. It won't be in the theaters long; anyone who sees it will tell everyone they know how horrible it is."

Hasty generalizations occur when a conclusion is formed based on too little evidence. It is also important to remember that while the conclusion may occasionally be true, the act of drawing a conclusion without enough evidence is still a logical error.

If A has characteristic X, then all things like A also have X characteristic.

If both my aunt and her friend hated the movie, then everyone will dislike the movie.

If Emad and Abel, who are both math majors, are nerdy, then all math majors must be nerdy.

Hasty generalizations can be particularly dangerous because they are difficult to spot. Some generalizations may initially sound reasonable. To identify a hasty generalization, pay attention to how many items were inspected, how many people were asked, or how many studies were cited. Ideally, enough information should be provided to show that the argument can be supported with multiple examples.

ERROR IN THOUGHT	DEFINITION	QUESTIONS TO ASK TO DETECT AN ERROR
Hasty Generalizations	Hasty generalization errors occur when a conclusion is based on too little evidence.	How many people were interviewed, or how many items were observed? Is there enough information to draw a conclusion or make a decision?

STUDENT EXAMPLE

Rene was asked to identify the generalizations in the song "Silly Eye-color Generalizations" by Regina Spektor and answer the questions below.

What generalizations are being made in the song? Were there enough men studied to make an accurate conclusion? Is there enough proof to support this generalization?

The lyrics of the song say that boys with dark brown eyes are sweet and well grounded. Boys with hazel eyes are deep and dangerous. Boys with blue eyes can't be trusted as they are changing and misleading, much like the singer's own eyes. It doesn't sound like Spektor's beliefs about eye color are based on very many people. The only proof we get is her description of each eye color and the effect the person had on her, which is not enough to serve as good evidence.

YOUR TURN

Search online for an example of a hasty generalization in an advertisement and answer the questions below. Consider advertisements for fast food restaurants or makeup products.

What hasty generalization is being made? Were there enough people or items examined to make an accurate conclusion? Is there enough proof to support the generalization?

False Dichotomy

Imagine your friend has just asked you to help him cheat on an upcoming test. When you voice your concern and argue that cheating doesn't sound like a good idea, he angrily replies, "You either help me, or we are no longer friends!"

A false dichotomy occurs when two choices are provided, even though more options are available. A dichotomy exists when things can be divided into two categories (e.g., dead / alive, up / down). If someone tries to suggest that a dichotomy exists when there are more than two possible categories, or more than two options, then they are presenting a *false dichotomy*.

There are only two choices: A or B.

Tonight, would you like to go to the movies, or would you rather play a game?

I must find the most unique costume, or I will not be able to go to the Halloween party.

Sometimes a false dichotomy can be presented in a threatening tone; if it takes this form, it might be appropriate to refer to it as an ultimatum. You may have heard the expression "It's my way or the highway." To avoid creating a false dichotomy in your academic writing, try to provide your readers with a variety of options. When you are presented with arguments, be conscious of any time you are given two options, and consider other options that might be available.

ERROR IN THOUGHT	DEFINITION	QUESTIONS TO ASK TO DETECT AN ERROR
False Dichotomy	False dichotomy errors occur when two choices are provided, even though several choices actually exist but are not given.	What options or choices are given? What other choices may be available? What does the speaker gain from each option?

STUDENT EXAMPLE

Rene's assignment is to find the false dichotomy error in a television show and answer the questions below. She chooses the episode "Ultimatum" from season six of the show *Numb3rs*.

What two choices are offered? What additional options could there be?

One character is explaining the ultimatum game, which contains a false dichotomy error, to another. In the game, one person gets to decide how to split one hundred dollars. The other participant can choose to accept the offer (presumably less than half) without question or reject it. If the offer is rejected, then neither player gets any money. While this is a game, the players are only given two options when more exist, a false dichotomy. Other options would be that they could change the rules of the game, discuss how to split the money, or one person could take all of the money without sharing.

YOUR TURN

Search online for the lyrics or video of The Clash's "Should I Stay or Should I Go." What two choices does the singer offer? What additional options could there be? Why might the singer give only two choices?

Practicing Finding Errors in Thought

Find as many logical errors as you can in the article "Should Students and Teachers Be Facebook Friends?" from *The Ledger*. Make notes in the article to identify each logical error you find, and explain why you marked each one.

"Should Students and Teachers Be Facebook Friends?" by Karen Matthews

The Ledger, April 18, 2012

Should students and teachers ever be friends on Facebook? School districts across the country, including the nation's largest, are weighing that question as they seek to balance the risks of inappropriate contact with the academic benefits of social networking.

At least 40 school districts nationwide have approved social media policies. Schools in New York City and Florida have disciplined teachers for Facebook activity, and Missouri legislators recently acquiesced to teachers' objections to a strict statewide policy.

In the New York cases, one teacher friended several female students and wrote comments including "this is sexy" under their photos, investigators said. A substitute teacher sent a message to a student saying that her boyfriend did not "deserve a beautiful girl like you."

Such behavior clearly oversteps boundaries, but some teachers say social media—in particular Facebook—can be a vital educational resource if used appropriately, especially because it's a primary means of communication for today's youngsters. "E-mail is becoming a dinosaur," said David Roush, who teaches media communications and television production at a Bronx high school. "Letters home are becoming a dinosaur. The old methods of engaging our students and our parents are starting to die."

New York Chancellor Dennis Walcott plans to release social media guidelines this month, saying recently that teachers "don't want to be put in a situation that could either compromise them or be misinterpreted."

Roush does not accept students as friends on his personal Facebook page but has created a separate profile to communicate with them—something that runs afoul of Facebook rules restricting users to a single profile. He used the page to get the word out quickly about a summer internship on a cable-access show, and a student who learned about it from the Facebook post won it. "If I would have e-mailed him, if I had tried calling him, he never would have got it," Roush said.

Nkomo Morris, who teaches English and journalism at a high school in Brooklyn, said she has about 50 current and former students as Facebook friends. That could be a problem if the new rules instruct teachers not to friend students.

In that event, "I'd send out a massive message, and I would unfriend them," Morris said.

In the meantime, Morris manages her privacy settings so neither current nor former students see her personal information but do see posts about current events. She also lets students know whether something on their Facebook pages raises a red flag, such as sexual content.

"They're not always as savvy as I am," Morris said. "They haven't really grasped the level of formality out in the real world."

Efforts like New York's have been subject to legal wrangling and resistance from teachers and their advocates.

Missouri legislators last year passed a law that barred teachers from using websites that allow "exclusive access" with students 18 years old or younger. Teachers complained that they would be banned from Facebook and Twitter.

A judge granted an injunction, declaring that the law "would have a chilling effect" on free-speech rights. The legislature then repealed the restrictions and passed a new law directing school districts to develop their own policies.

Some districts adopted a model policy by the Missouri School Boards Association, decreeing that staff members must use district-approved devices when communicating electronically with students. The guidelines are intended to make it easier for supervisors to monitor teacher-student interactions.

The Missouri State Teachers Association believes some of the local policies are too restrictive. Spokesman Todd Fuller said the association will support its members if they are disciplined under those new rules.

"We're prepared to deal with the first issue where a teacher's rights are being infringed," he said.

In New York City, a United Federation of Teachers spokesman said the union would not comment without seeing the district's new guidelines.

Donna Lieberman, executive director of the New York Civil Liberties Union, said she hopes the new policy considers First Amendment rights as well as "the enormous potential for benefiting students' education that is represented by technology."

Musical theater teacher Charles Willis was suspended in 2010 from Braden River High School in Florida for friending more than 100 students on Facebook and for allegedly posting sexually suggestive images and acronyms for profane words. He is now in a non-classroom job at another school, said John Bowen, a school board attorney.

The district still does not have a formal policy on social media use by teachers but is working on one, a district spokeswoman said.

Willis' lawyer did not return a call from The Associated Press, but in comments to the *Bradenton Herald* in March, he noted that students aren't innocents.

"For anyone who says that a teacher shouldn't curse in front of students, I say they haven't been on a football field or in the dugout in a baseball game," he told the newspaper. "If you could go incognito in those settings and somehow gather audio, you might be surprised at what is said."

Doctoral research at the University of Southern California found 41 districts nationwide that have approved social media policies.

Under a policy approved by the school board in Muscogee County, Ga., in November, school employees are "strongly discouraged" from allowing students access to personal websites. Districts in Tampa, Fla., and Norton, Mass., also have wrestled with the issue.

Nancy Willard, author of "Cyber Savvy: Embracing Digital Safety and Civility," believes school districts should set up their own online environments and use tools like Gaggle.net and ePals.com, which have been designed for educational purposes. There is also Edmodo, a Facebook-like network for teachers and students. The problem with Facebook, she said, is that it was set up for socializing.

"On Facebook, flirting is encouraged," she said. "You are encouraged to post your relationship status and your relationship interests. That's not appropriate for a relationship between teachers and students."

James Giordano, a guidance counselor at a Bronx high school, said that he makes a habit of waiting about four years after a student has graduated to friend one and that he's glad the district is discussing the issue.

"I hope that they distinguish between personal Facebook pages and pages that are professional," he said. "It would be a shame if Facebook altogether was banned from use by educators, because it's a valuable resource."

Assessing Your Knowledge

CHAPTER TARGETS	REMINDER	HOW WELL DID YOU UNDERSTAND THIS MATERIAL?	PAGE(S)
Identify and understand the logical error bandwagon	The **bandwagon** error would occur when an idea is considered correct because it is popular.	☐ I've Got It! ☐ Almost There ☐ Need More Practice	pp. 146–47
Identify and understand the logical error stereotyping	The **stereotyping** error occurs when assumptions or generalizations about a whole group are based on one trait or characteristic.	☐ I've Got It! ☐ Almost There ☐ Need More Practice	pp. 147–48
Identify and understand the logical error hasty generalization	A **hasty generalization** is an error that is made when a conclusion is formed without enough evidence.	☐ I've Got It! ☐ Almost There ☐ Need More Practice	pp. 148–49
Identify and understand the logical error false dichotomy	A **false dichotomy** error happens when an either/or choice is given; however, several more options are available but not mentioned.	☐ I've Got It! ☐ Almost There ☐ Need More Practice	pp. 150–51
Practice locating logical errors	This chapter provides an opportunity to practice finding logical fallacies in media examples and in an article.	☐ I've Got It! ☐ Almost There ☐ Need More Practice	pp. 146–53

Deepening Your Understanding

If you would like to go beyond the material in this chapter, explore additional connections, and get more practice, check out these related topics:

- **Vocabulary Development**: Knowing the meaning of words can help you understand a tricky or misleading passage more thoroughly. Defend yourself against errors in logic by building your vocabulary.

- **Argumentation**: In your classes, you will need to both create arguments and read the arguments of others. Understanding argumentation will assist you in finding the flaws in arguments you read in the future.

- **Critical Thinking**: Arguments don't always take the form of an article; some are visual, such as an advertisement or commercial. Visual arguments can also have logical errors and should be analyzed closely.

- **Research Process**: As you complete research, many of the arguments you encounter will offer evidence or examples as support. Evaluate each one for logical errors by paying close attention to the information presented and the reasoning provided.

PART II
Analyzing the Media

THE MEDIA ARE HARD to avoid in our daily lives. The previous chapters have touched on music videos, pictures, television show clips, and more. These are all types of media that you have probably encountered in your daily life. The upcoming chapters in Part II will focus on four specific types of media: social media, advertisements, the news, and television.

Social media are an ever-changing form of communication. Think of it as the modern version of people sitting around a campfire, chatting. Millions of people use social media to express feelings and ideas, share news, tell stories, and make new friends. Social media activities range from simply sharing a picture on Instagram or Tumblr, to tweeting about your favorite television show episode that just aired, to debating with strangers about the best gaming system on reddit.

Radio and television commercials, social media advertisements, billboards, and print advertisements in magazines—these are just a few of the many types of advertising. Advertisements allow companies to inform consumers about products and sell them. Advertisements also allow companies to compete with one another, thus giving the consumer a choice. This, however, also makes the companies rely heavily upon the ability to convince or persuade the viewer or reader to buy a product.

Keeping up with the news is important if we are to keep informed of local, national, and world events. There are several types of news, including press releases, newspapers, radio reports, and traditional television news. Many people rely on social media news feeds. Because there are so many options, we have a good deal of choice as to what sorts of news reaches us—although nowadays there is a great deal of controversy over how news media decide what news we see or read.

When televisions became widely available and popular in the 1950s, they were generally found only in living rooms. Families would gather around their one television set and watch together. This is no longer the case. We now watch television on our smart phones, in our cars, while we ride the bus, through the Internet, and at school. When we watch television, we can choose many different types of shows and programs, including comedies, reality television, news, talk shows, and dramas, among others. Television can provide us with endless hours of entertainment, and it can also give us a view of the world that would never be possible without it. Television even connects strangers by giving people a common subject to talk about. Yet many have also associated television with various negative trends; the term "couch potato" provides a vivid description of a very real phenomenon.

Before You Read

Before you read the chapters in Part II, answer the following questions:

1. Write down the social media sites you are aware of. Next, put a star next to the ones you personally use. Compare your list with your fellow students' lists. What sites had you never heard of until now? What is the most commonly used site in the class?

2. Make a list throughout your day of the advertising you encounter. Be sure to write down where you saw the ad and what it was for. Then look back at your day and reflect on the list you made. Which ad was the most convincing? Which was the least convincing? Which was the most memorable? To what extent were you aware of the advertisements around you?

3. Think of two ways in which you think social media and advertising are alike. Then think of two ways in which they are different.

4. How much television do you watch in a week? Keep a journal and record how long you watch television and what shows or programs you watch. Do you think you watch more or less television than other students in your class?

5. If you could get the news in any way or form you wanted, what would be your ideal news source? Use your imagination. Think about whether you would like to watch a show on television, listen to news on your phone or radio, or read about it online or in a newspaper. Describe in as much detail as possible what you would want the news to be like. What would it look or sound like? Who would you want to deliver your news? How would they look or sound? How long would it take to watch or listen to?

10 Social Media

"The question isn't, 'what do we want to know about people?'; it's, 'what do people want to tell about themselves?'"

—Mark Zuckerberg

Discovering Key Points

- Identify types of social media
- Recognize rhetoric in social media
- Understand the purposes of social media
- Apply what you've learned about social media in your writing

Social media are a vast and varied category of websites and mobile apps that allow individuals to communicate with others. Other forms of media provide information and entertainment to viewers but are not interactive; viewers may react to what they see or hear, but their reactions have no influence on the program being watched or heard. In contrast, social media encourage people to share their own information and to interact. These interactions can take many forms, including sharing status updates, providing personal messages, and even recommending movies, songs, restaurants, and articles. Through social media, multiple parties influence each other, and the direction of the conversation changes, depending on the information that is shared.

Why Are Social Media Important?

Social media affect how we live and how we view the world; they shape our world both directly and indirectly. We use social media to catch up with old friends, start new romances, gather news, share photos, upload videos, follow celebrities, and kill time. We are drawn to interact with others, and social media platforms provide us with a way to communicate with others who have similar interests. Like clubs and organizations, social media make it easy to identify and reach out to people who have shared opinions and passions. Not bound by a physical location or meeting place, social media allow us to meet people from all over the world, broadening our understanding of cultures, places, and ideas one interaction at a time.

Companies and advertisers have recognized social media as a vital way to connect with people. Sponsored posts that appear directly in feeds are a common and obvious way to advertise. Companies pay for space on social media platforms to try to ensure that those most likely to be interested in a service or product see the advertisement. Businesses create Facebook, Instagram, and Twitter accounts so they can interact with customers on a more personal level. Many websites, especially news sites, have embraced social media by encouraging viewers to share or like what they see. QR codes (quick response codes), handles, and other social media symbols are on almost everything, inviting you to learn more. The next time you see a clothing catalogue, commercial, political advertisement, or help wanted sign, look for social media symbols.

Examples of Different Types of Social Media

There are numerous social media platforms; below you will find a few representative examples.

Social Networks

The primary purpose of a general social networking site is to help people communicate with one another. These sites can be joined by anyone, and users choose the people with whom they want to interact. Facebook and Twitter are two of the most popular examples. Both are status-based, meaning users are encouraged to have large numbers of friends or followers. Unlike Facebook, Twitter restricts the length of each communication to a maximum of 280 characters, so longer streams of thought are often posted in the form of threads rather than in a single larger post.

Professional Networks

Some networks are more narrowly focused than the social networks mentioned earlier and limit themselves to a particular purpose. Professional networks such as LinkedIn help connect employers with job seekers and allow professionals to interact with others in their field. Others, like deviantArt, are specific to a type of career, in this case art, and allow users to showcase their work, connecting users with similar backgrounds.

Social News Aggregates

Some social media are designed to help you gather, or aggregate, more information. With the recommendations or posts from other users, reddit and Slashdot will help you find websites, pictures, videos, and articles that interest you. Digg's content is collected by editors and made available to users to view and organize.

Media Sharing

Some social media platforms put more emphasis on sharing information than on networking. YouTube shares videos that users post, either homemade or pulled from other sources. Last.fm tracks the music you listen to and recommends new music. Snapchat and Instagram allow users to share pictures, videos, or stories to their accounts and comment on others' posts. On Pinterest, pictures and short videos are often linked to websites where more information can be found.

Location-Aware Networks

Location-focused media help you locate what is near you and often give ratings or recommendations for businesses and restaurants. Some of them (such as Foursquare) also alert you to any people you know in the area. Shopkick shows stores near you, recommends popular items, and rewards you with points for entering a store and making a purchase. Yelp is one of several platforms that recommends restaurants in your area based on your preferences and allows you to post reviews of your experiences.

The Rhetorical Connection

Because there is so much content to take in across so many platforms, we tend to devote our energy to the posts that catch our attention. Sorting through the unending and fast-paced stream of content can be daunting. As a result, we often rely too heavily on a message's traffic or clout (how many times it has been viewed) to measure value. Examining rhetorical appeal offers a different way of understanding social media. In Chapter 8, you learned about three sorts of rhetorical appeal: ethos, logos, and pathos. How can we apply these concepts in the context of social media?

ⓘ
Need a review of rhetorical appeals? See Chapter 8.

Ethos—We are inclined to believe a post when we know or trust the person who made it. Is the person reputable or friends with others you know and trust? Do they have a history of reliable and helpful posts?

Pathos—How does the post or message make you feel? Do you think the post is cute, funny, shocking, or offensive?

Logos—On social media, information can come in many forms, including personal updates, tutorials, and even music recommendations. What kind of information is provided? Did the information satisfy your curiosity or answer your questions? If an argument is being made through a social media post, does it make sense?

YOUR TURN

Look for ethos, pathos, and logos appeals in the Facebook post from Future Farmers of America (FFA). Provide an explanation for each appeal you find.

The Purposes of Social Media

ⓘ
Want more information about purpose? See Chapter 3 or Chapter 5.

Creators of social media platforms may say that their sites are designed to connect people and allow us to share ideas, pictures, and videos. The public has found new and creative ways to use these platforms in addition to their original intended uses. We have adapted them to our own purposes: to persuade, to inform, to inspire, and to entertain. Specific platforms can serve several of these purposes depending on how, and by whom, they are used. Being aware of the purposes of the social media you engage with will help you to improve your experience and your understanding of what you see.

To Persuade—Persuasion in a social media community often takes the form of a recommendation. Other users may suggest websites or articles for you to read, or they might encourage you to go a restaurant. Persuasion also comes in the form of sponsored recommendations of products or experiences from influencers—people with large followings who are paid to post about a brand's products.

Examples: Yelp and Instagram

To Inform—Many social media platforms make it easy to inform or educate others. These communities are often a great place to hear about current events, discover new job openings, or learn how to redecorate your room.

Examples: reddit and LinkedIn

To Inspire—Some platforms are used to motivate others to improve their personal lives, skills, or surroundings.

Examples: Pinterest and deviantArt

To Entertain—Entertainment is a common purpose for media in general, and social media are no different. Social media can be used to amuse us with videos and games, as well as serve as a distraction or escape from our lives.

Examples: Snapchat and YouTube

YOUR TURN

Search online for a video tutorial. Consider looking for a tutorial explaining how to apply makeup, change the oil of a car, or how to build a tree house. What purposes can you find for this tutorial? You may find more than one purpose. Explain your reasoning for each purpose you find.

DISCUSSION TOPICS

1. As a class, make a list of your various interests, such as art, video games, or football. Break into small groups; each group should take several hobbies or interests from the list. Research online to see if there is a social media platform that connects people with the interests you have been given. Report which hobbies or interests you were able to find social media platforms for. What similarities can you find between the interests that had platforms available? What patterns can you find?

2. Bullying has always been a problem, but as the popularity of social media grows, so do the number of reported cases of bullying through social media. Have you been or do you know anyone who has been bullied through social media? How serious is social media bullying? What can be done to prevent bullying or improve the situation?

3. Ethos, pathos, and logos are important in any form of communication. Choose three social media communities. For each community, decide which rhetorical appeal is used

the most or is the most important. Explain your answers fully and provide examples as support. Explain why some communities might value one appeal over another.

CLASS DEBATE

1. Search online for information about the 2016 body-shaming post by Dani Mathers. Some argue that the comments and posts of celebrities are more influential because of their celebrity status and large number of followers. Split into two groups. Debate whether or not, and to what degree, celebrities should be held accountable for what they post on their social media accounts.

2. As a class, review Facebook's privacy policy. Does Facebook adequately protect the privacy of its users? What responsibilities should Facebook have concerning its users and their personal information?

BEFORE YOU READ

You're about to read an essay titled "My Daughter Asked Me to Stop Writing about Motherhood. Here's Why I Can't Do That" by Christine Tate. Before you read this essay, try to answer the following questions:

- Just based on the title, what do you think this essay is about?
- What do you already know about the subject?
- When was the essay written? Is it current (written within the last two years) or old?
- Where was the essay published (newspaper/magazine/textbook/etc.)? How do you know?
- Do you know anything about this author?

"My Daughter Asked Me to Stop Writing about Motherhood. Here's Why I Can't Do That," by Christine Tate

Washington Post, January 3, 2019

"This is the most epic Christmas ever," my fourth-grade daughter proclaimed from behind the new laptop we gifted her. After three years of her begging for a phone, tablet or computer, we capitulated with a basic laptop, complete with parental controls. We envisioned it primarily as a tool for schoolwork and learning how to use a keyboard. Based on her enthusiasm level, she envisioned it as a tool for binge-watching her favorite shows and keeping up with Zac Efron's love life. After enduring years of laments about how she was "the only kid" without her own device, it felt novel to soak in her gratitude and unalloyed joy.

That lasted almost 14 hours. The day after Christmas, she hunkered down to explore her laptop. First stop: an Internet-wide search on my name. Second stop: a furious march to my room, where she thrust the shiny new device in my face. "What's all this?" she said. The screen was covered with thumbnail sketches of her as a baby, a toddler and pre-schooler—each paired with an essay or blog post I'd written on the subject of parenting. "Why are all of these pictures of me on the Internet?" She wanted to know, and she had a right to know.

Years ago, when I began publishing essays and submitting family pictures to editors, I considered the day my children would confront me about what I'd written. At the time, I'd read articles by parents of older children who were weighing the ethics of using their children's stories or pictures for essay material, but my kids were too young to care what I shared about how they ate, how little they slept or how their taste in clothes was terrible. I remember thinking that one day I would have to answer for my work. Yet when the day finally arrived, I had no response prepared.

In the moment, I stammered, trying to buy time so I could go back and read what those sage parents had advised. When that failed, I told her the truth: that I write about our family in essays and that sometimes I include a picture. She was not comforted. "I wouldn't do that now without your permission," I promised. Could I take the essays and pictures off the Internet, she wanted to know. I told her that was not possible. There was heavy sighing and a slammed door. When I had pictured our first serious conversation about how the Internet is forever, I always thought we'd be talking about content posted by her, not me.

I read through some of my old pieces, and none of them seemed embarrassing to me, though she might not agree. A few years ago, I wrote about a disappointment in her social life—a girl she counted as her best friend abruptly stopped talking to her. While I wrote about the experience from the perspective of a mother trying to help her daughter through a rough patch without succumbing to anti-girl stereotypes about so-called mean girls, she might not appreciate seeing a painful episode from her past splashed across the Internet.

My impulse is to promise her that I'll never write about her again. In most of the articles I found on this subject, the writers eventually gave up writing about their children when they reached a certain age. They stopped to protect their children's privacy, or as Darlena Cunha explained, "to salvage their desire for such privacy so that as they become adults there is something there to preserve at all." I respect that approach and understand why it works for many writers, but it's not a promise I can make. Certainly, my daughter is old enough now that I owe her a head's up and a veto right on the pictures or on portions of the content, but I'm not done exploring my motherhood in my writing. And sometimes my stories will be inextricably linked to her experiences.

Promising not to write about her anymore would mean shutting down a vital part of myself, which isn't necessarily good for me or her. So my plan is to chart a middle course, where together we negotiate the boundaries of the stories I write and the images I include. This will entail hard conversations and compromises. But I prefer the hard work of charting the middle course to giving up altogether—an impulse that comes, in part, from the cultural pressure for mothers to be endlessly self-sacrificing on behalf of their children. As a mother,

I'm not supposed to do anything that upsets my children or that makes them uncomfortable, certainly not for something as culturally devalued as my own creative labor.

Writer Christine Organ has described how "we seem to be creating this unrealistic image of the mother as all-giving, all-knowing, selfless, superhuman who will gladly give up the last piece of apple pie to please her lip-smacking, big-eyed child." Surely, there's a way to cut the pie so that I can write about motherhood in a way that takes into account my daughter's feelings and respects her boundaries. But if I simply cordoned off motherhood as a forbidden subject for my writing, we would never know. My daughter didn't ask to have a writer for a mother, but that's who I am. Amputating parts of my experience feels as abusive to our relationship as writing about her without any consideration for her feelings and privacy.

For now, we have agreed that I will not submit a picture for a publication without her permission and that she has absolute veto rights on any image of herself. As for content, I have agreed to describe to her what I'm writing about, in advance of publication, and to keep the facts that involve her to a minimum. I have not yet promised that she can edit my work, but we acknowledged that is a future possibility. She also requested that instead of using her name, I call her by her self-selected pseudonym, Roshelle, and I'm taking that under advisement. One thing I did unequivocally say, however, was that I won't write anything mean about Zac Efron. That's a promise I intend to keep.

COMPREHENSION QUESTIONS

1. Describe what Christine Tate typically writes about.

2. Why is Tate's daughter upset?

3. How has Tate agreed to modify her writing in the future?

JOURNAL WRITING PROMPTS

1. What do you post about on your social media accounts? If you include pictures, what or who is featured in them? Have you ever posted a picture of someone without asking for his or her permission?

2. How do you try to protect your privacy on the Internet? Do you use the privacy settings on social media and web browsers? How concerned are you about posts you are tagged in?

DISCUSSION TOPICS/CLASS DEBATES

1. Tate says, "the Internet is forever." Explain what Tate means in this statement. Why is this such an important conversation for parents to have with their children? What kind of information is dangerous to share on the Internet?

2. At what age should children be allowed to decide what personal information is posted on the Internet? Discuss whether the age recommendation might be different for various social media sites.

1. Should Christine Tate avoid writing about her family, specifically her children? Develop your answer in an essay format.

2. In an essay, explore the complications and dangers that could be caused by parents' oversharing, or "sharenting," on social media.

Connecting the Pieces

Now that you've learned all about social media, you can apply what you've just learned. In this section, you'll find writing and discussion topics for you to practice your new skills.

1. Many sports leagues, both professional and collegiate, struggle to find balance with social media use. The National Football League's policy, which applies to players and staff, states, "No updates are permitted to be posted by the individual himself or anyone representing him during this prohibited time [before and during the game] on his personal Twitter, Facebook, or any other social media account." In a similar move, The National Basketball Association forbids players from posting 45 minutes before games through their post-game media commitments. Some teams have expanded these rules even further. Teams and owners want to avoid the media backlash from questionable social media posts. Write an essay discussing the potential effects of sports staff and players using social media. Consider the harms and benefits it can cause. Ultimately, decide if players and staff should be able to tweet what they think and feel.

2. Imagine you are a superhero. Create a profile for your alter ego on Facebook by answering the questions below. Then write an explanation of your profile. In your explanation, discuss who your friends would be and what you would highlight about yourself. Describe the photos you would post along with a reason you posted them. You should also discuss whether your profile would be public or private, and why.

	Name	
	Power	
	Email	
+ Add Profile Picture	City	
	Friends	

3. Most social media communities have basic guidelines for users that list behaviors that are not tolerated, such as Facebook's "Community Standards" or Pinterest's "Pin Etiquette," but few explain what people should do. Pick one social media community and write a set of instructions for new members that explains how they should behave. Think about advice that would help users effectively use the platform, become aware of safety precautions, and develop healthy personal interactions with other members.

DISCUSSION TOPICS

1. Researchers have found evidence to support a strong connection between spending time on Facebook and feelings of loneliness and unhappiness. Split into two groups and argue whether Facebook and other social media platforms do, on balance, tend to make users feel lonely and/or unhappy. If you are arguing that they do make us lonely and unhappy, how do they do so? Both sides should provide specific examples to support their arguments.

2. Sometimes people create fake accounts pretending to be celebrities, pets, or even completely made-up people. While this is sometimes entertaining, it can also cause problems, especially for people who interact with these fake profiles. Discuss what kind of problems may be caused by these attempts to be anonymous or deceitful. Decide whether people should be able to make fake profiles or accounts by pretending to be someone else. Is this more problematic for some social media communities than others? All of your answers should be fully explained. Use examples to support your opinion when possible.

Assessing Your Knowledge

KEY POINTS	REMINDER	HOW WELL DID YOU UNDERSTAND THIS MATERIAL?	PAGE(S)
Identify types of social media	There are many different types of social media. You are probably most familiar with **social networking**, **professional networking**, **social news aggregates**, **media sharing**, and **location-aware networks**.	☐ I've Got It! ☐ Almost There ☐ Need More Practice	pp. 158–59
Recognize rhetoric in social media	Rhetorical appeals can also be found in social media communications. We can use ethos, pathos, and logos to evaluate social media messages.	☐ I've Got It! ☐ Almost There ☐ Need More Practice	pp. 159–60
Understand the purposes of social media	Just like other types of media, social media have purposes which can be defined: to persuade, to inform, to inspire, and to entertain.	☐ I've Got It! ☐ Almost There ☐ Need More Practice	pp. 160–65
Apply what you've learned about social media in your writing	This chapter provides multiple opportunities for exploration through writing. Writing about social media will help you further understand its significance in our society.	☐ I've Got It! ☐ Almost There ☐ Need More Practice	pp. 160–66

Deepening Your Understanding

If you would like to go beyond the material in this chapter, explore additional connections, and get more practice, check out these related topics:

- **Subject-Verb Agreement**: Readers can have a hard time understanding your train of thought if they are confused about what is being described. Using subjects and verbs that agree in number and gender will help you keep your readers from getting distracted or confused, and proofreading your posts creates credibility with your readers.

- **Modifiers**: Discussing social media often requires a fair amount of detail. Using modifiers properly will make your explanations clear.

- **Narration**: Telling a story or narrating an event is common in papers about social media. Brush up on narration to get the most out of each paragraph.

- **Summary**: Use summaries in your social media posts to recount what others say. A summary can help you share the thoughts of others more efficiently when you are dealing with large amounts of information.

Advertisements

"Advertising is the greatest art form of the 20th century."
—Marshall McLuhan

Discovering Key Points

- Identify types of advertisements
- Recognize rhetoric regarding advertisements
- Identify target audience and placement in advertisements
- Identify techniques used in advertisements

"Satisfy your hunger."

"Just do it."

"The quicker picker-upper."

Recognize any of these slogans? If you do, advertising is the reason. An advertisement is a form of paid promotion by a company, designed to persuade consumers to purchase a particular product. Advertisements fill much of our daily lives. We hear them on the radio when we are traveling to work. We see them on the television when we are watching our favorite television show. We see them on the Internet when we are surfing the web. We see them on billboards and magazines. We see them on Facebook and Twitter.

The year's largest sports event in America is also the year's largest advertising event. Companies spend millions for a spot to place their commercial and spend months, even years, trying to prepare the "perfect" commercial. Many people tune in to the big game just to watch the advertisements. This event, of course, is the Super Bowl.

Advertisements can help us choose as consumers. We choose which movie to go see by watching trailers. We desire mascara when we see the beautiful model in the advertisement. We purchase a pizza when we receive a promotional email. Trailers, print ads, and promotional emails are all forms of advertisements. We even see advertisements in social media. For example, Twitter has Promoted Trends, where a musician, movie, or business can "get the word out" via tweeting from other users.

Examples of Different Types of Ads

Print Advertisements

Print advertisement are found in magazines and newspapers, like *Cosmopolitan*, *The New York Times*, *GQ*, or *The Wall Street Post*.

Radio Commercials

Radio commercials are found on both terrestrial radio (stations), satellite radio (for example, SiriusXM Radio), and Internet radio (for example, Slacker Radio). They rely heavily upon getting the audience's attention through sound.

Television Commercials

Television ads often play not only on television, but also on platforms such as YouTube and on company websites (for example, oldspice.com). Television commercials try to get the audience's attention through the use of visuals and sounds.

Social Media Advertisements

Advertisements found on social media can be either in a picture format (like a print ad from a magazine or newspaper) or in video form (like a television commercial).

Billboards

Billboard advertisements are found outside, often on the side of roads, and are quite large. Like print ads, billboards are visual in nature. However, they must be straightforward in their intention since their audience consists mainly of people in moving vehicles.

Political Advertisements

Political advertisements often occur during voting season and are made by politicians and political parties to reach a large audience and influence voters.

Other Types of Advertisements

Advertisements can also be found on park benches, buses, t-shirts, and many other places. Advertisements can take any form, including different shapes and sizes. A person can be a walking advertisement, even if he or she doesn't realize it. Simply walking around wearing Nike-branded gear promotes the brand.

The Rhetorical Connection

Advertisements are means of persuasion: advertisers try to influence you to buy their product, to motivate you to donate time or money, to encourage you to believe a certain position, or to sway you to vote a particular way. When you write an argumentative paper for class, you need to convince your audience of your argument; in the same way, advertisements must convince the audience to do something (in most cases, buy the product). This is their **purpose**. In fact, both argumentative papers and advertisements even use some of the same methods.

To review what purpose is, see Chapter 3.

Advertisements also use rhetoric, just as your essays will. Also, just like your writing, advertisements may be based on any or all of the three types of rhetorical appeals—**ethos**, **logos**, and **pathos**. These rhetorical appeals take slightly different forms in advertisements, though. Below are the appeals, and the questions you should ask yourself to see if those appeals are present:

Can't remember what ethos, logos, and pathos are? See Chapter 8.

Ethos—Is the company or product trustworthy? Do you trust the spokesperson?

Logos—Are there facts, figures, or statistics present in the advertisement? Do all claims in the advertisement seem reasonable?

Pathos—What might the audience feel when looking at this ad? What do I feel? What emotions did the company want to provoke?

One type of appeal is made more often than any other in advertisements—pathos. Advertisements typically try to appeal to our feelings as they try to motivate us to buy the product. Advertisements can be funny, sad, thought-provoking, or sexy.

YOUR TURN

Search online for two advertisements for Old Spice—one from the past few years and one from before 2016. What rhetorical appeals are found in these ads? Would both advertisements be considered rhetorically effective? Describe the similarities and the differences.

Target Audience and Placement

Just as every paper you write has a specific **audience** you are writing to, the **target audience** of an advertisement is the audience it is trying to sell to. To understand who the target audience is, it may be helpful to ask ourselves a few questions:

Can't remember how you know who your audience is or why they're important? See Chapter 3 or Chapter 5.

- What is the advertisement selling?
- Who generally uses this product?
- What age range would the audience be in?
- What else do we know about the audience?

STUDENT EXAMPLE

Josue is going to answer these same questions about a makeup advertisement.

- What is the advertisement selling?
  This advertisement is selling lipstick.

- Who generally uses this product?
  Women, because women generally wear makeup.

- What age range would the audience be?

  Women 25 to 60. This doesn't look like a brand a teenager would wear because it looks expensive.

- What else do we know about the audience?

  I know that women use lipstick to look good. I know that this lipstick ad looks like it is expensive because the packaging looks elegant and uses colors that look rich like gold, red, and black. I know that if a woman is wearing this lipstick, she likes to splurge on expensive things.

Placement

Placement goes hand in hand with target audience, so where the advertisement is placed may tell you a lot about the target audience. For example, an advertisement placed in *Vogue* will not have a target audience of men in the 65-and-older age group. One of the steps to figuring out the target audience is to determine the type of advertisement. If the advertisement is a video, the placement may be on a television channel or on social media platforms. If the advertisement is a print ad, like the Dior advertisement, the placement may be in a magazine or newspaper. Just like target audience, in order to know the placement, we have to ask ourselves a few questions:

- What type of advertisement is this (commercial, print ad, etc.)?
- Where would this type of advertisement generally appear (a magazine, television channel, etc.)?
- Refer to your answer to the previous question. Name a specific magazine, television channel, etc. where you would find this advertisement. (Sometimes, you have to make an educated guess about this one.)
- Who is the target audience?

Josue is going to answer these questions for the same Dior advertisement previously discussed.

- What type of advertisement is this (commercial, print ad, etc.)?

  This lipstick ad is a print ad because it is just a picture.

- Where would this type of advertisement generally appear (a magazine, television channel, etc.)?

  Lipstick ads are usually found in women's fashion magazines.

- Refer to your answer to the previous question. Name a specific magazine, television channel, etc. where would you find this advertisement. (Sometimes, you have to make an educated guess about this one.)

  I'm not too familiar with women's fashion magazines, so I had to Google it.
  After going to the sites of a few magazines, I think this one would be found in Glamour or Allure.

- Who is the target audience?

  I figured out the target audience would be women, 25–60, who like to look good and have money to spend on expensive lipstick.

A Breakdown of Techniques

To appeal to consumers, advertisements employ techniques. These varied techniques attempt to grab the audience's attention, influence their emotions, and persuade them. Here is a more detailed list of the sorts of techniques that may be used in advertisements.

See also Chapter 9 for errors in thought.

Bandwagon	The ad relies on the belief that something should be done or bought because this is what everyone else is doing.
Cartoons	A cartoon character (often a famous one) is connected with this ad.
Celebrities	The ad uses celebrities to sell the product. The ad may use testimonial (see below), an endorsement (spokesperson), or may promote a celebrity's brand.
The Cool Factor	The ad features people who are "cool" or could be seen as "cool."
Dreams and Insecurities	These ads play on the viewers' dreams (of being sexy, attractive, rich, etc.) and/or their insecurities (body image, lack of money, etc.).
Facts and Figures	The ad uses facts, figures, or statistics.
Family	The ad shows families being together or implies that this product will make your family happier.
Humor	The ad can be seen as funny to yourself or someone else.
Ideal People	Models in the ad appear to be perfect. They are fit, attractive, and cool looking. Women in these ads tend to be sexy and alluring, while the men tend to be tough and masculine.
Macho	The ad uses men that look masculine or uses manliness to sell the product (either the product will make you manlier or the product itself is manly).
Nature	The ad shows nature, or the product implies a connection with nature.

Nostalgia	The ad uses the feeling of nostalgia, a positive feeling about the past or one's childhood.
Sex Appeal	The ad uses sexual imagery to draw attention to the product.
Testimonial	The ad uses people (either celebrities or "average Joes") to provide their experience with the product ("I've used this product, and it worked for me!").
Wealth	The ad uses actors who look wealthy or associates wealth with the brand or buying the product.

YOUR TURN

Search online for a commercial for Werther's Original products. What sort of appeal(s) can you find in the commercial? (Refer to the chart above for a list of the techniques.)

DISCUSSION TOPICS

1. Split into groups. Each group should choose one of the ads presented in this chapter. Then, in the groups, answer the following questions:

   a. Is this advertisement rhetorically effective?
   b. If the advertisement is not rhetorically effective, how could you change it to make it more effective?
   c. What techniques are being used? Refer to the chart above for a list of techniques.
   d. Who is the audience for this ad?
   e. What is the placement of this advertisement?
   f. Would you buy this product based solely on the ad?

2. Can money truly buy happiness, or is Biggie right when he argues "Mo Money, Mo Problems"?

3. Make a list of the last five items you bought for yourself. These items cannot be bills, rent, or gas—just items strictly bought for you. What do these items say about who you are?

CLASS DEBATE

1. Many state that using sex appeal in advertisements is acceptable because "sex sells." Do you agree? Why or why not?

2. Is advertising aimed at children ethical? (Look, for example, at ads showing toys and what fun they can be to play with.)

3. In two groups, discuss ways in which the two types of tactics (using sex appeal and advertising to children) are similar, and ways in which they are different.

"What's in a Package," by Thomas Hine

Excerpt from *The Total Package: The Secret History and Hidden Meanings of Boxes, Bottles, Cans and Other Persuasive Containers*. Little, Brown and Company, 1995. Pages 1–9

When you put yourself behind a shopping cart, the world changes. You become an active consumer, and you are moving through environments—the supermarket, the discount store, the warehouse club, the home center—that have been made for you.

During the 30 minutes you spend on an average trip to the supermarket, about 30,000 different products vie to win your attention, and ultimately make you believe in the promise of the product. When the door opens, automatically, before you, you enter an arena where your emotions and your appetites are in play, and a walk down the aisle is an exercise in self-definition. Are you a good parent, a good provider? Do you have time to do all you think you should, and would you be interested in a shortcut? Are you worried about your health and that of those you love? Do you care about the environment? Do you appreciate the finer things in life? Is your life what you would like it to be? Are you enjoying what you've accomplished? Wouldn't you really like something chocolate?

Few experiences in contemporary life offer the visual intensity of a Safeway, a Krogers, a Pathmark or a Piggly Wiggly. No marketplace in the world—not Marrakesh or Calcutta or Hong Kong—offers so many different goods with such focused salesmanship as your neighborhood supermarket where you're exposed to 1,000 different products a minute. No wonder it's tiring to shop.

There are, however, some major differences between the supermarket and a traditional marketplace. The cacophony of a traditional market has given way to programmed, innocuous music, punctuated by enthusiastically intoned commercials. A stroll through a traditional market offers an array of sensuous aromas; if you are conscious of smelling something in a supermarket, there is a problem. The life and death matter of eating, expressed in traditional markets by the sale of vegetables with stems and roots and hanging animal carcasses, is purged from the supermarket, where food is processed somewhere else, or at least trimmed out of sight.

But the most fundamental difference between a traditional market and the places through which you push your cart is that in a modern retail setting, nearly all the selling is done without people. The product is totally dissociated from the personality of any particular person selling it—with the possible exception of those who appear in its advertising. The supermarket purges sociability, which slows down sales. It allows manufacturers to control the way they present their products to the world. It replaces people with packages.

Packages are an inescapable part of modern life. They are omnipresent and invisible, deplored and ignored. During most of your waking moments, there are one or more packages within your field of vision. Packages are so ubiquitous that they slip beneath conscious notice, though many packages are designed so that people will respond to them even if they're not paying attention.

Once you begin pushing the shopping cart, it matters little whether you are in a supermarket, a discount store or a warehouse club. The important thing is that you are among packages: expressive packages intended to engage your emotions, ingenious packages that make a product useful, informative packages that help you understand what you want and what you're getting. Historically, packages are what made self-service retailing possible, and in turn, such stores increased the number and variety of items people buy. Now, a world without packages is unimaginable.

Packages lead multiple lives. They preserve and protect, allowing people to make use of things that were produced far away, or a while ago. And they are potently expressive. They assure that an item arrives unspoiled, and they help those who use the item feel good about it.

We share our homes with hundreds of packages, mostly in the bathroom and kitchen, the most intimate, body-centered rooms of the house. Some packages—a perfume flacon, a ketchup bottle, a candy wrapper, a beer can—serve as permanent landmarks in people's lives that outlast homes, careers or spouses. But packages embody change, not just in their age-old promise that their contents are new and improved, but in their attempt to respond to changing tastes and achieve new standards of convenience. Packages record changing hairstyles and changing lifestyles. Even social policy issues are reflected. Nearly unopenable tamper-proof seals and other forms of closures testify to the fragility of the social contract, and the susceptibility of the great mass of people to the destructive acts of a very few. It was a mark of rising environmental consciousness when containers recently began to make a novel promise: "Less packaging."

For manufacturers, packaging is the crucial final payoff to a marketing campaign. Sophisticated packaging is one of the chief ways people find the confidence to buy. It can also give a powerful image to products and commodities that are in themselves characterless. In many cases, the shopper has been prepared for the shopping experience by lush, colorful print advertisements, 30-second television mini-dramas, radio jingles and coupon promotions. But the package makes the final sales pitch, seals the commitment, and gets itself placed in the shopping cart. Advertising leads consumers into temptation. Packaging *is* the temptation. In many cases it is what makes the product possible.

But the package is also useful to the shopper. It is a tool for simplifying and speeding decisions. Packages promise, and usually deliver, predictability. One reason you don't think about packages is that you don't need to. The candy bar, the aspirin, the baking powder or the beer in the old familiar package may, at times, be touted as new and improved, but it will rarely be very different.

You put the package into your cart, or not, usually without really having focused on the particular product or its many alternatives. But sometimes, you do examine the package. You read the label carefully, looking at what the product promises, what it contains, what it warns. You might even look at the package itself and judge whether it will, for example, reseal to keep a product fresh. You might consider how a cosmetic container will look on your dressing table, or you might think about whether someone might have tampered with it, or whether it can be easily recycled. The possibility of such scrutiny is one of the things that makes each detail of the package so important.

The environment through which you push your shopping cart is extraordinary because of the enormous amount of attention that has been paid to the packages that line the shelves. Most contemporary environments are landscapes of inattention. In housing developments, shopping centers, highways, office buildings and even furniture, design ideas are few and spread very thin. At the supermarket, each box and jar, stand-up pouch and squeeze bottle, each can and bag and tube and spray has been very carefully considered. Designers have worked and reworked the design on their computers and tested mock-ups on the store shelves. Refinements are measured in millimeters.

All sorts of retail establishments have been redefined by packaging. Drugs and cosmetics were among the earliest packaged products, and most drug stores now resemble small supermarkets. Liquor-makers use packaging to add a veneer of style to the intrinsic allure of intoxication, and some sell their bottle rather than the drink. It is no accident that vodka, the most characterless of spirits, has the highest profile packages. The local gas station sells sandwiches and soft drinks rather than tires and motor oil, and in turn, these products have been attractively repackaged for sales at supermarkets, warehouse clubs and home centers.

With its thousands of images and messages, the supermarket is as visually dense, if not as beautiful, as a Gothic cathedral. It is as complex and as predatory as a tropical rain forest. It is more than a person can possibly take in during an ordinary half-hour shopping trip. No wonder a significant percentage of people who need to wear eyeglasses don't wear them when they're shopping, and some researchers have spoken of the trance-like state that pushing a cart through this environment induces. The paradox here is that the visual intensity that overwhelms shoppers is precisely the thing that makes the design of packages so crucial. Just because you're not looking at a package, it doesn't mean you don't see it. Most of the time, you see far more than a container and a label. You see a personality, an attitude toward life, perhaps even a set of beliefs.

The shopper's encounter with the product on the shelf is, however, only the beginning of the emotional life cycle of the package. The package is very important in the moment when the shopper recognizes it either as an old friend or a new temptation. But once the product is brought home, the package seems to disappear, as the quality or usefulness of the product it contains becomes paramount. But in fact, many packages are still selling even at home, enticing those who have bought them to take them out of the cupboard, the closet or the refrigerator and consume their contents. Then, once the product has been used up, and the package is empty, it becomes suddenly visible once more. This time, though, it is trash that must be discarded or recycled. This instant of disposal is the time when people are most aware of packages. It is a negative moment, like the end of a love affair, and what's left seems to be a horrid waste.

The forces driving package design are not primarily aesthetic. Market researchers have conducted surveys of consumer wants and needs, and consultants have studied photographs of families' kitchen cupboards and medicine chests to get a sense of how products are used. Test subjects have been tied into pieces of heavy apparatus that measure their eye movement, their blood pressure or body temperature, when subjected to different packages. Psychologists get people to talk about the packages in order to get a sense of their innermost feelings about what they want. Government regulators and private health and safety advocates worry over package design and try to make it truthful. Stock-market analysts worry about how companies are managing their "brand equity," that combination of perceived value and consumer loyalty that is expressed in advertising but embodied in packaging. The retailer is paying attention to the packages in order to weed out the ones that don't sell or aren't sufficiently profitable. The use of supermarket scanners generates information on the profitability of every cubic inch of the store. Space on the supermarket shelf is some of the most valuable real estate in the world, and there are always plenty of new packaged products vying for display.

Packaging performs a series of disparate tasks. It protects its contents from contamination and spoilage. It makes it easier to transport and store goods. It provides uniform measuring of contents. By allowing brands to be created and standardized, it makes advertising meaningful and large-scale distribution possible. Special kinds of packages, with dispensing caps, sprays, and other convenience features, make products more usable. Packages serve as symbols both of their contents and of a way of life. And just as they can very powerfully communicate the satisfaction a product offers, they are equally potent symbols of wastefulness once the product is gone.

Most people use dozens of packages each day and discard hundreds of them each year. The growth of mandatory recycling programs has made people increasingly aware of packages, which account in the United States for about forty-three million tons, or just under 30 percent of all refuse discarded. While forty-three million tons of stuff is hardly insignificant, repeated surveys have shown that the public perceives that far more than 30 percent—indeed, nearly all—their garbage consists of packaging. This perception creates a political problem for the packaging industry, but it also demonstrates the power of packaging. It is symbolic. It creates an emotional relationship. Bones and wasted food (13 million tons), grass clippings and yard waste (thirty-one million tons), or even magazines and newspapers (fourteen million tons) do not feel as wasteful as empty vessels that once contained so much promise.

Packaging is a cultural phenomenon, which means that it works differently in different cultures. The United States has been a good market for packages since it was first settled and has been an important innovator of packaging technology and culture. Moreover, American packaging is part of an international culture of modernity and consumption. At its deepest level, the culture of American packaging deals with the issue of surviving among strangers in a new world. This is an emotion with which anyone who has been touched by modernity can identify. In lives buffeted by change, people seek the safety and reassurance that packaged products offer. American packaging, which has always sought to appeal to large numbers of diverse people, travels better than that of most other cultures.

But the similar appearance of supermarkets throughout the world should not be interpreted as the evidence of a single, global consumer culture. In fact, most companies that do business internationally redesign their packages for each market. This is done partly to satisfy local regulations and adapt to available products and technologies. But the principal reason is that people in different places have different expectations and make different uses of packaging.

The United States and Japan, the world's two leading industrial powers, have almost opposite approaches to packaging. Japan's is far more elaborate than America's, and it is shaped by rituals of respect and centuries-old traditions of wrapping and presentation. Packaging is explicitly recognized as an expression of culture in Japan and largely ignored in America. Japanese packaging is designed to be appreciated; American packaging is calculated to be unthinkingly accepted.

Foods that only Japanese eat—even relatively humble ones like refrigerated prepared fish cakes—have wrappings that resemble handmade paper or leaves. Even modestly priced refrigerated fish cakes have beautiful wrappings in which traditional design accommodates a scannable bar code. Such products look Japanese and are unambiguously intended to do so. Products that are foreign, such as coffee, look foreign, even to the point of having only Roman lettering and no Japanese lettering on the can. American and European companies are sometimes able to sell their packages in Japan virtually unchanged, because their foreignness is part of their selling power. But Japanese exporters hire designers in each country to repackage their products. Americans—whose culture is defined not by refinements and distinctions but by inclusiveness—want to think about the product itself, not its cultural origins.

We speak glibly about global villages and international markets, but problems with packages reveal some unexpected cultural boundaries. Why are Canadians willing to drink milk out of flexible plastic pouches that fit into reusable plastic holders, while residents of the United States are believed to be so resistant to the idea that they have not even been given the opportunity to do so? Why do Japanese consumers prefer packages that contain two tennis balls and view the standard U.S. pack of three to be cheap and undesirable? Why do Germans insist on highly detailed technical specifications on packages of videotape, while Americans don't? Why do Swedes think that blue is masculine, while the Dutch see the color as feminine? The answers lie in unquestioned habits and deep-seated imagery, a culture of containing, adorning, and understanding that no sharp marketer can change overnight.

There is probably no other field in which designs that are almost a century old—Wrigley's gum, Campbell's soup, Hershey's chocolate bar—remain in production only subtly changed and are understood to be extremely valuable corporate assets. Yet the culture of packaging, defined by what people are buying and selling every day, keeps evolving, and the role nostalgia plays is very small.

For example, the tall, glass Heinz ketchup bottle has helped define the American refrigerator skyline for most of the twentieth century (even though it is generally unnecessary to refrigerate ketchup). Moreover, it provides the tables of diners and coffee shops with a vertical accent and a token of hospitality, the same qualities projected by candles and vases of flowers in more upscale eateries. The bottle has remained a fixture of American life, even though it has always been a nuisance to pour the thick ketchup through the little hole. It seemed not to matter that you have to shake and shake the bottle impotently, until far too much ketchup comes out in one great scarlet plop. Heinz experimented for years with wide-necked jars and other sorts of bottles, but they never caught on.

Then in 1992 a survey of consumers indicated that more Americans believed that the plastic squeeze bottle is a better package for ketchup than the glass bottle. The survey did not offer any explanations for this change of preference, which has been evolving for many years as older people for whom the tall bottle is an icon became a less important part of the sample. Could it be that the difficulty of using the tall bottle suddenly became evident to those born after 1960? Perhaps the tall bottle holds too little ketchup. There is a clear trend toward buying things in larger containers, in part because lightweight plastics have made them less costly for manufacturers to ship and easier for consumers to use. This has happened even as the number of people in an average American household has been getting smaller. But houses, like packages, have been getting larger. Culture moves in mysterious ways.

The tall ketchup bottle is still preferred by almost half of consumers, so it is not going to disappear anytime soon. And the squeeze bottle does contain visual echoes of the old bottle. It is certainly not a radical departure. In Japan, ketchup and mayonnaise are sold in cellophane-wrapped plastic bladders that would certainly send Americans into severe culture shock. Still, the tall bottle's loss of absolute authority is a significant change. And its ultimate disappearance would represent a larger change in most people's visual environment than would the razing of nearly any landmark building.

But although some package designs are pleasantly evocative of another time, and a few appear to be unchanging icons in a turbulent world, the reason they still exist is because they still work. Inertia has historically played a role in creating commercial icons. Until quite recently, it was time-consuming and expensive to make new printing plates or to vary the shape or material of a container. Now computerized graphics and rapidly developing technology in the package-manufacturing industries make a packaging change easier than in the past, and a lot cheaper to change than advertising, which seems a far more evanescent medium. There is no constituency of curators or preservationists to protect the endangered package. If a gum wrapper manages to survive nearly unchanged for ninety years, it's not because any expert has determined that it is an important cultural expression. Rather, it's because it still helps sell a lot of gum.

COMPREHENSION QUESTIONS

1. Why does Hine say that a supermarket "is as complex and as predatory as a tropical rain forest"?

2. How has the ketchup bottle changed? Why did Heinz choose to change it?

3. Hine argues there is a "power of packaging" that is "symbolic" and "creates an emotional relationship." Do you agree with this or not? Why? Provide specific examples.

JOURNAL WRITING PROMPTS

1. What is one item you've bought solely based on the packaging? What was it about the packaging that made you want to buy it?

2. Name one instance of a product where packaging is important and one where it is not. Explain your answers with specific reasons.

DISCUSSION TOPICS/CLASS DEBATES

1. Why are Americans less likely to want packaging to change?

2. In groups, choose an existing product. Then, decide how you would change the packaging in order to appeal to more people. Present the old packaging, as well as how your group chose to change the packaging. Explain your decisions to the class as well.

WRITING TOPICS

1. Write a paper where you compare/contrast a product with two different types of packaging (for example, cereal in a box vs. cereal in a bag). Be sure to describe both types of packaging, the similarities, and the differences. Finally, argue which packaging is the best and why.

2. Many people would argue that people package themselves. In an essay, argue whether or not this is true and why. Be sure to give specific examples to prove your point.

Connecting the Pieces

Now that you've learned all about advertising, you can apply what you've just learned. In this section, you'll find writing prompts and discussion topics for you to practice your new skills.

WRITING PROMPTS

1. Write an essay where you compare and contrast two ads relating to milk. In your essay, describe both ads, as if your reader had not seen them before. In your description, be sure to include not only what is in the ad but also the audience, possible placement, rhetorical appeals used, and techniques used. Then you should compare and contrast the ads, giving two reasons for each (Hint: Think about how the ad looks, how the ad is set up, and the emotions it might evoke). Lastly, argue which advertisement is most effective and why.

2. Select a problematic advertisement campaign, such as that of an oil company trying to regain consumers' trust after an oil spill. Imagine that you are an account executive in charge of advertising for the campaign, and that a major problem has arisen: Consumers have begun to protest the ethical problems involved in the campaign's current advertising strategy, and public protests and boycotts have caused sales or donations to drop. In response to this problem, write an essay that proposes a new direction for the campaign and present it to the company for approval. Ultimately, the task is to make an argument about what new direction this campaign should take and why. Be very specific in your proposal; discuss what elements in the company's ads should change, what techniques should be used, what sorts of images or slogans should be employed, etc. Think about your rationale. *Why* will your proposed campaign be a more effective way to sell the product/company?

3. For this paper, you will create an advertisement for a brand-new product (one that does not exist). After your advertisement is created, you can begin focusing on the essay. This essay will focus on arguing why the advertisement is an effective one. Here are things you should think about:
   - Why is your advertisement effective (and what sort of rhetorical appeal does it make)?
   - Who is your audience? (Be specific! Don't just say "people" or "women.")

- What techniques will you use? Refer to the chart on pages 174–75 for a list of techniques.
- How do you want your audience to respond to your ad?
- What emotions do you want to use to sell your product?
- How do you want to create your ad?
  - poster board
  - video
  - PowerPoint
- What is the best way to advertise your product?

1. Work in groups. Then, based on one of the topics below, create an advertisement with a spokesperson. Remember to consider all of the ethical dilemmas you may face with this advertisement. Also remember that you have been hired by the company, so the advertisement needs to be an effective one that would make people want to buy this product. Write a paragraph explaining why you made the choices you did and why your advertisement is effective. Remember, your advertisement must include all three rhetorical appeals.
   - Imagine you live in a jurisdiction in which marijuana is legal and work at an advertisement agency that has been hired to promote a new marijuana cigarette for ambitious, white-collar businesspeople.
   - Grand Theft Auto: Broads & Bordellos has been released for the PlayStation 5 and Xbox Series X. You work at an advertisement agency, and you need to promote this game for teenage girls and young women, ages 13–26.
   - There is a new 1,000-acre resort hotel off the tropical coast of Costa Rica that is hiring children, ages 3–12, to be on the hotel staff. You work at an advertisement agency, and you need to promote this resort to families with small children.
   - You are the head of a large advertising agency that has been hired by a car manufacturer to sell a self-driving car to teens and parents of teens.

2. Work in groups, and create an advertisement based on "a very bad ad." In other words, locate an advertisement that is not rhetorically effective and completely redesign the advertisement so that it is more effective in reaching its target audience, conveying its message, and achieving its purpose. You may choose a print advertisement from a magazine or a commercial; however, you must revise it using the same medium. This means if you choose a Nike commercial, you will need to revise the advertisement by making another commercial (video, not PowerPoint or poster board). You must start from scratch—everything must be newly generated; no trace of the original advertisement may remain, except the product name. In addition, all images and copy must be

generated by you (no stock photos, no clip art). Present the "bad" and revised advertisement to the class, and as a group, write a paragraph describing what was wrong with the "bad" ad, what you changed, and why you changed it.

Assessing Your Knowledge

KEY POINTS	REMINDER	HOW WELL DID YOU UNDERSTAND THIS MATERIAL?	PAGE(S)
Identify types of advertisements	There are many types of advertisements: print ads found in **magazines**, **radio commercials**, **television commercials**, **social media advertisements**, **billboards**, **political advertisements**, and other ads, such as those found on buses.	☐ I've Got It! ☐ Almost There ☐ Need More Practice	pp. 170–71
Recognize rhetoric regarding advertisements	Successful advertisements use all three rhetorical appeals—**ethos** (making their brand/product trustworthy), **logos** (presenting facts/statistics), and **pathos** (evoking an emotion from the audience).	☐ I've Got It! ☐ Almost There ☐ Need More Practice	pp. 171–72
Identify target audience and placement in advertisements	The **target audience** for an advertisement is the specific group it is selling the product to. The **placement** is where that ad could be found. These two elements work hand in hand as well, because where the advertisement is placed will tell you a good deal about the target audience.	☐ I've Got It! ☐ Almost There ☐ Need More Practice	pp. 172–74
Identify techniques used in advertisements	**Techniques**, such as the "cool" factor and sex appeal, are used to evoke emotion, or pathos, in the audience. These techniques help the advertisement become more effective.	☐ I've Got It! ☐ Almost There ☐ Need More Practice	pp. 174–75

Deepening Your Understanding

If you would like to go beyond the material in this chapter, explore additional connections, and get more practice, check out these related topics:

- **Adjectives**: Advertisements use descriptive words to explain what the product is like to the viewer. These expressive words are known as adjectives.

- **Using Precise Language**: Companies know that using the right words is important in advertisements. Choosing the right words can affect the ethos of the product and company.

- **Argumentation**: All advertisements argue or persuade us to buy the product. Ethos, logos, and pathos all influence whether the advertisement is argumentative or how argumentative it is.

- **Description**: Advertisements rely heavily upon description, as they must communicate what the product is, does, and looks like. An advertisement with detailed, specific description can help a consumer decide whether to buy the product.

12 News

"People can get their news any way they want. What I love about what's happened is that there are so many different avenues, there are so many different outlets, so many different ways to debate and discuss and to inquire about any given news story."

—Jim Lehrer

FACT OR FICTION?
All news programs are biased and can't be trusted.

FICTION.
Bias, the influence or preferences of those providing the news, is often unavoidable. Acknowledging the presence of bias, however, can help neutralize the effects. If you are aware of bias, you can sift through the information for the facts you need.

Discovering Key Points

- Identify types of news
- Recognize errors in thought within the news
- Understand fact and opinion within the news
- Understand bias within the news

The news, in its various forms, keeps us informed or educated about our local communities and communities around the world. Knowing what is going on in the world around you will provide you with perspective. Not only will you have more to talk about, but if you are well informed, you will be better able to make decisions, vote, and even write essays for class.

Recent advances in technology allow us to receive our news in ways that we couldn't have dreamed of ten or twenty years ago. While we still have more traditional forms of news, such as newspapers and traditional television news shows, we can also receive news through social media and the Internet on our laptops and phones. The rapid increase in options has provided us with alternatives, but it has also given us more responsibility. Being aware of bias, opinion, and accuracy has always been important, but additional media sources have brought with them new problems. No matter where your news comes from, you are still responsible for critically evaluating the information.

Examples of Different Types of News

Below are a few examples of the various types of news programs you may find.

Press Releases

Press releases are announcements given to members of the press. They can be issued by governments, corporations, sports teams, charitable bodies, or by any other sort of organization. Reporters are often able to ask questions after the announcement has been made.

Newspapers

Newspapers focus largely on current news stories. Some newspapers focus on national and international news; others cover local or regional news. The popularity of printed newspapers has declined as more people prefer to get their news online or from social media. As a result, some newspapers are now found only online.

Radio News

News found on radio programs can vary greatly in subject matter. Generally, each show or host has a theme, such as politics, sports, or entertainment. Some stations offer news every half hour, while others air news programming for most of the day.

Social Media News

Twitter, Facebook, reddit, and other social media platforms have become a primary source of news for many people. Specific news sources can be followed or liked, and many people appreciate the speed with which they receive breaking news through live feeds and instant updates.

Traditional Television News

Many major television networks have daily news programs, and other networks are completely dedicated to news programs. Regional news can often be found on local television channels. These programs generally project a formal tone and attempt to remain neutral.

Comedy News

Comedy news looks like traditional television news but uses comedy and humor to comment on current events. These shows often use clips from traditional television news shows to further their stories, but they add their own commentary and interpretation.

Specialized News

Some news programs, websites, and radio programs are very specialized and discuss only certain topics. Entire shows are dedicated to the in-depth coverage of topics such as sports, weather, or finance.

Entertainment News

News about celebrities, entertainment, and gossip is a very informal type of news. Entertainment news can be found on television, radio, and on the Internet. While entertainment news sources are not taken as seriously as other types of news, they do provide current information about high-interest people and topics.

Connection with Errors in Thought

In Chapter 9, you learned about errors in thought. Such errors can occur in any type of message, including the news. Accepting everything you see or hear to be true is dangerous. While errors may be made by those reporting the news, they may also be made by those being interviewed or giving eye-witness reports. Being aware of logical errors in any communication you receive will help you defend yourself against misinformation and faulty thinking.

> **ⓘ**
> Want more information about errors in thought? See Chapter 9.

ERROR IN THOUGHT	DEFINITION	QUESTIONS TO ASK TO DETECT AN ERROR
Bandwagon	Bandwagon errors are based on the reasoning that an idea is true because many people believe it to be true.	Are you being asked to join a larger group? Are you made to feel left out?
Stereotyping	Stereotyping errors are an assumption or generalization about a whole group based on a trait or characteristic.	What assumptions about an individual are being made based on his or her being part of a larger group?

Hasty Generalizations	Hasty generalization errors occur when a conclusion is based on too little evidence.	How many people were interviewed, or how many items were observed? Is there enough information to draw a conclusion or make a decision?
False Dichotomy	False dichotomy errors occur when two choices are provided, even though several choices actually exist but are not given.	What options or choices are given? What other choices may be available? What does the speaker gain from each option?

Even though logical errors are not found in all news programs or reports, looking for these errors is still a necessary part of processing the information they provide.

YOUR TURN

Search online for the episode of *Last Week Tonight with John Oliver* about multilevel marketing. What logical error(s) can you find in this episode? Explain how each error you find in the episode is made.

Fact and Opinion

While the definition of facts and opinions may be clear, identifying them in a news broadcast can be tricky. Hosts, announcers, reporters, and even those being interviewed can insert opinions about a person or issue into their reports. Coming up with your own conclusions is easier when you can separate the facts from opinions. You are less likely to be unfairly swayed by the unproven beliefs of others if you practice evaluating the information you receive.

	DEFINITION	EXAMPLE
Fact	A piece of information that can be confirmed as accurate or correct	Barack Obama was the 44th president of the United States. The high temperature today was 98 degrees.
Opinion	A feeling, belief, or judgment; cannot be verified	The best presidents come from Virginia. It was too hot to go to soccer practice.

YOUR TURN

Search online for a clip from the site TMZ. As you watch, record the facts you hear, as well as the opinions.

Understanding Bias

You may have heard people say that all news is biased. **Bias** in the media is the influence of the reporter, publication, or news network's opinion on a topic. In many ways, bias is unavoidable, but many involved in presenting the news try to remove as many of their opinions as possible.

Bias through Placement and Selection

Bias may be evident not only in opinions that are expressed (or implied) but also in the choice of what is covered and how much prominence is given to each item. Time constraints and page limits force producers and editors to choose some stories over others. While people in these jobs don't write the material, they do choose what gets published. These decision-makers try to pick stories they feel are current and important. The stories and information that make it into the news have been shown preference just by being chosen. The most important stories will be put in a place of significance. In a print newspaper or news website, the stories deemed by the editors to be most important are on the front page or at the top of the screen to catch the readers' attention. On a television program, it is common for some of the most important stories to be saved until the end of the program to keep viewers from changing the channel.

Bias by Association or Regionalism

Bias can also be caused by a close affiliation to a program, group, organization, or even an affinity for an area of the country. In general, people are most concerned with issues that directly affect them. As a result, local news stations will give preference to stories about local issues. Additionally, a strong feeling of belonging can affect how information is interpreted. Just as a person is unlikely to believe negative rumors about someone they care for, many people show preference for sports teams, politicians, or local businesses when compared to those perceived as outsiders or different.

Bias through Word Choice and Tone

To tell a news story, many descriptive words must be used. Creating a vivid picture of an event without using words with connotations is nearly impossible. The words that are chosen can have a profound effect on how an audience understands the story. Some words have positive associations. When you hear the words "sweet" and "warm," you are likely to remember good feelings and memories. Reporters can't avoid using descriptive words; still, they must try to be as fair as possible. When reading or viewing the news, be aware of the words that are chosen. For example, protesters could be described as "waiting peacefully" or "sitting with a defeated air," as "forceful and determined" or as "hostile and aggressive." Nouns are important too; one news network may describe as "activists" a group that another network describes as "terrorists." With each word or phrase, a reporter's feelings about a subject may affect the perspective of an unsuspecting audience.

DISCUSSION TOPICS

1. Split into groups in class. Each group should find a news clip and look for evidence of bias in the clip. After answering the following questions, decide if a specific type of bias is present.

   a. Does the news clip use descriptive words with strong connotations? List all that you find.

   b. What feelings or ideas do you normally associate with these words?

   c. Does the news clip show a preference or positive feelings toward a local area, person, business, or group? Explain your answer.

   d. Does the news clip show bias by covering some stories first or for a longer period of time? Explain your answer.

2. Watch a broadcast of traditional television news. Pay attention to what the reporter says. Does the speaker seem trustworthy? Explain why or why not. Make sure to provide examples to support your opinion.

3. In the past, the news was expected to give only the facts of a story. Should that still be the aim? Can opinions offered by newscasters and reporters be helpful? Explain why or why not. Make sure to provide examples to support your opinion.

CLASS DEBATE

1. Some people would argue that entertainment news has no value and can even be harmful. In two groups, discuss whether entertainment news has value. Does it provide our society with any benefits or anything we need?

BEFORE YOU READ

You're about to read an essay titled "That's News to Me" by Robert Schmuhl. Before you read his essay, try to answer the following questions:

- Just based on the title, what do you think this essay is about?
- What do you already know about the subject?
- When was the essay written? Is it current (written within the last two years) or old?
- Where was the essay published (newspaper/magazine/textbook/etc.)? How do you know?
- Do you know anything about this author?

"That's News to Me," by Robert Schmuhl

Notre Dame Magazine, June 19, 2005

When the Television Critics Association selected *The Daily Show* on Comedy Central as the outstanding news and information program for 2004, the host of the nightly satire, Jon Stewart, acted mystified. Winner the year before for best achievement in comedy, Stewart worried the award might be a case of mistaken identity.

Outside observers had their own concerns. Were critics engaging in their own frivolity by choosing "The Most Trusted Name in Fake News" (as *The Daily Show* bills itself) over such nominees as ABC's *Nightline*, CBS's *60 Minutes* and PBS's *Frontline*? Or has traditional journalism in America reached a crossroads, with novel forms arresting our attention and becoming influential in contemporary affairs?

A cartographer intending to map today's media world needs to work in pencil and keep a sizable eraser handy. As the communications revolution that began in the 20th century keeps accelerating, the landscape for receiving messages seems unrecognizable from the past. New forms (via cable, satellite and the Internet) compete with ink-on-paper publications and over-the-air broadcasts not only for a person's time but also for the way that person becomes informed.

Numbers help explain why yesterday's maps look outdated. Newspaper circulation dropped 1 percent each year from 1990 to 2002. Since 1975, across the country 300 daily papers have gone out of business. According to a 1994 survey by the Pew Research Center for the People and the Press, 58 percent of respondents said they'd read a newspaper the day before. A decade later, the number was down to 42 percent, with those ages 18 to 29 at a mere 23 percent.

Television news, particularly at the major network level, is in sorrier shape. From peak ratings in the late 1960s, the 30-minute nightly news broadcasts on ABC, CBS and NBC have lost 59 percent of their collective audience. Between 1993 and 2004, Pew Center researchers found that regular watching of an evening network report declined from 60 percent of those surveyed to 34 percent.

American population is steadily increasing—203 million in 1970 to 295 million in 2005—but the consumer base of traditional news outlets is contracting. New information alternatives offer such an array of choices it's often difficult to know where to turn. In the current media world, the concept of "mass"—as in "mass audience" or "mass medium"—loses much of its prior meaning because the environment is so cluttered. Journalistic sources that didn't exist a few years ago flourish at the expense of long-established outlets.

In the same Pew Center study charting the decline in frequency for reading newspapers and watching television news, 38 percent of Americans say they regularly tune to cable news and 29 percent go to Internet news sites at least three days per week—a rise in online usage from a miniscule 2 percent in 1995. Popularity of news magazines and radio news remained fairly constant over the past decade—but neither form's current status could be confused with bygone glory days.

Then, of course, there's *The Daily Show*. What the public considers news today is vastly different from the era of "mass" outlets. Jon Stewart and his talented sidekicks focus on current subjects and journalism vulnerabilities, including network coverage, producing "fake news" that's funny and telling. Younger viewers in particular find *The Daily Show* approach engaging, ranking it highly as an influential source of what they know about contemporary affairs.

That Stewart actually interviews authentic newsmakers means that a viewer is constantly shifting back and forth between satire and some semblance of news. (John Edwards, for instance, announced his candidacy for the 2004 Democratic presidential nomination on *The Daily Show*.) The program takes delight in violating traditional journalistic canons, and in a rapidly changing information arena it wins awards....

What makes *The Daily Show* different is not only its bull's-eye reliance on newsy matters (momentous or momentary) but also its deliberate appearance as a television news production. The program blurs the lines dividing journalism from entertainment. What we're watching is parody, ersatz news, yet it's certainly about real news.

To a certain extent, nationally aired radio talk programs share similarities with *The Daily Show*. In high-tech symbiosis, they live off of what's being reported as news while the host provides a point of view that combines commentary and crowd-pleasing delivery. A Rush Limbaugh or an Al Franken comes across as an ideological true believer, but an impulse to amuse often animates the words. News becomes part of the personality's shtick. Is the result journalistic commentary or news-driven entertainment? Again, distinct lines aren't apparent....

In today's tangled and thorny media world, older mainstream sources (newspapers, magazines, broadcast networks and the like) compete with newer alternative outlets—and increasing numbers rely on the tributaries rather than the mainstream. Ready access to these new media and their messages is but one reason they're selected.

Another factor is the precipitous decline in trust and credibility experienced by traditional news organizations in recent years. Back in the 1970s, CBS news anchor Walter Cronkite led opinion surveys as "the most trusted figure" in American public life, and newspaper reporters Carl Bernstein and Bob Woodward were regarded as heroes for their investigation of Watergate. Such admiration didn't last. In the fall of 2004, a Gallup Poll found just 44 percent of Americans confident of the media's ability to report news accurately and fairly.

Whether it be Jayson Blair's fabricated dispatches for *The New York Times*, the ill-sourced and irresponsible report on CBS's *60 Minutes* about President George W. Bush's National Guard service or any of the other outrages exposed lately, flagrant unprofessionalism propels dubious citizens to other sources. The beneficiaries of mainstream media malfeasance are often the nontraditional outlets. Bloggers, in particular, can—and do—point out blatant errors, as they did with the *60 Minutes* report, and gain followers in the process.

Valuable as alternative sources might be, they pose potential problems. In most cases, serious shoe-leather reporting is secondary to commentary, and the new outlets are highly dependent on a particular point of view. Is it possible to understand different sides of an issue or problem if most of what someone knows originates at a source with a definite slant? ...

As the news and information universe continues to expand, the discriminating citizen will need to be purposefully indiscriminate, actively selecting what's available as daily communication. One way of minimizing misunderstanding is to scrutinize several sources from varying viewpoints, encompassing traditional *and* alternative outlets....

Bias of some kind is inherent in human communication, but that doesn't mean every news organization thinks alike. Viewing the media as a monolith of similarly slanted messages draws into question the independent operations existing at each outlet and the competitive impulses that enliven and inspire newsrooms....

Ari Fleischer, former presidential press secretary to George W. Bush, provides context for understanding media orientation. In his just-published memoir, *Taking Heat*, Fleischer explains: "Many Republicans, especially conservatives, believe the press are liberals who oppose Republicans and Republican ideas. I think there's an element of truth to that, but it is complicated, secondary, and often nuanced. More important, the press's first and most pressing bias is in favor of conflict and fighting. That's especially the case for the White House press corps."

As Fleischer suggests, media bias is more complicated than political or ideological preference. Structural, attitudinal and institutional factors come into play—and carry more weight. Above all, mainstream news values a good story—one that's novel, timely, consequential and engaging, if not compelling. The old chestnut that American journalism tries to comfort the afflicted and afflict the comfortable adds a distinct attitude—civic compassion and public accountability—to the work.

Especially when it comes to power and authority, the establishment media can be probingly skeptical. Naturally critical, these hounds of hypocrisy try to sniff out whether words match deeds and whether a figure's image conforms, as much as possible, to reality....

Claims of bias always depend on personal interpretation and point of view. Although those on the right tend to be more organized and vocal in their criticism, many on the left consider the establishment media as profit-obsessed operations of corporate conglomerates. In their opinion, a searching story that draws into question the larger status quo or runs the risk of alienating a sizable audience won't receive exposure for economic reasons. It's safer for the sake of the bottom line to carry an abundance of soft news and features—about celebrities, health treatments, fads and the like.

Consistent political partiality across the mainstream media is largely mythical. If traditional journalism is so overwhelmingly slanted and influential, as some rightist critics argue, you'd think that conservative politicians would have more trouble than they do winning elections and that more than 18 percent (according to a 2004 Harris Poll) would identify themselves as liberal.

Be that as it may, representatives of both ends of the political spectrum agree the news reporting about certain social and cultural issues generally reflects liberal orientation. Abortion, affirmative action, gay rights, gun control and the environment tend to receive more positive coverage, and in this sense indirectly help like-minded politicians.

Yet, serious as this situation is, other factors take precedence in explicitly political and governmental reportage. When Monica Lewinsky became a household name overnight in 1998, President Clinton's political and social views didn't make an iota of difference in the free-for-all mania to reveal sordid specifics of their relationship.

The debate over bias has become both more complicated and less meaningful in recent years. It's more complicated because the argument took root during the late 1960s, when only a few nationally significant channels of information were available. Today there are many more sources from which to choose, including some that take sides and don't aim for impartiality.

The multitude of information voices vying for attention often means a journalistic outlet takes a considered, even calculating approach to set itself apart from competitors. Some newspapers and magazines might encourage prose that features know-it-all, look-at-me "attitude," with the writer's viewpoint rivaling the subject treated. Even Associated Press, the 156-year-old wire service noted for its who-what-when-where-why reporting, recently began offering newspapers the choice of two leads for stories. While one emphasizes basic facts in straight news fashion, AP says it wants to offer the second one to "draw in the reader through imagery, narrative devices, perspective or other creative means."

On radio and television, full-throated, at times raucous, discussion frequently replaces any semblance of civil discourse. It's as though the loudest, most combative voice will stand out from the others—and thus get heard. Although such programs are carried on all-news outlets, the proximity to genuine journalism is remote. Part personal prejudice, part ego gratification, heat rather than light usually results.

With the media multiplying like kudzu and the mainstream shrinking, there might seem less at stake in the controversy over bias. In an era of deep political divisions, however, messengers carrying political messages are as vulnerable to criticism as partisan politicians. Indeed, the media bias debate feeds political polarization in the United States by making the public suspicious of what they read, see and hear from the left, right and center.

Consider the titles of recent books about the media, several of which became national bestsellers: *Bias: A CBS Insider Exposes How the Media Distort the News* by Bernard Goldberg; *Slander: Liberal Lies about the American Right* by Ann Coulter; *What Liberal Media? The Truth about BIAS and the News* by Eric Alterman; *Lies (And the Lying Liars Who Tell Them): A Fair and Balanced Look at the Right* by Al Franken; *Big Lies: The Right-Wing Propaganda Machine and How It Distorts the Truth*, by Joe Conason; and *Weapons of Mass Distortion: The Coming Meltdown of the Liberal Media* by L. Brent Bozell III....

Although the media bias debate (in books, articles, talk shows and elsewhere) often appears as a sideshow to the center-ring argument between conservatives and liberals over the nation's direction and political issues, it's taking place as the public tries to figure out how best to navigate through all the available news and information.

In this new milieu, the mainstream media no longer exert the hold they once did. Other voices are being heard, and some of those voices critique media performance and perceived slanting for whatever motivation.

Fox News Channel might promote "fair and balanced" news coverage, but that slogan is about as truthful and self-serving as the one published on every edition of *The New York Times*: "All the News That's Fit to Print." Fox News found its niche by defining its messages differently from others in TV journalism. Begun in 1996 and inspired in part by the success of talk-radio, the channel wasn't afraid to be perceived as having a point of view. That style attracted viewers, propelling Fox News into the lead of cable news organizations. Significantly, during the 2004 Republican National Convention, Fox News had a larger audience than any of the three broadcast networks (ABC, CBS, NBC) and over three times the viewership of either MSNBC or CNN. By taking a point of view, the channel is building a following that's worth watching on its own.

To what extent does the success of Fox signal a return to a partisan press in America? In the nation's early years, newspapers made no effort to be neutral, a practice that continues in Britain, Europe and elsewhere. If the news audience expects a particular slant, charges of bias become meaningless. This, however, comes at the expense of not learning certain aspects of a story or never hearing a contrary opinion about a subject.

With ideologically oriented information, the content has a predictability that puts it in the category of preaching to an already assembled and faithful choir. What's reported might introduce new information, but the larger objective involves reinforcing someone's viewpoint and opinions. The approach also tends to deepen political and social divisions— and to stifle more comprehensive inquiry. Instead of fostering fuller understanding, sides are taken, fingers are pointed and blame is assessed.

What complicates any discussion of today's media environment in the United States is the variety of different messages circulating at a given time. A newspaper, for example, might try to present its reportage with (in Irish writer and statesman Edmund Burke's phrase) "the cold neutrality of an impartial judge," but commentary columns and editorials frequently make readers think they detect a distinct perspective. In news magazines and on broadcast media, analysis and interpretation often seem to mingle with personal opinion. Trying to keep types of journalism and different sources straight becomes difficult for the public.

Most media don't take enough care to explain their work or to make the necessary distinctions among different journalistic forms. How many faithfully follow the famous dictum "fact is sacred, opinion is free"? Compounding the problem are the new, alternative sources of information that rely on the news for their content but follow their own agendas and prejudices. In this increasingly crowded and noisy arena, distinguishing between journalism and entertainment or journalism and "parajournalism" can be difficult.

There are no bright, bold lines marking off balanced, complete reporting (of just-the-facts school) from selective, slanted opinion offerings.

To be sure, a citizen's access to a wide range of fact and opinion has never been greater. For example, through cable outlets (including C-SPAN) and Internet sites, it's now relatively easy to watch or read the entirety of speeches, news conferences and other presentations, allowing someone to evaluate and judge a source without outside interference.

But that admirably independent approach now openly competes with its opposite: Point-of-view reporting and analysis that originates with an agenda or purpose. These sources can be valuable—bloggers, say, can keep a story alive by investigating it from other angles and by pushing the traditional media to correct an original account—but the trick is to avoid what media theorists call "information segregation."

When this happens, people rely on outlets with which they already agree. They don't seek contrasting information. This method of media selection—and personal bias—results in the possibility of never understanding an issue as completely as possible or even very well.

Different technologies now make it possible to receive personally designed, tailor-made collections of reportage, analysis and commentary that observers have dubbed "The Daily Me." But if the "Me" too narrowly defines the information provided—a preponderance of entertainment or sports news, political information from one perspective, economic or business reports but little else—there's the danger of not receiving a thorough, reliable picture of America or the world.

The Daily Show and "The Daily Me" challenge conventional thinking about news, but they symbolize our times and future—with definitions changing, traditions ending, lines blurring. With the media world teeming with choice, our relationship to it will be radically different, as we try to deal with the endless welter of messages. "Keeping up" with contemporary affairs (a civic notion of an earlier era with far fewer sources) will demand a conscious effort of constant scrutiny. The age-old worry over gaining access to information is over. Now it's a matter of selection and attention—and assuming new obligations of 21st-century citizenship.

COMPREHENSION QUESTIONS

1. According to Schmuhl, who is the biggest beneficiary of the mistakes made by traditional news sources?

2. What are the negative consequences of providing intentionally biased news to viewers? How concerned should we be about these consequences?

3. What is media segregation? Why is it important?

JOURNAL WRITING PROMPTS

1. List the types of news that you watch. What kind of news do you like the best? What do you like most about this news?

2. Do you think that humor has a place in the news? Would you watch news that was presented in a humorous manner? Explain why or why not. Give specific examples to support your opinion.

DISCUSSION TOPICS/CLASS DEBATES

1. Why have so many people stopped watching traditional news sources?

2. Schmuhl points out that 44 percent of Americans feel the news can give fair and accurate news. In two groups, debate whether the news can be considered fair and accurate. Support your opinions with specific examples.

WRITING TOPICS

1. Write an essay where you divide and classify the various types of news. Be sure to describe each type of news, and give specific examples of each type.

2. Schmuhl argues that being well informed is one of our modern civic obligations. In an essay, argue whether this is true. Explain your position completely, and give specific examples to prove your point.

Connecting the Pieces

Now that you've learned all about news, you can apply what you've just learned. In this section, you'll find writing prompts and discussion topics for you to practice your new skills.

WRITING PROMPTS

1. Write an essay where you compare and contrast traditional news and comedy news. In your essay, describe both types of news show in detail. In your description, be sure to mention the typical audience member, the setting or stage, the use of technology, the appearance of the reporter, and the use (or lack of) humor. Lastly, argue which type of news show is the more effective and why.

2. Choose a national news program, such as *ABC World News* or *CBS Evening News*. Imagine you are the show's producer. You are worried that the number of viewers is decreasing, and you are responsible for attracting new viewers by making your show more appealing to either a wider audience or a new one altogether. First, consider the current audience. What is their approximate age? Are they mostly male or female? Do they have anything else in common, such as a personal interest or economic status? Next, decide how you will change your show to attract new audience members. You may consider changing the set, slogan, reporter, tone, even the subject matter. In order to get approval from

the network, write an essay that includes the changes you would make to the show. Be very specific as you describe your improvements. Explain how each change will appeal to the desired audience.

3. Imagine you are a journalist for a traditional news program. To prepare for your broadcast, write a news story about a current event that includes both sides of the issue. Describe the arguments or concerns of each group involved. Make sure you provide equal time, or space in your paper, for each side. Attempt to stay as neutral as possible in your word choice.

DISCUSSION TOPICS

1. Split into small groups of two or three. Each group should have a copy of a current, printed newspaper or access to an online newspaper. With your group, look through the paper for stories that contain bias. Highlight the words or phrases you believe contain bias or introduce bias into the story. For each article containing bias, write a paragraph answering the questions below. Articles can also be cut out and attached to the corresponding paragraph.
   - In what section of the paper is the article found? Why might this be important?
   - What kind of bias can be identified? Be specific in your answer. Explain how the highlighted words or phrases create bias.
   - Does the author make a recommendation or offer a judgment on the topic of the article? Provide examples, and explain how each specific case is a form of bias.

2. Imagine you are creating your own news program. From a list of approximately 20 current events, either provided by your teacher or made as a class, your group should decide which stories will be covered in your news program, the order in which they will be given to the audience, and the length of time each story will be discussed. As your show is only 15 minutes long, you will need to determine whether some stories will be left out of your program. All of your choices should be made for a reason and will need to be explained. Present the list of current events that will be on your show, and explain to the class how you made your decision. Write a paragraph explaining your decision-making process.

Assessing Your Knowledge

KEY POINTS	REMINDER	HOW WELL DID YOU UNDERSTAND THIS MATERIAL?	PAGE(S)
Identify types of news	Thanks to technology, there are many types of news: **press releases**, **newspapers**, **radio news**, **social media news**, **traditional television news**, **comedy news**, **specialized news**, and **entertainment news**.	☐ I've Got It! ☐ Almost There ☐ Need More Practice	pp. 188–89
Recognize errors in thought within the news	**Errors in thought** can occur in any type of information. In the news, logical errors may be made by a journalist or by someone being interviewed.	☐ I've Got It! ☐ Almost There ☐ Need More Practice	pp. 189–90
Understand fact and opinion within the news	A **fact** is a piece of information that can be confirmed as accurate or correct. An **opinion** is a feeling, belief, or judgment. Understanding that you can find opinions in the news will help prevent you from being unfairly influenced.	☐ I've Got It! ☐ Almost There ☐ Need More Practice	p. 190
Understand bias within the news	**Bias** is the influence of the journalist's opinion on a subject. This chapter provides activities to encourage a better understanding of common types of bias found in the news: bias though placement and selection, bias by association or regionalism, and bias through word choice and tone.	☐ I've Got It! ☐ Almost There ☐ Need More Practice	pp. 191–92

Deepening Your Understanding

If you would like to go beyond the material in this chapter, explore additional connections, and get more practice, check out these related topics:

- **Exact Language**: Using the right words is just as important in the news as it is in your papers. Choosing exactly the right words inspires confidence and trust.

- **Narration**: The skill of narrating helps reporters provide information in a way that is helpful and easy to follow.

- **Comparison and Contrast**: While there are many similarities between the various types of news, there are also a few very important differences. Make sure you know how to structure your discussion and communicate clearly.

- **Cause and Effect**: When logical errors, bias, and opinions are present in the news, they can have a profound effect on the audience. Understanding how these relationships work will help you navigate mass amounts of information safely.

Television

"TV is chewing gum for the eyes."

—Frank Lloyd Wright

FACT OR FICTION?
Television is just a means of entertainment.

FICTION.
Television has many purposes, only one of which is entertainment. While television can be entertaining, it may also be persuasive, informative, and inspiring.

Discovering Key Points

- Understand why television is important
- Understand and identify the four different purposes of television shows
- Identify different genres of television shows
- Apply what you've learned about television to a specific show

Television is a medium that can reach millions of people. It is one means through which we can all be connected; news, information, and entertainment can reach viewers, no matter who we are or where we come from. Also, people across the world can be linked through watching the same television show. This gives people a common ground through which we can communicate with one another—even with people who are quite different from us. We can share the experience of watching a television show, yet we all take away something very different due to our personal backgrounds.

The Purposes of Television

Essays also have multiple purposes. Want to find out more? See Chapter 3 or Chapter 5.

Television is a vital part of the media. It provides us with a broad array of programs to choose from, and it helps fulfill some of our needs, such as a need for education and a need for entertainment. When we write, we write with a purpose in mind. We want to educate our readers about a subject, to argue for a particular point, or to entertain our readers. Television shows, like essays, have **purposes**. There are four purposes of television: to **inform/educate**, to **entertain**, to **persuade**, and to **inspire**. A television show can have more than one purpose. For example, many children's television shows can be categorized as both informative/educational and entertaining.

To Inform/Educate

You'll notice that the titles of television shows are in italics. Want to know what else to put in italics? See Chapter 16: MLA/APA Documentation.

These shows make us aware of what's going on around us or teach us about something specific (like a historical event, faraway place, etc.).

Examples:

- News stations/the news
- The Weather Channel
- *Sesame Street*
- *River Monsters*
- *Top Gear*
- *Cook Like an Iron Chef*
- *Sixty Minutes*

To Entertain

These shows make us feel emotions when we watch them. They allow us to escape from "real life" into imaginary worlds. These are the shows we watch when we come home from a hard day of work or school; we relax, distract our mind, and de-stress with television.

Examples:

- *Sons of Anarchy*
- *Big Bang Theory*

- *The Voice*
- *Spartacus*
- *Storage Wars*

To Persuade

These try to convince us to do something, buy something, or believe something. Typically, these are commercials and infomercials.

Examples:

Want to know more about advertisements? See Chapter 11.

- The presidential debates
- All commercials
- All infomercials
- *Mad Money with Jim Cramer*
- *Penn & Teller: Bullshit!*

To Inspire

These shows allow us to learn more about how to do something and/or how to better ourselves.

Examples:

- *30 Minute Meals with Rachel Ray*
- *How Do I Look?*
- *The 700 Club*
- *Cook Like an Iron Chef*
- *Bath Crashers*

The Rhetorical Connection

Television shows can use any (or all) of the three sorts of rhetorical appeal—**ethos**, **logos**, and **pathos**. While you've learned previously what these appeals are, the definitions are somewhat different when applied to television shows. Below are some questions you may ask yourself:

Ethos—Is the television show or broadcasting channel trustworthy? Do you trust the actors or writers? Do you find the plot believable?

Logos—Are there facts, figures, or statistics present in the television show? Do all claims in the television show seem reasonable?

Pathos—What could the audience feel when watching this television show? What emotions did the writers or actors want to provoke?

Not all appeals may be found in all television shows; however, you'll find that most make some appeal to our emotions. Television shows are made to provoke a reaction. The actors and the plot can make us feel excitement, terror, sadness, humor, and other emotions.

YOUR TURN

Search online for a video at least five minutes long from a television show about food and/or cooking. What sorts of rhetorical appeals are being made? Support your answer with examples from the video.

Examples of Different Types of Television Shows

There are many different categories of television shows. Seven of the most common are listed here.

Children's Shows

Children's shows include cartoons, puppetry, etc., and are meant for a population of children. Often, their purpose is to educate and/or entertain.
Examples:

- *SpongeBob SquarePants*
- *The Wiggles*
- *Bob the Builder*

Comedies

Comedies are television shows that tell a story that's light-hearted in tone; we know a comedy will have a happy ending. The characters and story material of comedies tend to be humorous. Some comedies—such as the half-hour situation comedies (or sitcoms) that are common in American television—are structured to make the audience laugh frequently.
Examples:

- *Veep*
- *It's Always Sunny in Philadelphia*
- *Modern Family*

Dramas

Dramas are serious television shows. Their purpose, like sitcoms, is to entertain. Within the broad category of drama there are several sub-genres, including soap opera, police drama, crime drama, medical drama, and horror.

Examples:

- *General Hospital*
- *CSI*
- *The Vampire Diaries*

How-To Shows

How-To shows teach us how to do something. Their purpose is to inform and also to entertain.

Examples:

- *Hometime*
- *Barefoot Contessa*
- *The Martha Stewart Show*

News

News tells us what's going on around us and in the world. Their purpose is to inform, but often they also aim to entertain. There are three sub-genres of news shows: traditional news, entertainment news, and comedy news.

Examples:

- *The Daily Show with Trevor Noah*
- *CBS This Morning*
- *Access Hollywood*

ⓘ
Want to learn more about the news? See Chapter 12.

Reality Television

Reality television presents unscripted (or supposedly unscripted) life and/or competition on film. Their purpose is mostly to entertain, although some reality television shows can be informative or inspirational. Reality television has four sub-genres: competition reality shows, self-improvement reality shows, documentary shows, and social experiment shows.

Examples:

- *The Challenge*
- *Dancing with the Stars*
- *The Biggest Loser*

Talk Shows

Talk shows feature a host (or multiple hosts) and guests who discuss current issues. Late night talk shows and daytime talk shows tend to have substantial differences both in tone and content.

Examples:

- *The View*
- *Conan*
- *Dr. Phil*

DISCUSSION TOPIC

1. In groups, look at the list of the four purposes of television shows and come up with a new example (one that isn't mentioned in this chapter) for each purpose. Then answer the following questions:
   a. What show did you choose for each purpose? What was your reasoning for choosing each show?
   b. Look at your list of four shows. What genre(s) do these television shows fall into? How do you know?

   Then, as a class, compile what you've found as groups. Look at the examples the class found for each purpose, as well as what genres the examples belong to. Can you find a connection between purpose and genre? In other words, do shows in a particular genre tend to have a similar purpose?

2. Look at the list of genres of television shows again. What genre do you most enjoy on television? Why? Compare your classmates' answers to your own. What five genres did the class find the most enjoyable? Why do you think these genres were chosen?

3. Make a list of your five favorite television shows (these can be either current programs or programs no longer being produced). What genre(s) and purpose(s) can you find in common with each show? What do these commonalities say about what type of television viewer you are?

CLASS DEBATE

1. As a class, divide into two groups. Then work with your group to answer the following question: Does reality television do more harm or good for viewers? One half of the class should focus on the "For" side (or, in other words, arguing that reality television shows are doing more good for viewers). The other half should focus on the "Against" side, where the focus is on how and why these shows are harmful to viewers. Come up with your arguments for or against, but be sure to provide specific television shows as your examples. Feel free to research online clips from the shows as examples.

BEFORE YOU READ

You're about to read an essay titled "*South Park* Is Still Our Most Consistently Fair Political Satire" by Joshua Axelrod. Before you read his essay, try to answer the following questions:

- Just based on the title, what do you think this essay is about?
- What do you already know about the subject?
- When was the essay written?
- Where was the essay published (newspaper/magazine/textbook/etc.)? How do you know?
- Do you know anything about this author?

"*South Park* Is Still Our Most Consistently Fair Political Satire," by Joshua Axelrod

Fansided, May 2019

Let's start off with a hot take that's really just an observation from someone with eyes and ears: *South Park* as of 2018 is better than *The Simpsons* and *Family Guy*.

While both of those shows have seen a notable dip in quality as they struggle to stay relevant to modern audiences, Trey Parker and Matt Stone's construction paper Comedy Central series has not only displayed an ability to be reliably hilarious, but also has kept its place in the pop culture zeitgeist in a way its competition has not.

While *The Simpsons* has recently become more notable for bungling the criticism of one of its longest-running characters and *Family Guy* for just kind of being there (though that might change with its upcoming movie), *South Park* is still as sharp as ever. Neither of those shows have reached anything resembling the level of virality "Do you like fish sticks?" achieved in the last decade.

More importantly, *South Park* has never wavered in its efforts to be an equal opportunity offender to everyone deserving of criticism. It's the rare piece of political satire that has consistently been able to see the bigger picture, skewering both sides of the aisle and everyone in-between.

And yes, that includes even folks generally regarded by much of Hollywood as "the good guys."

As the show becomes old enough to legally buy a drink, it's worth taking a minute to reflect on where *South Park* started and the role it currently plays in the American comedy landscape.

In a 1998 interview with Parker and Stone, *Rolling Stone*'s David Wild described the then-one-year-old *South Park* as "the only TV show from the latter half of 1997 that made a dent critically or commercially."

Wild continued: "The cable smash instantly upgraded Comedy Central's ratings and, according to the network, has moved more than a million T-shirts and $30 million in merchandise since the show debuted last August."

Right out of the gate, *South Park* was clearly a cultural phenomenon. Who knew all it would take to put Comedy Central on the map permanently was a few animated 10-year-olds with foul mouths and a propensity for finding themselves in the middle of world-altering conspiracies?

As the animation improved and the show began tackling the pressing cultural issues of the day, *South Park* became ubiquitous for its portrayal of celebrities like Jennifer Lopez and Ben Affleck, political figures like Al Gore, and arguably most infamously, its epic two-part takedown of Seth MacFarlane's comedic sensibilities on *Family Guy*.

As with any boundary-pushing show, *South Park* has earned its fair share of criticism. Recently, that criticism has involved a condemnation of the show's loyal fanbase. Some have even gone as far as to posit that *South Park*'s laissez-faire attitude toward political correctness, as The *Financial Times*' Janan Ganesh put it, "foreshadowed the counter-elite mood of today."

The A.V. Club's Sean O'Neal echoed that sentiment: "*South Park* may not have 'invented' the 'alt-right,' but at their roots are the same bored, irritated distaste for politically correct wokeness, the same impish thrill at saying the things you're not supposed to say, the same button-pushing racism and sexism, now scrubbed of all irony."

Of course, comments like those only seemed to inspire Parker and Stone to double down on their general disdain for societal BS in whatever form it takes. For example, one of the most recent seasons of *South Park* introduced a character named P.C. Principal who was designed to be the logical extreme of political correctness.

They also seemed to make a point to go after Donald Trump and Hillary Clinton in equal measure during the lead-up to the 2016 presidential election. This faux debate is as smart and scathing a commentary on Clinton as you will find anywhere, and it came straight from "liberal Hollywood."

Connecting an intentionally broad satire to the rise of an actual political movement is a pretty giant leap, but Parker and Stone seem to have internalized that criticism based on the show's last season, which heavily featured a storyline about the dangers of trolling and the cascading effect it can have on public discourse.

South Park's 22nd season will premiere on Sept. 26, and as usual it's anyone's guess as to what Parker and Stone will do. The show is famous for being able to produce episodes on turnarounds of less than a week, allowing it to take on whatever is weighing on Americans' minds at a given moment.

It has, however, recently delved into serialization, weaving season-long arcs that do their best to take a funny snapshot of the world as Parker and Stone see it in a given year. Combine that with its quick episode-generation process and its continued efforts to satirize anything that movies [sic], and you have the recipe for why *South Park* has maintained its cultural relevance for 21 years.

As the *New York Times*' James Poniewozik put it, *South Park* has successfully "revitalized itself by telling a more ambitious, serialized story and by asserting that it takes an outrageous comedy to capture an era of outrage."

COMPREHENSION QUESTIONS

1. At issue in this and various other essays about *South Park* is whether its "time has passed." The show was first introduced in 1997. Do you believe that the show's "time has passed" and that it is "less culturally relevant" today to viewers? Why or why not?

2. How has *South Park* evolved or "grown up" over the years? How do you think the show has changed since 1997?

3. The article quotes Sean O'Neal's claim that *South Park* shares some of the same roots as the "alt-right." Do you agree or disagree? Why? Be sure to provide specific examples.

JOURNAL WRITING PROMPTS

1. Would you (or do you) watch *South Park*? Why or why not? Would you let your children watch *South Park*? Why or why not?

2. Watch one of the episodes mentioned in the essay. What are your thoughts on the episode? Did you enjoy it? Why or why not?

DISCUSSION TOPICS/CLASS DEBATES

1. Is *South Park* more than just potty humor? Does the show offer more to the viewers?

2. Matt Stone, one of the *South Park* creators, said that the show's episodes "center on a really solid story involving one of the characters." Split into two groups and argue whether the show does focus on an individual character, rather than an event or conflict.

WRITING TOPICS

1. Compare and contrast an episode of *South Park* with an episode of *Family Guy* or *The Simpsons*. How are the two similar? How are the two different? Remember to be specific with your examples.

2. Imagine you've been asked by Stone and Parker to create a new character for the show. What gender would this character be? What would this person look like? What would his/her personalities and characteristics be? Why did you choose this character?

Connecting the Pieces

Now that you've learned all about television, you can apply what you've just learned. In this section, you'll find writing prompts and discussion topics for you to practice your new skills.

WRITING PROMPTS

1. Imagine you are a writer for *South Park*. Lately, both viewers and the studio are unhappy with the show. You have been asked to rewrite the show and take it in a new direction, one where the viewers and the studio would be happy. In order to make sure you are the right writer for the job, they want you to write a proposal about the changes you would make and why. They are giving you free rein to change the characters in the show, the formula, the purpose, and the plot. However, you may not change the genre (in other words, *South Park* must remain a cartoon comedy).

2. Write an essay reviewing your favorite television show. In the essay, argue why the show is your favorite, giving lots of specific examples. Be sure to explain what genre the television show is, as well as the purpose. Next, describe the main characters and how they are portrayed. Include a one-paragraph summary of one of your favorite episodes of the show, being sure to be specific about the main story line. Lastly, evaluate the show by arguing what type of viewer might enjoy this television series, how it compares to other shows in the same genre, and, overall, why someone should watch the show.

3. Find a television show that has been adapted either for the United States from the UK or for the UK from the United States. The original versions of *The Office*, *Top Gear*, *Hell's Kitchen*, and *Being Human* were all British. The British have had their own versions of *Dancing with the Stars* (UK: *Strictly Come Dancing*), *American Idol* (UK: *Pop Idol*), and *America's Got Talent* (UK: *Britain's Got Talent*). Pick one show. Then compare and contrast the American version with the British version. What are the similarities? What are the differences? Which do you prefer, and why?

DISCUSSION TOPICS

1. Work in small groups. In your groups, pick one of the following shows: *The Simpsons*, *Glee*, *Modern Family*, *Leave It to Beaver*, *Fresh Prince of Bel-Air*, *The Sopranos*, *Star Trek*, *House*, *Scooby Doo*, or *Sex in the City*. What stereotypes are presented in this show? Are these positive or negative stereotypes? Could they be considered harmful to a group of people? Why or why not? Then gather as a class and share your observations. Are any of the stereotypes found in multiple television shows? If so, what are they? Why do you think they are the most prevalent stereotypes found on television?

2. Television shows have a rating system put in place by a monitoring board. Do you think this rating system is fair? Does this rating system need to be stricter? What do you see as the possible problems with this rating system?

Assessing Your Knowledge

KEY POINTS	REMINDER	HOW WELL DID YOU UNDERSTAND THIS MATERIAL?	PAGE(S)
Understand why television is important	Television is one of the most important forms of media because it reaches so many people. It is also powerful because it allows viewers to make emotional connections with the content due to its strong audio-visual nature.	☐ I've Got It! ☐ Almost There ☐ Need More Practice	p. 204
Understand and identify the four different purposes of television shows	There are four purposes of television shows: ▪ To inform/educate—to tell or teach you about something specific ▪ To entertain—to make you feel emotions and help you "escape the real world" ▪ To persuade—to convince you to do or buy something ▪ To inspire—to make you want to better yourself or teach you how to do something	☐ I've Got It! ☐ Almost There ☐ Need More Practice	pp. 204–05
Identify different genres of television shows	There are many different genres of television shows. Seven were discussed here in this chapter: ▪ Children's Shows ▪ Comedies ▪ Dramas ▪ How-To Shows ▪ News ▪ Reality Television ▪ Talk Shows	☐ I've Got It! ☐ Almost There ☐ Need More Practice	pp. 206–08

Apply what you've learned about television to a specific show	Here in this chapter, you read an essay on a specific television show, *South Park*. You then had the chance to apply the elements that you learned previously in this chapter to this show, as well as to another of your choice.	☐ I've Got It! ☐ Almost There ☐ Need More Practice	pp. 209–13

Deepening Your Understanding

If you would like to go beyond the material in this chapter, explore additional connections, and get more practice, check out these related topics:

- **Reading and Understanding Visuals**: Being able to examine visuals is key when dealing with television shows. Knowing what to look for and how to analyze the visuals will help you understand them better.

- **Process Analysis**: "Do It Yourself" television shows are a great media example of process analysis. These shows provide instructions on how to complete a task.

- **Argumentation**: Commercials and infomercials use argument to persuade you to buy their product. In your own essays, you must use argument to persuade your readers by using specific examples and sources.

- **Description**: Television shows use the senses to show the viewers the scenery and characters. In your essays, you must describe using strong and expressive adjectives and adverbs to appeal to your readers' senses.

PART III
Exploring Academic Writing

WHEN YOU WRITE ESSAYS for your college classes, you will need to use academic writing. Academic writing requires you to communicate your ideas clearly, concisely, and effectively in a formal setting. Sometimes academic writing will entail conducting scholarly research, which will require you to be a close critical reader.

There are many characteristics of academic writing. An academic essay will entail selecting a topic, creating a well-structured argument, and supporting it with examples. The conventions of academic writing generally require you to avoid contractions, slang, profanity, and first and second person pronouns. In contrast, informal writing does not have as many rules. In informal writing you can use slang and many of the same sort of expressions you use in conversation. Grammatical correctness is less important in informal writing.

In academic writing, you will want to consider your content, tone, and audience as well. Your content should be appropriate for a formal paper. Your tone should generally be serious in nature; an academic essay is not the place to tell jokes or be sarcastic.

Many students are apprehensive when faced with academic writing. All the rules may seem daunting. Students may be afraid of rejection, especially if they have not practiced much academic writing. Some students have a fear of academic writing because they feel that they have nothing to add to the conversation about a scholarly topic—that "it's all been said before." To others, academic writing is boring, uninteresting, and difficult to read and understand. They feel it's something only stuffy scholars write and read.

Think of academic writing as a way of deepening your understanding, challenging conventional thoughts and ideas, proposing solutions to problems, and arguing an opinion that is important to you. Academic writing follows the same writing process you've already learned in the previous chapters of this book. Every opportunity for academic writing is an opportunity to learn something. Don't let academic writing be boring: choose a topic that genuinely interests you. There is rarely anything worse in writing than writing begrudgingly on a topic you don't care about. If you are engaged in your writing, your writing will come to you more easily and your ideas within the essay will be more impassioned. Thus, your reader will be more involved and interested while reading your essay.

Before You Read

Before you read the chapters in Part III, answer the following questions:

1. In your opinion, what is the most difficult part of academic writing? Why?

2. Which type of writing do you think you are likely to prefer: academic writing or informal writing? Why?

3. Imagine you are asked to write an academic essay on some aspect of energy consumption in America. How would you start? What rules and strategies would you follow for your essay?

The Research Paper Process

14

"Research to me is as important as or more important than the writing. It is the foundation upon which the book is built."

—Leon Uris

Discovering Key Points

- Understand how to make a schedule
- Understand how to find a research paper topic
- Understand how to narrow a topic
- Understand how to generate research questions
- Understand how to define purpose and audience
- Understand how to create a working thesis statement
- Understand how to locate sources for a research paper
- Understand how to organize and take notes about sources
- Understand how to start your draft

As a student, you will be asked to write numerous research papers over the course of your college career. Research papers are used as a way to assess your knowledge of a subject and to encourage you to learn through research and writing. A research paper will require you to formulate an argument or investigate a topic. The research you do for your paper will provide you with background information and allow you to build on the ideas of others. Unlike more informal types of writing, research papers take a lot of preparation. Writing a successful research paper starts with good planning and a few easy steps. Following the process below will encourage you to stay focused.

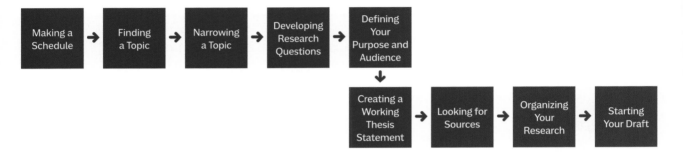

While the majority of your research will be done after you have narrowed your topic and developed a working thesis statement, you will need to research and gather information about your topic at every stage of the process. The information you find while doing your early research will help you narrow your topic, answer your research questions, and create a working thesis.

Making a Schedule

As soon as you are assigned a research paper, you should create a schedule. Because there are often several weeks between when the paper is assigned and the due date, you may be tempted to procrastinate. A schedule allows you to keep track of your progress and of your important due dates. Start by noting due dates set by your instructor. Then set additional dates for when you plan to complete other steps in the process. Carefully consider how long it will take you to complete each step. Here is an example schedule for a paper due May 30th.

MY RESEARCH PAPER

Activity/Assignment	Due Date
Assignment Given	April 1st
Find a Topic	April 2nd

Narrow My Topic	April 4th
Develop Research Question	April 7th
Define My Purpose and Audience	April 10th
Create a Working Thesis	April 12th
Look for Sources	April 13th
Organize My Research	April 20th
Start My Draft	April 25th
Prewriting	April 28th
First Rough Draft Due	May 9th
Do a Little More Research	May 14th
Visit the Writing Center	May 18th
Second Rough Draft Due	May 23rd
Research Paper Due Date	**May 30th**

Finding a Topic

All research papers start with the initial assignment and a topic. In some courses, you may be given a general topic. In a sociology course, you might be given topics such as childhood obesity, homelessness, or online dating. In a history course, you might be given topics such as the Civil War or the Industrial Revolution. In some courses, you may be given some freedom to choose your own topic within the scope of a course theme. In a criminal justice course, you might choose juvenile crime or prison overpopulation, for instance. If your general topic is assigned, make sure you follow the instructions and topic guidelines you are given. When you choose your own topic, you have several factors to consider: your interest, the assignment requirements, and the amount of resources available.

Your Interest

Being interested in the topic of your research paper is helpful because you will spend more time reading about and working with the research paper topic than you might with other types of papers. Generally, the more interested you are in the paper's topic, the more creativity and effort you will put into the paper. If you cannot think of a topic, try talking to a friend or doing a quick search on the Internet for ideas.

The Assignment Requirements

The assignment requirements will give you an idea of your limitations. For instance, most classes will expect that a research paper will relate to the general theme of the course. Some courses will specify a page length and the number of sources that should be used. In order to satisfy these requirements, you should choose a topic that can be narrowed to the assigned page length.

One of the key components in a research paper is the research itself. Do a quick search for information on your topic. If you can't find any information about your topic on the Internet or from your library's resources, then you should consider choosing another topic. You should also consult a librarian or your instructor if you have trouble finding information. Think of writing a research paper as jumping into a conversation. There should already be researchers and scholars discussing your topic. Once you understand the complexities of the topic, you are going to gather the best information and then communicate your own position in your research paper. Accordingly, you should choose a topic that scholars and researchers have already published information about.

Narrowing a Topic

All of the general topics mentioned previously in this chapter are far too broad to be discussed thoroughly in a research paper. Whether you are assigned a topic or you get to choose your own, it will need to be narrowed further. **Narrowing a topic** will focus your thinking and research. Topics should be narrowed to a controversy or issue that can be explained and discussed within the page length of your assignment. Narrowing a topic is an important step toward creating a thesis statement. Below are a few examples of general topics that have been narrowed.

General Topics		Narrowed Topics
Childhood Obesity	➜	Solutions and prevention strategies for childhood obesity through public schools
Homelessness	➜	The effectiveness of shelters and work programs in reducing homelessness
Juvenile Crime	➜	The prevention of gang violence in urban areas
Landfills	➜	Green waste and recycling programs managed by local governments
Online Dating	➜	Safety precautions for online dating
Prison Overpopulation	➜	Prison population reduction through early release and parole programs
Industrial Revolution	➜	Social and economic changes in US caused by the mass production of automobiles
American Literature	➜	Gender identity in *The House on Mango Street*

If a topic is too narrow or too broad, it will make writing and researching difficult. Below is an example of a topic that has been narrowed too much and an example of the same topic that has not been narrowed enough.

General Topic	Juvenile Crime
Too Narrow	Length of sentences for drug-related crimes of female, juvenile Roma people in Virginia
Problem	A topic that is too narrow will not have enough research published for you to gather a reasonable amount of information. Since the process of conducting research is part of a research-paper assignment, this is a serious concern. Topics with too narrow a scope or too little published about them also run the risk of not seeming interesting or important to your audience. The topic above can be improved by removing one or more specific qualifications: location, culture, or gender.
Too Broad	Juvenile crime rates in the United States
Problem	Most assignments will require you to write about a specific issue. A topic that is too broad cannot be discussed in detail. The topic above can be improved by focusing on a type of juvenile crime, the reason for the juvenile crime, or strategies for the prevention of juvenile crime.

MEDIA EXAMPLE OF NARROWING A TOPIC

Narrowing a topic for a research paper is the act of making your topic more specific. Examples can also be found in the media. Search online for a Dos Equis commercial featuring the "Most Interesting Man in the World."

Identify the general topic of the commercial. Then, explain how the topic is narrowed or becomes more specific. What details are included as the commercial progresses?

STUDENT EXAMPLE

Kadience has been assigned a research paper in her Introduction to Biology course. She is able to pick her own topic and has chosen cloning as her general topic. She knows she must narrow her topic. After talking with a few friends and her roommate, she develops a couple of options. She draws a star next to the one she likes the best.

General Topic		**Narrowed Topics**
Cloning	→	*The cloning of animals for medical research*
	→	*The ban on cloning humans* ★

Imagine you are assigned a research paper in your Introduction to Psychology course. You have been given the general topic of social media addiction. How would you narrow the topic? Give two options for how this topic might be narrowed. Draw a star next to the option you like the best.

General Topic   **Narrowed Topics**

Social Media Addiction   ➜
                         ➜

Developing Research Questions

Need to review the 5 *W*s and 1 *H*? See Chapters 3 and 5.

You may know some basic information about your narrowed topic, but it is unlikely that you have considered all of the concerns surrounding it. As a responsible writer, you should take into account a variety of perspectives and solutions. Explore your narrowed topic by asking **research questions**. Start by asking the 5 *W*s and 1 *H*. The list of questions below offers examples of the kinds of questions you should ask. Developing your own research questions that are specific to your topic will be even more helpful.

- Who is affected by this topic?
- What is the problem, controversy, or situation?
- What caused this problem, controversy, or situation?
- What are some alternative views or opinions?
- When did this situation begin?
- Where did the problem, controversy, or situation occur?
- Why is this topic important?
- How can the problem be solved?

MEDIA EXAMPLE OF RESEARCH QUESTIONS

Research questions allow you to learn more about your topic. Questioning can also be found in the media. Search online for any one of a series of Charles Schwab Wealth Management commercials that encourage people to ask questions.

What kinds of questions are being asked in the commercial? What does the commercial suggest about why questions are important?

STUDENT EXAMPLE

Kadience is ready to explore her narrowed topic, the ban on cloning humans. She uses the questions to develop ideas and uncover more questions.

Narrowed Topic: *The ban on cloning humans*

- Who is affected by this topic?
  Eventually, everyone could be affected.

- What is the problem, controversy, or situation?
  From a medical perspective, cloning is risky. Human clones could be harmed during an experiment. Would private companies be able to conduct experiments or only the government? Will there be legal restrictions? There is also a social aspect. Society also doesn't agree on the legal status of human clones. Discrimination could be a problem.

- What caused this problem, controversy, or situation?
  Advancements in technology have progressed to make human cloning possible.

- What are some alternative views or opinions?
  Some people are for human cloning because they believe there can be great advances in medicine if it is pursued. Others are firmly against it because of their religious views or because they think we are socially unprepared.

- When did this situation begin?
  The conversation became popular in 1997 when the world learned that a sheep, named Dolly, had been successfully cloned.

- Where did the problem, controversy, or situation occur?
  Human cloning can technically occur anywhere. England, Germany, and the United States seem to be interested in cloning science.

- Why is this topic important?
  This topic is important because our laws and conversations about our social expectations are not keeping up with the speed of technology.

- How can the problem be solved?
  The dangers can't really be avoided, but we can talk about human cloning more.

YOUR TURN

Practice using research questions by answering the questions for your narrowed topic on social media addiction.

Narrowed Topic:

- Who is affected by this topic?
- What is the problem, controversy, or situation?
- What caused this problem, controversy, or situation?

- What are some alternative views or opinions?
- When did this situation begin?
- Where did the problem, controversy, or situation occur?
- Why is this topic important?
- How can the problem be solved?

Defining Your Purpose and Audience

Understanding your audience and purpose is important for any paper you write. For a research paper, you should define these early on in the process, as they will shape how you approach your paper.

For more information about audience and purpose, see Chapter 3.

Audience

In a research paper, the tone is generally formal, and your audience will expect you to use academic language and write as a knowledgeable author. To help you discover what your potential audience might feel or know, talk to some fellow students in the course. You should also ask your instructor what his or her expectations are.

How much background information does your audience know? You should provide enough background information to educate your readers on important parts of your argument. Anything your audience might be confused about or not have prior knowledge of should be explained and defined. Topics that are technical, mechanical, uncommon, or very current may require more explanation.

What are the audience's general feelings about your topic? If a topic is widely discussed, your audience may already have strong opinions about the matter. You may even need to dispel common misconceptions your readers might have. If your audience is indifferent, it may be because they do not know much about the topic. In this case, one of your goals may be to show them why your topic should be important to them as well.

Purpose

Research papers can have more than one purpose. Generally, research papers are meant to inform and/or persuade. Entertainment is sometimes an added benefit, but it is not a requirement. Check the assignment requirements to see what the purpose of your research paper should be. If you are not sure, ask your instructor.

Does your paper need to inform? Informative research papers are designed to help you and your reader learn about a topic or issue. Think about the information your audience needs to know about your topic.

Examples include definitions, background information, statistics, and data.

Does your paper need to persuade? Persuasive research papers use information, examples, and reasons to convince readers that the argument being presented is reasonable.

What kind of proof might you need? Think about what your readers might already believe about the topic. Most persuasive papers will also ask you to provide information for your readers.

Examples include interviews, statistics, data, and multiple viewpoints from outside sources.

Does your paper need to entertain? Entertaining papers engage the readers' attention. Think about what your audience might find interesting, funny, or touching.

Examples include fictional stories, personal narratives, satire, and songs.

MEDIA EXAMPLE OF PURPOSE AND AUDIENCE

Any time we communicate with others, we should consider the purpose and audience. The media are no exception, as they are a form of communication. Search online for a clip of *Reading Rainbow* with LeVar Burton.

Who is the target audience for this show? How can you tell? What is the purpose of the show? Explain your answer.

STUDENT EXAMPLE

After a little bit of research, Kadience is ready to think about her audience and purpose. She analyses her audience and purpose separately.

Audience   How much background information does your audience know? What are the audience's general feelings about your topic?

My professor said to write the paper for her and my classmates. My classmates have heard of cloning, but might have some misconceptions, too. I expect most of them to have made up their minds either for or against the cloning of humans, even though they may not know much, other than some general information they heard on the news.

Purpose   Does your paper need to inform, persuade, and/or entertain? What specific examples can you use to fulfill this purpose?

I will need to both inform and persuade. While I have been asked to make an argument, I will also need to include background information on how cloning works. I would like to also include quotes from scientists about their perspectives.

YOUR TURN

Following Kadience's example, think about the audience of your paper on social media addiction. What is the purpose of this paper?

Audience   How much background information does your audience know? What are the audience's general feelings about your topic?

_____

_____

_____

_____

Purpose   Does your paper need to inform, persuade, and/or entertain? What specific examples can you use to fulfill this purpose?

_____

_____

_____

_____

Creating a Working Thesis Statement

Want a review of thesis statements? See Chapter 4.

The thesis statement of your research paper is the main idea or claim made in your paper. As the blueprint for your paper, it should let the reader know what the topic of the paper is and what will be discussed. The thesis will help you to further narrow your topic. A working thesis statement is one that may undergo several revisions as you develop your paper. However, your thesis should always accurately reflect the information and arguments presented in your paper.

Argumentative—Persuasive research papers make a claim or judgment and will need an argumentative thesis statement. Most research papers are persuasive.

> More tax dollars should be devoted to back-to-work programs because they are more effective than homeless shelters in reducing homelessness.

Analytical—If your paper is meant to inform and not persuade, you can use an analytical thesis.

Local governments have reduced the amount of landfill waste by sponsoring green waste and recycling programs.

While thesis statements occur only in written papers, they are very similar to the main idea in various forms of media. Search online for a commercial for *freecreditscore.com*. It contains a specific main idea that is much like a thesis statement.

What is the main idea of the commercial? What ideas are presented to support the main idea?

STUDENT EXAMPLE

Now that she has narrowed her topic, used research questions, and considered her audience and purpose, Kadience writes out an argumentative thesis statement.

Narrowed Topic: *The ban on cloning humans*

Thesis Statement: *Although cloning offers the potential to advance lifesaving medicine, human cloning should remain illegal because of the physical and social dangers.*

YOUR TURN

Create an argumentative thesis statement for your narrowed topic on social media addiction. Write it in the space below.

Narrowed Topic: _____

Thesis Statement: _____

_____

_____

Looking for Sources

One of the ways of making your research experience more successful is to use a good search strategy and develop **key terms**. Before you begin an in-depth search using search engines, online catalogues, and electronic databases, you will need to have your key terms ready.

- **Pick out key terms from your thesis statement**. Key terms are important words or phrases. In the following thesis statement, the key terms are bolded.

  More **tax** dollars should be devoted to **back-to-work programs** because they are more effective than **homeless shelters** in **reducing** homelessness.

- **Find synonyms for your key terms**. Because researchers and scholars may use slightly different words in their research, also think of synonyms, words with the same or very similar meanings. Come up with additional words and phrases that have a closely related meaning, or association.

Key Terms	Synonyms
tax	money, revenue
back-to-work programs	employment, training, job program
homeless	impoverished, needy, vagrant
homeless shelter	rescue mission, housing shelter, homeless program
reducing	eliminate, diminish, minimize

- **Use "and," "or," and "not" to manipulate your results**. Use your key terms and synonyms in pairs or groups to narrow the results from search engines, online catalogues, and electronic databases to a reasonable number.

  - **Use "and" to include sources with both terms.**

    Example: homeless and vagrant

    Tip: This combination will provide you with fewer sources. The sources you get will contain both terms.

  - **Use "or" to include sources with either term.**

    Example: homeless or vagrant

    Tip: This combination will provide you with more sources. The sources you get will either contain the word "homeless" or they will contain the word "vagrant." The presence of both words in a source is not required.

  - **Use "not" to exclude a term altogether.**

    Example: homeless not vagrant

    Tip: This combination can help you eliminate sources that are not as helpful. The sources you get will contain the word "homeless," but any source that also contains the word "vagrant" will not be included.

If you end up with too many or too few sources, vary the combination of your key terms. Here "and" is used to narrow the number of sources to a manageable amount.

Key Terms	Number of Sources in Results
homeless	762,342,796
shelter	348,252
homeless and shelter	12,998
homeless and shelter and employment	841

MEDIA EXAMPLE OF KEY TERMS

Key terms are used for research, but important or key words are found in most conversations and interactions with others. Search online for a clip from the show *MythBusters*.

What key term(s) did you find? Explain why each term is important.

STUDENT EXAMPLE

Ready to conduct in-depth research, Kadience underlines key terms in her thesis statement. She then thinks of synonyms and related words for her key terms, so she has a variety of words and phrases to use in her search for sources.

Thesis

Although <u>cloning</u> offers the potential to advance <u>lifesaving medicine</u>, human cloning should remain <u>illegal</u> because of the <u>physical</u> and <u>social</u> <u>dangers</u>.

Key Terms	Synonyms
cloning	clone, identical DNA
lifesaving medicine	medical advances, breakthrough
Illegal	banned, restricted, outlawed
physical danger	experiment, harm
social danger	discrimination

YOUR TURN

Copy your thesis statement below and underline the key terms in the thesis. Then copy the key terms into a list. Lastly, think of synonyms and closely related words and phrases for each term.

Thesis

_____

Key Terms   **Synonyms**

_____   _____

_____   _____

_____   _____

_____   _____

Types of Sources

When looking for sources to support your working thesis statement, you should be choosy. You want to include only sources that are directly relevant to your paper. The sources you include should be fairly recent, be relevant to your topic, and add something important. Having a variety of sources will show that you have done thorough research and have a well-supported thesis. Below is a description of some of the basic types of sources you might include in your paper.

Books

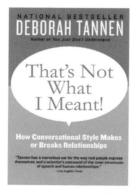

Where to Find Them—The easiest place to find books is in your school's library. Use your library's online catalogue to search for books that contain information about your topic. Some books will be written by one author, while others may be a collection of writings gathered together by an editor and published as a book. Many books are likely to be available in electronic form through your library. If your library doesn't have a book you want, there may be a way to get it from another library through an interlibrary loan system. Ask a librarian if this is an option for you. An electronic version of the book might also be available.

Concerns—If you are writing about a very new topic, such as a new type of medicine or a recent discovery, you may not be able to find a book that is specifically about your topic. You may, however, still be able to find a book that contains background information that will add valuable information to your paper.

Factors to Evaluate—Because books take time to publish, the information might be outdated. Try to choose books with publication dates that are within the last five years.

Periodicals

Where to Find Them—The word periodical is used to describe sources that are published periodically or regularly. Periodicals can be found in your library either in a print copy or

in electronic form. Many libraries subscribe to electronic databases that contain a large selection of periodicals. Periodicals include several types of sources: journals, newspapers, and magazines.

Journals are often published once a month, four times a year (quarterly), or yearly. Articles in journals are written by scholars and researchers and generally present research findings, discoveries, or new ways of thinking about a topic.

Newspapers are generally published daily or weekly. The articles in newspapers are written by

journalists who report on a variety of topics but are not considered experts or scholars. Newspaper articles report what is currently happening or what is currently known.

Magazines are usually published monthly or weekly. The articles in a magazine, like those in a newspaper, are written by journalists

who may report on a variety of topics but are not considered experts or scholars. Magazine articles may provide more details than newspaper articles due to the length and purpose of the article.

Concerns—Newspaper and magazine articles do not carry as much respect or credibility as journal articles because they are written by journalists or reporters rather than scholars.

Factors to Evaluate—The reputation of the periodical can be used to help evaluate the source. Well-known and respected journals such as the *Journal of the American Medical Association* are better to include in your paper than a local newspaper. Sometimes, the title of the source can help you determine which periodicals are newspapers, magazines, or journals. Because periodicals are published so frequently, look for articles that have been published within the last three to five years.

Websites

Where to Find Them—Websites may contain a wide variety or information that can prove helpful in your research. Websites can be found through a search on a web browser.

Concerns—The credibility of websites is always a concern. Because websites are not regulated, you should be extremely careful when adding them to your list of sources.

Factors to Evaluate—There are several ways to evaluate a website. Check all of the factors below before using a website.

- **Date**—Websites are more trustworthy if they have a date, and the more recent the date, the better. To find the date, you may need to scroll to the bottom of the page or visit the "About Us" page. If there is no date, you can't be sure how old the information is.
- **Author**—In general, websites are more trustworthy if they have an author listed. However, some sites, like corporate, government, and educational sites, may not list an author. This is typical, as the whole organization takes credit for the site. Either way, the individual or group should be credible (experienced and trustworthy).
- **Type of Site**—Education, government, organization, and news websites are generally credible; however, you should still evaluate them carefully. Be cautious of most commercial (.com) websites, as the purpose is usually to sell you a product. Avoid using personal sites, blogs, message boards, and wikis unless approved by your instructor.
- **Contact Information**—Credible websites should provide viewers with contact information. This information is often on the "About Us" or "Contacts" page. Look for a name, email address, physical address, and phone number. Websites that only ask for your information should be evaluated closely.
- **Documentation**—Information on a website should be documented just like any other source. Websites that publish their own findings and information may cite their own organization. Look for citations, references, and links to other credible websites and groups. Newspaper articles on websites are the exception to this rule, as they do not normally publish their sources.

Media

Where to Find Them—Media are a broad category; they include, but are not limited to, television programs, movies, songs, social networking platforms, advertisements, and posts to websites like YouTube.

Concerns—These sources are not considered academic and should be used in research papers only when the assignment calls for them. Paper topics in this textbook will often reference media sources, but you should ask if they can be used in other courses.

Factors to Evaluate—Like most sources that can be found online, careful attention should be taken to ensure that the media sources come from a reputable, if not original, source.

Organizing Your Research

You will find more sources than you will need to use in your paper. In order to keep track of these sources, you will need to follow a system to keep you organized.

Keep a list of all the sources you find. This list will allow you to see at a glance what sources you have. Each entry in your list should contain the author, title, and publishing information for the source. Record the information for each source, so it can be documented correctly when you are ready to incorporate it into your paper.

Make sure you have a record of all the sources you are considering using. Never rely on just your memory or try to copy down a whole source by hand. Accuracy is incredibly important when you are using sources, and you may realize that you want to see the whole source at a later time. While books can be checked out of the library, not all sources can be. You may need to make a photocopy of an entry in a reference book or a journal article that is not allowed out of the library. Print or save copies of electronic sources.

Take thorough notes about each source. Taking good notes will help you learn more about your sources and will provide you with an effective way of referencing important information within each source as you start your draft. Record information that will be needed when you document the source and refer to your notes about the content or argument presented. Put the notes for each source on a separate page.

Author(s) and/or Editor(s) _____

Title
(Chapter, Article, Essay,
Webpage, Post, Song, or Update) _____
_____
_____

Name of Source, if
Different Than Title Above
(Journal, Book, Website, or
Magazine Title) _____
_____
_____

Type of Source
☐ Whole Book
☐ Chapter in a Book
☐ Article in a Newspaper, Magazine, or Journal
☐ Article or Page from a Website
☐ Television Program
☐ Movie
☐ Advertisement
☐ Social Media
☐ Song
☐ Other _____

Where did you find the
source?
☐ Library (print copy)
☐ Library (online database) _____
☐ Website_____
☐ Other_____

Citation Information

_____
_____
_____
_____

Why is this source helpful?
What kind of information does it provide?

_____
_____
_____
_____

Important Quotes to Remember

Note—Record important information and page numbers so you can find quotes again later.

_____
_____
_____
_____
_____
_____

MEDIA EXAMPLE OF ORGANIZING YOUR RESEARCH

Organizing and note taking can be used on numerous occasions. Note taking has been encouraged for decades, both in schools and through the media. Search online for "How to Take Notes in Class: The 5 Best Methods" by Thomas Frank.

According to the video, what are the five best styles of note taking? Which styles does the speaker use the most?

STUDENT EXAMPLE

Kadience has found several good sources. While searching online, she found a helpful webpage from the Genetic Science Learning Center's Website, _Learn. Genetics_. The information from the webpage is printed below. Taking notes allows her to become familiar with the source and helps her keep track of the information within the source.

Cloning Humans

Genetic Science Learning Center. (7 January 2015) _Learn. Genetics_. Retrieved 17 November 2017 from http://learn.genetics.utah.edu/content/cloning/whyclone/

The prospect of cloning humans is highly controversial, and it raises a number of ethical, legal, and social challenges that need to be considered.

The vast majority of scientists and lawmakers view human reproductive cloning—cloning for the purpose of making a human baby—immoral. Supporters see it as a possible solution to infertility problems. Some even imagine making clones of geniuses, whose work could advance society. Far-fetched views describe farms filled with clones whose organs are harvested for transplantation—a truly horrific idea.

For now, risks and technical challenges—as well as laws that make it illegal—will probably keep human reproductive cloning from becoming a reality. Even though many species have been cloned successfully, the process is still technically difficult and inefficient. The success rate in cloning is quite low: most embryos fail to develop, and many pregnancies end in miscarriage.

Current efforts at human cloning are focused on creating embryonic stem cells for research and medicine, as described above. However, many feel that this type of therapeutic cloning comes dangerously close to human reproductive cloning. And once techniques become more streamlined and efficient, they fear that some may be tempted to take that next step.

From a technical and moral standpoint, before human cloning becomes routine, we need to have a good idea of the risks involved.

Author(s) and/or Editor(s)	*Genetic Science Learning Center*
Title *(Chapter, Article, Essay, Webpage, Post, Song, or Update)*	*"Why Clone?"*
Name of Source, if Different Than Title Above *(Journal, Book, Website, or Magazine Title)*	*Learn. Genetics.*

Type of Source

☐ Whole Book
☐ Chapter in a Book
☐ Article in a Newspaper, Magazine, or Journal
☑ Article or Page from a Website
☐ Television Program
☐ Movie
☐ Advertisement
☐ Social Media
☐ Song
☐ Other _____

Where did you find the source?

☐ Library (print copy)
☐ Library (online database) _____
☑ Website   *Google*
☐ Other_____

Citation Information	*Genetic Science Learning Center.*
	Published on 7 January 2015.
	"Why Clone?" <u>Learn. Genetics</u>.
	Found on 17 November 2017. http://learn.genetics.
	utah.edu/content/cloning/whyclone/
Why is this source helpful? **What kind of information does it provide?**	*This source gives me specific information on how cloning can be used. It also warns that caution should be taken. It offers a few statistics and comes from a reputable source.*
Important Quotes to Remember Note—Record important information and page numbers so you can find quotes again later.	*"Even though many species have been cloned successfully, the process is still technically difficult and inefficient" (paragraph 3).* *The source also says there could be therapeutic uses, but there are too many risks to try human cloning at this point (paragraph 4).*

YOUR TURN

Practice taking good notes for a source. Use the form to record your notes for the article provided.

"Is This the Beginning of a Like-Less Instagram?" by Lauren Rearick

MTV News, May 13, 2019

Showing your Instagram affection through a double-tap could soon be a thing of the past.

In recent weeks, Instagram has been testing out a version of its app that hid a photo's total number of likes, CNN reports. Users were still be [sic] able to view their own likes and statistics on any photos they had posted, but those numbers were kept private when viewing photos posted by friends, celebrities, or anyone else on the platform. The altered Insta experience debuted in Canada at the beginning of May, and users were notified of the change through a message displayed within Instagram, according to HuffPost.

The move comes following continued criticism about Instagram and its parent company, Facebook, for the impact the services have on users' daily lives. Of the shift, Facebook founder Mark Zuckerberg said on April 30 that the company believes "The future is private," and will be rolling out changes throughout its platforms, including Facebook, Instagram, and WhatsApp.

Adam Mosseri, the head of Instagram, told Buzzfeed News the change was about "creating a less pressurized environment where people feel comfortable expressing themselves." He said that users have expressed concern that they aren't getting enough likes.

Although Instagram likes aren't the only measure of success in the world, social media platforms remain frequent subjects of focus for professionals exploring potential negative impacts on mental health. Studies, including one conducted by the University of Pennsylvania and another from UK's Royal Society for Public Health and the Young Health Movement found that Instagram usage can have a detrimental effect on one's mental health.

Users that limited their time on the platform reported feeling less depressed and lonely, the University of Pennsylvania discovered. Additionally, the platform's "image-focused" feed led to feelings of "inadequacy and anxiety" among the 1,500 teens surveyed for the UK's Royal Society for Public Health and the Young Health Movement's study. (Some Instagram users do operate their online presence as a means of encouraging others, but their effect on a user's overall platform experience is harder to quantify.)

Social media usage will not necessarily have a negative impact on all users, Ana Radovic, MD, Division of Adolescent and Young Adult Medicine, UPMC Children's Hospital of Pittsburgh, told MTV News. However, those predisposed to feelings of low self-esteem may find that Instagram likes do serve as "another currency of self-comparison," and by hiding these likes, people are essentially able to "filter out the negative and enhance the positive."

"If they don't receive likes, they have nothing to fall back on in terms of their own feelings of self-worth," she said. "Specifically when someone has high concerns about their body image, then the social comparison deals with appearance and may cause them to feel more negatively about their body image." Ultimately, Dr. Radovic suggests remaining mindful of how you're using social media, and how much time you're spending on those platforms. If you do begin to notice that certain applications are having a negative impact on your self-esteem or mental health, she suggests talking about that with your healthcare provider.

"Keep an emotional pulse," she said. "Think about how you are feeling when you are using social media. Think about what you did, and why did it make you feel better or worse." She also suggests opening a new account where you only follow uplifting posters or consider unfollowing accounts that make you feel worse.

For now, those on Instagram, including Kylie Jenner and her record-breaking egg rival, don't have to worry about any of their likes disappearing. Mosseri didn't confirm that private likes would one day roll out to everyone, but he did tell Buzzfeed News that it wasn't "off the table."

Author(s) and/or Editor(s) _____

Title
(Chapter, Article, Essay, _____
Webpage, Post, Song, or Update) _____
_____

Name of Source, if
Different Than Title Above _____
(Journal, Book, Website, or _____
Magazine Title)

Type of Source
☐ Whole Book
☐ Chapter in a Book
☐ Article in a Newspaper, Magazine, or Journal
☐ Article or Page from a Website
☐ Television Program
☐ Movie
☐ Advertisement
☐ Social Media
☐ Song
☐ Other _____

Where did you find the
source?
☐ Library (print copy)
☐ Library (online database) _____
☐ Website _____
☐ Other _____

Citation Information _____
_____
_____

Why is this source
helpful? _____
What kind of information _____
does it provide? _____

Important Quotes to
Remember
Note—Record important infor- _____
mation and page numbers so
you can find quotes again later. _____

Starting Your Draft

Once you have collected enough research, review your notes and group like ideas together. Look for patterns that emerge; a pattern could be an argument that is mentioned by several sources or a commonly reoccurring concern. Reading your resources will give you additional insight into your topic and provide you with more ideas that you can build upon. At this point, try several different methods of prewriting to explore your topic further and organize your thoughts. Try creating an outline or use Post-it Notes or index cards to organize your ideas. The length requirements for a research paper may be longer than other papers you have been asked to write, but the process of creating a draft is the same.

Before you begin your draft, determine if you have sources to support each idea you plan on including in your paper. Your paper should be made up of mostly your writing, but you want your points to be well supported by reliable and credible sources. If you think you need more information, you can always continue your research. Many students find that in the process of writing, a little additional research is necessary.

i Need to review prewriting strategies? See Chapter 3.

i Find out how to incorporate sources into your paper effectively. See Chapter 15.

Assessing Your Knowledge

KEY POINTS	REMINDER	HOW WELL DID YOU UNDERSTAND THIS MATERIAL?	PAGE(S)
Understand how to make a schedule	**Making a schedule** is important to ensure you don't procrastinate. A schedule can help you stay on task and keep track of your progress.	☐ I've Got It! ☐ Almost There ☐ Need More Practice	pp. 218–19
Understand how to find a research paper topic	When choosing your topic, consider (1) your interests, (2) the assignment requirements, and (3) the amount of research available.	☐ I've Got It! ☐ Almost There ☐ Need More Practice	pp. 219–20
Understand how to narrow a topic	**Narrowing your topic** is an important step. The topic should be narrowed to a specific problem, controversy, or issue that can be discussed within the requirements of the assignment, especially page length.	☐ I've Got It! ☐ Almost There ☐ Need More Practice	pp. 220–22
Understand how to generate research questions	Generating **research questions** for your narrowed topic will help you understand the complexities of your topic better.	☐ I've Got It! ☐ Almost There ☐ Need More Practice	pp. 222–24

Understand how to define purpose and audience	**Audience** and **purpose** will inform decisions you make about your paper. The knowledge and background of your audience will determine how you approach your topic. The purpose of the paper can be to inform, persuade, and/ or entertain.	☐ I've Got It! ☐ Almost There ☐ Need More Practice	pp. 224–26
Understand how to create a working thesis statement	The thesis statement is the main idea or claim made in your paper. It is the blueprint of your paper and should let your readers know what your topic is and what to expect in your paper. Thesis statements can be **argumentative** or **analytical**.	☐ I've Got It! ☐ Almost There ☐ Need More Practice	pp. 226–27
Understand how to locate sources for a research paper	Locate sources by identifying **key terms** from your thesis statement. Once you have key terms, you can begin to look for sources from your library and the Internet.	☐ I've Got It! ☐ Almost There ☐ Need More Practice	pp. 227–30
Understand how to organize and take notes about sources	Without a good organizational strategy and thorough note taking, the hard work you invest in finding your sources might be lost. Keep track of the sources you find, and note the location of important information within each source.	☐ I've Got It! ☐ Almost There ☐ Need More Practice	pp. 232–38
Understand how to start your draft	Begin forming your draft by trying several types of prewriting. Reviewing your sources will help you identify patterns and arguments.	☐ I've Got It! ☐ Almost There ☐ Need More Practice	p. 239

Deepening Your Understanding

If you would like to go beyond the material in this chapter, explore additional connections, and get more practice, check out these related topics:

- **Prewriting**: Understanding your audience and purpose is critical when beginning your research paper. Your argument will be more effective if you have accurately assessed what your readers know about your topic.
- **Thesis Statement**: Create a strong and focused thesis statement for your research paper. Formulate a thesis early in the research process to guide your writing.
- **Organization**: Outlines and other forms of prewriting will help you determine the best organization for your research paper. More attention should be given to the organization of longer papers.
- **Argumentation**: Most research paper assignments will require you to make a judgment or claim. Arguments for research papers may be longer and more complex than arguments in other papers, but the basic parts are the same.

Using Sources

> "If we knew what it was we were doing, it wouldn't be called 'research,' would it?"
>
> —Albert Einstein

FACT OR FICTION?
When I use my sources, I can just stick them in my essay wherever I'd like.

FICTION.
When you incorporate sources into your essays, you will need to properly introduce and cite them, as well as explain and connect the source to your main idea/thesis statement.

Discovering Key Points

- ➔ Identify and practice writing a summary
- ➔ Identify and practice writing a paraphrase
- ➔ Identify and practice how to quote directly
- ➔ Identity and practice how to use ICE (introduce, cite, and explain)
- ➔ Understand the types of plagiarism and how to avoid plagiarism

Any time you are asked to write a research paper, you will have to use your sources clearly and effectively. In order to do this, you must integrate what you are taking from each source into your own argument. It must be clear to your audience *what* the source is doing in your essay. Why did you choose the source? Why is it important to your ideas and overall essay?

There are four ways to incorporate your sources properly into your essay:

- writing summaries
- writing paraphrases
- quoting directly
- using ICE (introduce, cite, and explain)

You are responsible for using and citing sources properly. You must avoid plagiarism, both intentional and accidental. In this chapter, you will learn the types of plagiarism and how to avoid it altogether.

Writing Summaries

A **summary** is an overview of the main ideas of the source. A source is the text you are working with. This could be a book or chapter from a book, an essay or article, a website, or even a film or television show. In a summary, you put the relevant part of the source concisely into your own words. Think of it as giving the plot of a film or book. If someone asked you what *Thor: The Dark World* was about, you would give a brief overview of the film, going over the key characters and plot points. You wouldn't give every single detail about the film, but just the important parts. The same is true for a summary of a source. You should be concise and select the most important points.

A summary tests your ability as a reader to pick out the significant parts and express them in your own words. This means you should not rely on the author's words or on quotations.

Steps for Writing a Summary

- **Read the essay**. During your first reading, just try to understand the text's main point and look up any concepts, terms, or words you don't know.
- **Put the source away and write an outline**. Without referring to the source, try to remember the main points and create an outline of them. By not looking at the source, you will be less likely to copy from the source or use quotes.
- **Take the outline and write your summary**. From the outline you've written, begin writing your summary. You can present the information in the order it is presented in the original source, or you can present the ideas in a different order (from the most to least important, for example). After you've written the summary, you'll want to make sure that none of the wording is too close to the original.

- **Reread the text**. During your second reading, try to fill in any gaps. Is there anything you've missed in your outline that you think your audience needs to know about the text?

- **Properly introduce the source**. Imagine your readers have never read this source. The first thing you should provide for them is a description of the source, which could also be the first sentence of your summary. You'll want to provide three pieces of information for your readers in the introduction:

You can tell if a source is an article or a book based on whether the title is enclosed in quotation marks. For more information, see Chapter 25.

AUTHOR'S FULL NAME	if there isn't an author, be sure to note that
SOURCE'S FULL TITLE	remember formatting for source titles
WHAT THE SOURCE IS ABOUT	offers the main point of the source

Try to put these three items in the first sentence of your summary, so as to properly introduce your audience to the source. The three items do not have to appear in that particular order, however. See the student example at the end of this section for an example.

- **Eliminate any opinion**. Read through your summary for any of your own judgments about the source. Summaries contain the facts about the source, and only the facts. What is the source about? What is the source's "plot" or main idea?

- **Think about your audience**. Since we should assume that your audience has never read the text, your job is to briefly sum up the main points. What would your readers need to know about the source? What don't they need to know? Is there jargon that you need to define for your audience?

- **Be clear and concise**. Most summaries are about a paragraph in length. Your source might be several pages long; you need to identify its essential points.

- **Know what to cut out**. If you find your summary is too long, be prepared to cut things out. Don't try to include every single example in your summary. Focus on the main points of the source.

- **Revise/Edit**. Make sure you have transitions between your ideas to help your reader understand your summary. Also look at your grammar and mechanics and ensure your language is specific, but easily grasped by your audience.

- **Add an in-text citation**. In some citation styles, summaries should end with an in-text citation for the original source. Follow the rules for your chosen documentation format.

STUDENT EXAMPLE

Lindsae has been asked to write a summary of the essay titled "Pepsi's Kendall Jenner Ad Was So Awful It Did the Impossible: It United the Internet." First, she needs to read the essay.

"Pepsi's Kendall Jenner Ad Was So Awful It Did the Impossible: It United the Internet," by Angela Watercutter

Wired, April 5, 2017

In case you've just awakened from a brief coma, Pepsi is taking a lot of heat for its latest ad. The broad strokes: Its official title is the word salad "Live for Now Moments Anthem"; it features reality star/model Kendall Jenner (if your coma was not-so-brief, that's a whole other thing, which we don't have time to get into right now); its gist is that we should all unite and "join the conversation." In that way, the soft drink ad succeeded. It did indeed provoke conversation—about Pepsi's tone-deafness.

In the 2-minute-39-second "short film," Jenner throws off the chains of the modeling industry by taking off her wig, then leaving a photoshoot to join a protest. After sharing some knowing nods and #woke-ass fist bumps with her fellow protestors, the *Keeping Up with the Kardashians* star manages to bring everyone together by ... handing a cop a Pepsi. The message is clear: All those Women's Marches, Black Lives Matter protests, and demonstrations outside Trump Tower would be much more effervescent—and effective!—if someone had just brought some soda.

The internet, as you might suspect, disagreed. Within 48 hours the video got nearly 1.6 million views on YouTube (five times as many downvotes as upvotes), and Twitter and Facebook lit up with people pointing out just how gauche the whole thing was. Activist DeRay Mckesson called it "trash," adding "If I had carried Pepsi I guess I never would've gotten arrested. Who knew?" People made memes (some even reaching back and evoking Pepper Spray Cop). And, rightfully, many folks pointed out that using protest imagery in order to peddle soda—particularly images that evoked the photo of Ieshia Evans facing down police in Baton Rouge, Louisiana last year—was pretty tasteless. It was one of the few times the internet ever agreed on anything.

And that, in and of itself, is noteworthy. For years, conversation online has brought out the best and worst in everyone. But this ad, with its effortlessly cool politically aware millennials in color-coordinated denim outfits, was the one thing everyone agreed to oppose. A Twitter search for "Pepsi" reveals that virtually no one is coming to the commercial's defense. In fact, not even Pepsi is defending it anymore. Earlier today, the company pulled the ad. "Pepsi was trying to project a global message of unity, peace and understanding. Clearly, we missed the mark and apologize," Pepsi said in a statement. "We did not intend to make light of any serious issue."

Soda companies sell harder to young consumers than to anyone else, and they've been pitching that coveted demographic messages of global unity for years. The most well-known of these attempts is Coca-Cola's peace-for-all 1971 "I'd like to buy the world a Coke" spot. (The one Don Draper dreamed up in the series finale of *Mad Men*.) But even before that, Pepsi was targeting youth culture with slogans like "Pepsi Generation" and "For those who think young"—both of which launched in the 1960s. Soda companies continued to aim for hip kids throughout the ensuing decades with celeb-packed ads featuring everyone from Michael Jackson to Drake to a truck-driving P. Diddy. Now Pepsi has tried to cross the streams, pairing a millennial mega-celebrity with what the company clearly thought was a fun spin on young people's ability to change the world. Between 1971 and now, though, people got the tools to respond to the misguided mashup on a mass scale—in 140 characters or less.

From Black Lives Matter to the Women's Marches, politically active people are already effecting change all over the world, and they're not doing it with soda and supermodels. Now, they've used the same tools that organized those movements to express how ill-advised it was to use their work to sell carbonated beverages. The reaction to Pepsi's ad, not the ad itself, brought people together. *That's* refreshing.

Once Lindsae has finished reading the essay, she writes her summary. Lindsae has chosen MLA formatting for her documentation style.

The essay "Pepsi's Kendall Jenner Ad Was So Awful It Did the Impossible: It United the Internet," written by Angela Watercutter, discusses the Pepsi ad featuring Kendall Jenner. The ad was quite controversial, causing significant backlash. Viewers felt the company was being insincere and that they were belittling the seriousness of the Black Lives Matter and Women's Rights movements. Because of this public outcry, Pepsi pulled the ad (Watercutter par. 1–6).

YOUR TURN

Read the following excerpted essay and then write a summary. Be sure to look at the tips for writing a summary as you write it.

"McDonald's Ad Accused of Exploiting Childhood Grief to Sell Sandwiches," by Amy B. Wang

The Washington Post, May 17, 2017

Throughout the years, McDonald's has used numerous tactics to sell its food, from luring kids in with Happy Meal toys to enlisting the help of celebrities such as Michael Jordan and the *Space Jam* cast. Last week, the international fast-food behemoth tried another approach: by debuting a commercial in the United Kingdom that featured a child wanting to know more about what his deceased father was like.

But the ad backfired, prompting accusations that McDonald's was using childhood grief to sell fast food—and forcing the company, days later, to apologize and pull the campaign. "It was never our intention to cause any upset," a McDonald's representative told *The*

Washington Post in a statement Tuesday. "We are particularly sorry that the advert may have disappointed those people who are most important to us—our customers."

In the 90-second commercial, a young boy walks alongside his mother as she runs through a list of his father's traits and hobbies: "Never scruffy. Always smart. And his shoes, so shiny, you could see your face in 'em." His father was captain of the football team, she adds.

With each quality, the boy seems disappointed to realize he doesn't seem to have much in common with his late parent. They arrive at a McDonald's. By now, the boy has stopped asking his mother questions. Soon after, they sit down at the table, the boy gets ready to take a bite out of his Filet-O-Fish sandwich. "That was your dad's favourite, too," his mother mentions offhand. The boy looks up, startled but pleased.

The ad seemed to divide those who watched it. Shortly after it aired, many people took to social media to say they were not loving it. Some said they had lost a parent as a child and were offended at the suggestion that a McDonald's meal would have lessened the pain. "You always wonder how many people had to sign off on an ad like this," tweeted Martin Belam, an editor at *The Guardian* in London.

Summaries of Short Passages

A summary can be provided for material of almost any length. The above examples involved summaries of articles several paragraphs in length. You might also be asked to summarize a much longer piece—or to summarize a short passage. As an example, let's take a single paragraph from one of the articles we have already looked at.

STUDENT EXAMPLE

Lindsae has been asked to write a summary of a specific paragraph from the essay she wrote the summary of earlier. Her instructor provides her with the following paragraph:

> The soda companies sell harder to young consumers than to anyone else, and they've been pitching that coveted demographic message of global unity for years. The most well-known of these attempts is Coca-Cola's peace-for-all 1971 "I'd like to buy the world a Coke" spot. (The one Don Draper dreamed up in the series finale of *Mad Men*.) But even before that, Pepsi was targeting youth culture with slogans like "Pepsi Generation" and "For those who think young"—both of which launched in the 1960s. Soda companies continued to aim for hip kids throughout the ensuing decades with celeb-packed ads featuring everyone from Michael Jackson to Drake to a truck-driving P. Diddy. Now Pepsi has tried to cross the streams, pairing a millennial mega-celebrity with what the company clearly thought was a fun spin on young people's ability to change the world. Between

1971 and now, though, people got the tools to respond to the misguided mashup on a mass scale—in 140 characters or less.

After Lindsae has read the paragraph, she writes the following summary:

Pepsi isn't the only one to try this approach in advertisements. Young people are crucial consumers for soda companies, and the companies try hard to reach them in their ads (Watercutter par. 5).

YOUR TURN

Look at the paragraph below, taken from the same essay on McDonald's advertising you wrote the summary about previously. Then write a summary of the paragraph.

> The ad seemed to divide those who watched it. Shortly after it aired, many people took to social media to say they were not loving it. Some said they had lost a parent as a child and were offended at the suggestion that a McDonald's meal would have lessened the pain. "You always wonder how many people had to sign off on an ad like this," tweeted Martin Belam, an editor at *The Guardian* in London.

Writing Paraphrases

To paraphrase a passage of someone else's writing is to put it in your own words. How is that different from a summary? It's simple: in a paraphrase you are not trying to select only the most important points so as to provide something much shorter than the original. Indeed, a paraphrase tends to be roughly the same length as the original. The aim of a paraphrase is to convey the meaning of the original as fully and as clearly as possible, but to express that meaning with different words—usually, words that are somewhat simpler for an audience to understand. Again, let's look at an example.

STUDENT EXAMPLE

Lindsae has been asked to write a paraphrase of the following sentence:

> The soda companies sell harder to young consumers than to anyone else, and they've been pitching that coveted demographic message of global unity for years.

That's the sort of sentence that some readers may not easily take in at first. Elementary-level readers may not immediately understand the meaning of "sell harder to young consumers" or "pitching that coveted demographic message." If you had uttered such a sentence and you were met by blank looks, you might then say, "let me provide a paraphrase in order to help you understand what I mean."

After Lindsae has read the sentence carefully two or three times, she sets it to one side where she can't see it, and writes the following paraphrase:

Companies that sell soda have been directing their advertising energy towards young people for a long time—and in doing so they have often tried to associate their products with ideas about peace and world-wide unity (Watercutter par. 5).

Lindsae then reads what she has written, and compares it to the sentence she is trying to paraphrase. She notices that her paraphrase is quite a bit longer than the original—and she realizes too that, despite the added length, she hasn't captured the meaning of the sentence as well as she'd like to. Here is her revised version:

Companies that sell soda pay special attention to young people—and in so doing have often tried to associate their products with the idea of world-wide harmony (Watercutter par. 5).

Steps for Writing a Paraphrase

Examine the original. Look at the sentence(s) you have been asked to paraphrase. Read the sentence(s) over a couple of times, first focusing on any words or concepts that you don't understand, and then reading for full understanding of the sentence(s).

- **First, put it away**. As with the summary, you'll want to put away the source while you try to express in your own words the meaning of the sentence(s) you have read. The reason for doing this is so that you won't be tempted to look at the source and copy some of the wording of the original.
- **Afterwards, check back**. After you've written the paraphrase, look back at the source to make sure that none of your wording was too close to the original—and that you have expressed as much of the meaning of the original as you can, as faithfully as you can.
- **Eliminate any opinion**. As with a summary, a paraphrase should not normally convey any of your own opinions about what the source says.
- **Be clear**. It is often difficult to find ways of clearly expressing in your own words what someone else has written or said—especially if they have used difficult words or expressed themselves in complicated sentence structures. In order to come up with a paraphrase that is clear and easy to understand, you may have to revise what you have written more than once.
- **Edit**. Be sure to look at your grammar and mechanics to make sure your ideas are presented clearly.

- **Add an in-text citation.** Like summaries, paraphrases should end with an in-text citation for the original source. Follow the rules for your chosen documentation format.

Directly Quoting

When you use sources inside your essay, you can summarize, paraphrase, or use the source by directly quoting it. **Directly quoting** involves including some of the exact words used in your source within your own essay. These word-for-word quotations should be placed inside quotation marks. Quotations can add weight to your own argument. By using them, you can present specific examples and show that other people also share the same viewpoint. However, when you directly quote, you need to make sure that you fit the quotation into the flow of your argument; it's important not to just dump quotations into your paper anywhere. You also need to introduce the source to your audience and properly document it by providing a citation after the quotation. After you have added the quote, check again to be sure that it supports your main point or thesis.

There is an easy method to remember for incorporating sources into your essays with direct quotes. This is called the **ICE method**, and it is described in detail later in this chapter.

When you directly quote a source, you'll want to make sure you have three parts. These three parts can come in any order, but you must have all three.

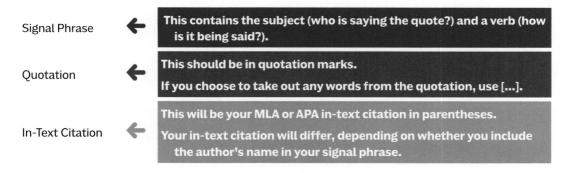

Signal Phrase ← This contains the subject (who is saying the quote?) and a verb (how is it being said?).

Quotation ← This should be in quotation marks.
If you choose to take out any words from the quotation, use [...].

In-Text Citation ← This will be your MLA or APA in-text citation in parentheses.
Your in-text citation will differ, depending on whether you include the author's name in your signal phrase.

Signal Phrase

A signal phrase is just a word, phrase, or clause that leads into a quotation. Generally, a signal phrase includes the author's name and a verb that tells *how* the author stated the information. Appropriate word choice here is crucial. You don't want to say that an author is "describing," when he or she is "arguing." Once you have an appropriate signal phrase, add in the quotation you are using and end it with a citation in parentheses.

EXAMPLES OF SIGNAL PHRASES
- As the article emphasizes, "
- When Luna analyzes this problem, she concludes that "

Want to know how to use commas properly with signal phrases and quotations? See Chapter 22.

- Jones points to this contrast when he argues that "
- She argues, "
- In Howlett's view, "
- He states, "

Quotation

After your signal phrase comes your quotation. Be sure to quote only what you need. You can take out any words or phrases you don't want by adding in [...]. A word of advice about taking out words: if you choose to take any words or phrases out, make sure you don't change the meaning of the quote.

Citation

For more examples of in-text citations, see Chapter 16.

After your quotation comes your citation. The citation provides your readers with the information they need if they wanted to refer back to the original source. This will be in parentheses. What is included in your citation will depend on what format you choose to use (MLA or APA).

Putting It Together with Punctuation

Remember the in-text citations in these examples are in MLA format; for in-text examples in APA format, see Chapter 16.

Punctuation for the direct quotation depends on which order you choose. Here are some formulas for direct quoting, along with punctuation. Notice the use and placement of commas. Also notice that there is no period at the end of the quote. The period ends the sentence after the citation. The examples below are in MLA format. For more examples in MLA and APA formatting, see Chapter 16.

AUTHOR'S LAST NAME IN SIGNAL PHRASE

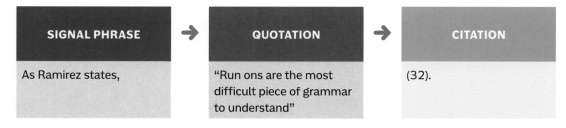

AUTHOR'S LAST NAME NOT IN SIGNAL PHRASE

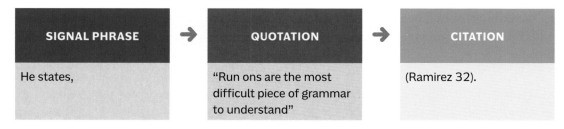

BEGINNING WITH QUOTATION AND AUTHOR'S LAST NAME IN SIGNAL PHRASE

BEGINNING WITH QUOTATION AND AUTHOR'S LAST NAME NOT IN SIGNAL PHRASE

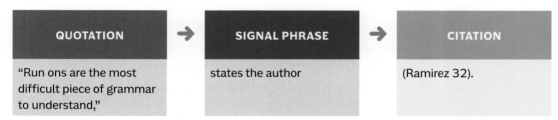

STUDENT EXAMPLE

Lindsae now has to try directly quoting from the essay she wrote the summary of earlier. Her instructor gives her a paragraph from the essay she can choose her quote from. She looks in Chapter 16 to find out how to cite this special source in text. She is using MLA documentation format.

Paragraph 4: And that, in and of itself, is noteworthy. For years, conversation online has brought out the best and worst in everyone. But this ad, with its effortlessly cool politically aware millennials in color-coordinated denim outfits, was the one thing everyone agreed to oppose. A Twitter search for "Pepsi" reveals that virtually no one is coming to the commercial's defense. In fact, not even Pepsi is defending it anymore. Earlier today, the company pulled the ad. "Pepsi was trying to project a global message of unity, peace and understanding. Clearly, we missed the mark and apologize," Pepsi said in a statement. "We did not intend to make light of any serious issue."

After Lindsae reads the paragraph, she decides on a direct quote:

As Watercutter tells it, "this ad, with its effortlessly cool politically aware millennials in color-coordinated denim outfits, was the one thing everyone agreed to oppose" (par. 4).

YOUR TURN

Read again the two paragraphs below (taken from the source about the McDonald's advertisement that you wrote the summary and paraphrase for) and compose a sentence in which you quote directly from the source. Be sure to use the correct punctuation and to provide your in-text citation.

Paragraph 1: Throughout the years, McDonald's has used numerous tactics to sell its food, from luring kids in with Happy Meal toys to enlisting the help of celebrities such as Michael Jordan and the *Space Jam* cast. Last week, the international fast-food behemoth tried another approach: by debuting a commercial in the United Kingdom that featured a child wanting to know more about what his deceased father was like.

Paragraph 5: The ad seemed to divide those who watched it. Shortly after it aired, many people took to social media to say they were not loving it. Some said they had lost a parent as a child and were offended at the suggestion that a McDonald's meal would have lessened the pain. "You always wonder how many people had to sign off on an ad like this," tweeted Martin Belam, an editor at *The Guardian* in London.

Using ICE

The ICE method can be used when quoting directly or when writing paraphrases or summaries. The ICE method has three parts and should be done for *every* source used in your essay.

Introduce: The very first time you ever want to use a source in your essay, you must introduce it, so that your readers will be familiar with the sources in your essay. After you use the source for the first time, you can start with the citation part of ICE. The introduction contains three parts, and these parts can go in any order, as long as all three are presented together.

AUTHOR'S FULL NAME	provides the first and last name of the author (if there isn't an author, be sure to note that)
SOURCE'S FULL TITLE	gives the title of the source (remember formatting for source titles)
WHAT THE SOURCE IS ABOUT	offers the main point of the source

Cite: When you want to directly quote the source, you'll need to include a signal phrase, the quotation, and an in-text citation. Remember that for your direct quotation, you need the following:

A SIGNAL PHRASE (WHO & HOW)

THE QUOTATION (IN QUOTATION MARKS)

A CITATION (IN PARENTHESES)

Explain: The last part of ICE is where you'll take the quotation that you used in the citation portion of ICE and then explain the quotation a bit further. This is also where you can connect the quotation directly back to your own ideas and thesis statement. This might include your opinion about the quote or a reflection upon it.

EXAMPLE OF THE ICE METHOD

Full Name of the Author	Full Title of the Source	Main Point/Argument of Source

Thomas Buckingham, author of the essay "Cat Breeds of Today," argues that the most interesting breed of cat is the munchkin. He states, "It is a conspiracy that the cutest cat isn't even recognized by the Breed Associations" (Buckingham 26). While Buckingham may believe that the munchkin is the "cutest," the breed is merely a genetic concoction, a mutation, and it should never be allowed with other purebreds by the Breed Associations.

Quotation

Citation (in MLA formatting)

Signal Phrase

Explanation of Quotation

STUDENT EXAMPLE

Lindsae now has to incorporate the source referring to the Pepsi advertisement using ICE. She uses the quotation she chose earlier and adds in the introduction and explanation parts of ICE.

Paragraph 4: And that, in and of itself, is noteworthy. For years, conversation online has brought out the best and worst in everyone. But this ad, with its effortlessly cool politically aware millennials in color-coordinated denim outfits, was the one thing everyone agreed to oppose. A Twitter search for "Pepsi" reveals that virtually no one is coming to the commercial's defense. In fact, not even Pepsi is defending it anymore. Earlier today, the company pulled the ad. "Pepsi was trying to project a global message of unity, peace and understanding. Clearly, we missed the mark and apologize," Pepsi said in a statement. "We did not intend to make light of any serious issue."

The essay "Pepsi's Kendall Jenner Ad Was So Awful It Did the Impossible: It United the Internet" written by Angela Watercutter discusses the Pepsi ad featuring Kendall Jenner. The ad was quite controversial, causing significant backlash. Viewers felt the company was being insincere and that they were belittling the seriousness of the Black Lives Matter and Women's Rights movements. Because of this public outcry, Pepsi pulled the ad. As Watercutter says, "this ad, with its effortlessly cool politically aware millennials in color-coordinated denim outfits, was the one thing everyone agreed to oppose" (par. 4). Even though Pepsi certainly believed they were creating a relatable and current ad, the audience was not pleased at how inconsiderate and unaware their ad really was.

> **YOUR TURN**

Use ICE for the source of the McDonald's advertisement that you wrote the summary, paraphrase, and direct quotation for. Try to change your introduction sentence from the one you wrote in your summary.

Paragraph 1: Throughout the years, McDonald's has used numerous tactics to sell its food, from luring kids in with Happy Meal toys to enlisting the help of celebrities such as Michael Jordan and the *Space Jam* cast. Last week, the international fast-food behemoth tried another approach: by debuting a commercial in the United Kingdom that featured a child wanting to know more about what his deceased father was like.

Paragraph 5: The ad seemed to divide those who watched it. Shortly after it aired, many people took to social media to say they were not loving it. Some said they had lost a parent as a child and were offended at the suggestion that a McDonald's meal would have lessened the pain. "You always wonder how many people had to sign off on an ad like this," tweeted Martin Belam, an editor at *The Guardian* in London.

What Is Plagiarism?

Plagiarism comes from the Latin word *plagiarus*, which means "kidnapper." In your essays, plagiarism means using another person's words or ideas without properly documenting and recognizing them. Plagiarism is unethical, and it is a serious offense. Plagiarism may be **intentional** or **accidental**. Intentional plagiarism is plagiarism that is deliberate. When you intentionally plagiarize, you are blatantly choosing to cheat. Often, those who intentionally plagiarize have poor time management skills and do not think they will get caught. Accidental plagiarism is plagiarism that is unintended. When you accidentally plagiarize, you may not be familiar with the documentation requirements, or you may have simply been careless. Often, those who accidentally plagiarize may not know how to take notes properly or how to properly integrate sources into an essay.

In many cases, of course, it is not possible for someone marking a paper to tell whether plagiarism is intentional or not. But instructors can distinguish between more and less serious forms of plagiarism—and they are remarkably good at sensing when students submit work that is not their own.

MORE SERIOUS FORMS OF PLAGIARISM	LESS SERIOUS FORMS OF PLAGIARISM
Buying your paper	Taking phrases or sentences from a source, changing only a few words, and presenting it in your paper without quotation marks and an in-text citation
Copying from sources and presenting the wording as your own	Presenting someone else's ideas without citing them
Downloading a paper from the Internet	Directly quoting a source, but not putting quotation marks around it
Copying from/Sharing with another student	Directly quoting a source and putting quotation marks around it, but not citing it in-text afterwards
Cutting and pasting from several sources without properly introducing and citing the sources	Paraphrasing or summarizing too closely to the source's original wording

Common Knowledge

Widely known facts are considered to be common knowledge and do not need to be cited. In order to be considered common knowledge, a fact must meet three criteria:

1. You must be able to find the same information in numerous other sources.

2. You think it is information your audience should already know.

3. A person could easily find the information with a general reference book.

If you are not sure whether an idea is common knowledge, cite it.

COMMON KNOWLEDGE (NO NEED TO CITE)	NOT COMMON KNOWLEDGE (MUST CITE)
Jupiter is the largest planet in the Earth's solar system.	Some researchers believe that the planet Jupiter was formed quickly.
The only animal with four knees is the elephant.	According to American law, a member of "an endangered species cannot be harmed, harassed, wounded, injured, or killed."
From 1881 to 1885, Chester A. Arthur was vice president of the United States.	Republicans didn't like Arthur's humanitarian streak; because of this, he didn't strongly campaign for their votes.

Common Plagiarism Myths

- **"I can't remember where the quotations or ideas came from, so I didn't cite them."** You must keep track of the sources and keep impeccable notes as to where each idea and quote originally came from.
- **"I only need to cite direct quotes and statistics."** You do need to cite direct quotes and statistics, but you also need to cite ideas or unique phrases from the original source.
- **"I included a Works Cited/References page. Isn't that really all I need to do?"** Just having the citations on a Works Cited or References page isn't enough. The second part of citing your source is citing it at the sentence level. This way, you are showing which words and ideas are yours and which belong to another person.

Avoiding Plagiarism

Here are a few steps to avoiding plagiarism:

- **Give yourself time**. Many students who intentionally plagiarize do so because they are writing the paper at the last minute and panic. Don't get yourself in a situation where you might be tempted to plagiarize. Talk to your instructor, or go to the tutoring center on your campus.
- **Print or copy sources and write down documentation info**. When you find a website you want to use as a source, print it out; at the top of the copy, write down all of the important citation information. You should do the same for any book or periodical that you find at the library. Make sure you write down all the information you will need for the citation.
- **Use notecards or Post-it Notes**. Notecards or Post-it Notes can help you when you are trying to incorporate sources. They are easy to shuffle around and rearrange, which can help you think about how you might organize and present the sources in your essay. They also allow you to write down all the pertinent information from a source you will need, as well as a quote or short summary of the source.
- **When in doubt, cite**. If you are ever unsure if your writing is too close to the source's ideas or wording, cite it.

YOUR TURN

First, summarize the whole essay that appears below in your own words. Next, pick a paragraph from the essay and summarize that paragraph as well. Then choose a quotation to use when you write ICE for this source.

"Study: Industry's Found Sneaky Way to Keep Advertising Junk Food to Kids," by Katy Bachman

AdWeek, August 3, 2011

Food and beverage advertisers may have found a handy way to dodge their own guidelines restricting the marketing of junk food to children, according to a new study from the Rudd Center for Food Policy and Obesity at Yale University. While companies have cut back on TV ads aimed at children, and in some cases cut out TV ads for candy altogether, they've also upped the use of product placement, the study found.

That's a loophole that the Council of Better Business Bureaus' Children's Food and Beverage Initiative, the industry's self-regulatory program, should close, the study concluded. "We want to recognize the food industry has changed how they market to children. We just want to make sure there isn't other stuff going under the radar," said Marlene Schwartz, deputy director of the Rudd Center and one of the authors of the study.

The study comes at a rotten time for food and beverage advertisers, which are in a heated battle over the federal government's new proposed voluntary guidelines on marketing to children, which, if followed, would affect every marketing tactic from advertising to packaging to sponsorships.

Opponents to the feds' proposed guidelines wrote off the Rudd Center study as more of the same. "It's the usual thing. They set up their own grading system and then they give us an 'F,'" said Dan Jaffe, executive vice president of the Association of National Advertisers. "The government has set up very clear criteria that we meet. They aren't looking at advertising directed to kids, but all advertising that might be seen by kids."

The authors analyzed Nielsen product placement data during prime time in 2008. On average, children 2–11 are exposed to 281 product placements for junk food during prime time, per the study released Tuesday. Adolescents 12–17 are exposed to 444 product placements.

The worst offender was soft drinks, which accounted for two-thirds of product placement appearances. Coca-Cola alone accounted for 71 percent of product placement occurrences viewed by children. It was also the only company where the product placement exposure exceeded the number of TV ads viewed by children. Children saw almost 10 times as many Coke brand occurrences as ads and nearly all of them—192 out of 198—were in one program, *American Idol*, which reached 2 million children 2–11 a year.

"Soft drinks have switched their [marketing] strategy," said Schwartz. "Coca-Cola said they were not going to market to children under 12. By sheer numbers, they are reaching massive numbers of children. That's the loophole. Whether they mean to or not, the kids are seeing that. If they really want to be sure, then put it on an adult show that's on at night, a drama where adults make up the audience. *Idol* is a family show. It's disingenuous."

Only 8 percent of the audience for *American Idol* is children 2–11, according to Nielsen. "Prime time isn't a daypart an advertiser wanting to reach children would look at," said Brad Adgate, senior vice president of corporate research for Horizon Media. Weekday afternoons and Saturdays make more sense, as that's when children make up between 13 percent and 18 percent of the TV viewing audience, according to an analysis of Nielsen data by Horizon.

"The CFBAI is directed at changing the ads that are directed to children, and the participants are doing an outstanding job of complying," said Elaine Kolish, the CFBAI's director. Kolish noted that data from the Georgetown Economic Services found that carbonated beverage advertising in children's programming decreased by nearly 100 percent between 2004 and 2010. "Our program focuses on child-directed advertising," she said. "We respect the rights of advertisers to advertise to adults."

Assessing Your Knowledge

KEY POINTS	REMINDER	HOW WELL DID YOU UNDERSTAND THIS MATERIAL?	PAGE(S)
Identify and practice writing a summary	A **summary** is where you recap all of the main ideas from a source in your own words. A summary should not include quotations, and the summary should begin with an introduction of the source. A summary should end with an in-text citation for the source used.	☐ I've Got It! ☐ Almost There ☐ Need More Practice	pp. 242–47
Identify and practice writing a paraphrase	A **paraphrase** is where you rephrase a specific section or paragraph of a source in your own words. A paraphrase should not include quotations. A paraphrase should end with an in-text citation for the source used.	☐ I've Got It! ☐ Almost There ☐ Need More Practice	pp. 247–49
Identify and practice how to quote directly	When you **directly quote** a source in your essay, you are borrowing word-for-word from the source. You'll also want to make sure that you use the proper citation at the end.	☐ I've Got It! ☐ Almost There ☐ Need More Practice	pp. 249–52
Identify and practice how to use ICE in an essay	When you use a source in your essay, you'll want to use the **ICE method**: ▪ **Introduce** the author's full name, the source's full title, and what the source is about ▪ **Cite** the source using the correct in-text citation format ▪ **Explain** the source and connect it back to your main ideas/thesis statement	☐ I've Got It! ☐ Almost There ☐ Need More Practice	pp. 252–54

| Understand the types of plagiarism and how to avoid plagiarism | **Plagiarism** is the use of someone else's words or ideas without acknowledging and documenting them. There are two types of plagiarism: **intentional** and **accidental**. In order to avoid plagiarism, you need to know when you have to document and when you don't have to. | ☐ I've Got It!
☐ Almost There
☐ Need More Practice | pp. 254–58 |

Deepening Your Understanding

If you would like to go beyond the material in this chapter, explore additional connections, and get more practice, check out these related topics:

- **The Research Process**: Before you can use your sources in your essays, you must first begin looking for sources. Knowing the ins and outs of completing research can help you find scholarly and useful sources.

- **Argumentation**: Often, when you use sources in your essays, you will be using them as examples to further your own argument. Reviewing how to write argumentative papers can help you improve how you incorporate your examples.

- **Quotation Marks**: When you use a source in your essay by directly quoting it, you will want to use quotation marks properly.

- **Using Precise Language**: When you write an essay with sources, you will want to use the most clear and concise language possible. This will allow you to write better summaries and paraphrases and to properly explain your quotations so that your audience better understands.

MLA/APA Documentation

"Research is formalized curiosity. It is poking and prying with a purpose."

—Zora Neale Hurston

Discovering Key Points

- Use **MLA** or **APA** to cite books
- Use **MLA** or **APA** to cite periodicals
- Use **MLA** or **APA** to cite websites
- Use **MLA** or **APA** to cite forms of media
- Recognize a paper written in **MLA** or **APA**

You may use borrowed information to support your argument, challenge an idea, or provide background. Any time information is borrowed, it must be properly documented: this includes summaries, paraphrases, and direct quotations. In order to make it clear which ideas and words are yours and which belong to others, you will need to follow a documentation style.

Documentation Styles

When we are driving, we all benefit from having rules and guidelines to follow. These rules help us anticipate the actions of other drivers and avoid accidents. The two documentation styles, **Modern Language Association (MLA)** and **American Psychological Association (APA)**, discussed in this textbook will provide you with guidelines for citing borrowed information in a way that your readers will understand. While both MLA and APA have different formatting rules, they both require (1) in-text citations for each piece of borrowed material and (2) a bibliography at the end of a paper. In MLA, the bibliography is called **Works Cited**; in APA, the bibliography is called **References**.

The MLA documentation style is the style most students learn in high school. In college, many of your general education classes may allow you to use MLA when writing papers that require sources. However, there are numerous discipline-specific documentation styles, such as Chicago Manual of Style, Institute of Electrical and Electronics Engineers (IEEE), and American Medical Association (AMA), and your instructor may require you to use a documentation style specific to the course. If you are an English, languages, art, theater, music, or religious studies major, you will probably be asked to use MLA regularly. APA documentation is used in psychology and several other disciplines in the behavioral and social sciences. While you may initially hesitate to learn a new documentation style, the popularity of APA documentation makes it worthy of study and practice. Like MLA, APA is a system that contains patterns. Once you recognize the patterns, using this formatting style becomes easier.

In-Text Citations

In-text citations are found within the paragraphs of your essay and give the readers information about the sources being used. As you learned in Chapter 15, you must give credit to an author if you include a summary, paraphrase, or direct quote of his or her ideas. The in-text citation allows you to provide your readers with a way to match the borrowed material in your paper to the citations on your Works Cited page or References page. Below are a few examples showing how readers should be able to connect the in-text citation with the entry in the Works Cited or References page based on the author's last name. Make sure that you follow only the examples for the documentation style you plan on using.

MLA

In Margaret Sampson's article "How Our Children Were Corrupted by Television," she argues that children's programming has changed since its invention in a way that stunts our children's social and educational growth. The main change is that "shows aimed at children are only meant for entertainment and not education" (Sampson 40). In order to enhance growth during these crucial years, children should substitute television viewing with educational games or activities that will increase motor learning.

> Sampson, Margaret. "How Our Children Were Corrupted by Television." *Media Today*, vol. 54, no. 2, Mar. 2006, pp. 33–41.

APA

In Margaret Sampson's article "How Our Children Were Corrupted by Television," she argues that children's programming has changed since its invention in a way that stunts our children's social and educational growth. The main change is that "shows aimed at children are only meant for entertainment and not education" (Sampson, 2006, p. 40). In order to enhance growth during these crucial years, children should substitute television viewing with educational games or activities that will increase motor learning.

> Sampson, M. (2006, March). How our children were corrupted by television. *Media Today, 54*(2), 33–41.

As an alternative, you may use the author's name in the signal phrase. However, the author's name must be in the same sentence as the parenthetical in-text citation. The connection between the in-text citation and the citation on the Works Cited or References page should still be clear to your readers. As you learned in Chapter 15, signal phrases lead into a quote and contain a verb that helps show how the original author stated the information. The example below shows the author's name in the signal phrase.

ℹ️
Want to know more about signal phrases? See Chapter 15.

MLA

Sampson argues that "shows aimed at children are only meant for entertainment and not education" (40).

Sampson, Margaret. "How Our Children Were Corrupted by Television." *Media Today*, vol. 54, no. 2, Mar. 2006, pp. 33–41.

APA

Sampson argues that "shows aimed at children are only meant for entertainment and not education" (2006, p. 40).

Sampson, M. (2006, March). How our children were corrupted by television. *Media Today*, 54(2), 33–41.

Basic In-Text Citations

MLA

The basic in-text citation for MLA requires the author's last name and the page number the borrowed material was originally taken from.

> Some workers argued, "The agreement between the company and the labor union was broken when everyone got a pay cut" (Brown 58).

> Samuel Brown estimates that "each worker will lose about $5,000 a year" (67).

APA

The basic in-text citation for APA requires the author's last name, the year the source was published, and the page number. Place a comma between the author's name and the year, as well as between the year and the page number.

> Some workers argued, "The agreement between the company and the labor union was broken when everyone got a pay cut" (Brown, 2008, p. 58).

Samuel Brown estimates that "each worker will lose about $5,000 a year" (2008, p. 67).

In-Text Citations for Sources with Multiple Authors

MLA

TWO AUTHORS

For two authors, give their last names separated by "and." Do not use an ampersand (&).

> Executives dispute the allegations "raised by fans who said the movie did not accurately reflect the author's original vision" (Le and Wilson 21).

> Le and Wilson contend, "the only way to satisfy a cult following is stay as true to the original story and characterization as possible" (24).

THREE OR MORE AUTHORS

If the source has three or more authors, list the first author. Then, use *et al.* to represent the other authors. "Et al." is Latin for "and others."

> Many parents blame "video games with first-person shooter perspective for the violence their children demonstrate toward others" (Ramsey et al. 99).

In the signal phrase, you can give all of the authors or offer the first author's name along with the words "and others."

> Studies conducted by Ramsey and others show that "violence is more likely associated with long hours of television viewing instead of video games" (99).

 APA

TWO AUTHORS

For two authors, separate the names with "&" instead of the word "and" inside the parentheses.

> Executives dispute the allegations "raised by fans who said the movie did not accurately reflect the author's original vision" (Le & Wilson, 2010, p. 21).

In the signal phrase, use "and" to separate the authors' names.

Le and Wilson contend, "the only way to satisfy a cult following is stay as true to the original story and characterization as possible" (2010, p. 21).

THREE OR MORE AUTHORS

After the first author, use "et al." to represent the other authors.

One parent at the meeting said, "It is hard to have faith that our failing school system will improve if no one is willing to make dramatic changes" (Martinez et al., 2012, p. 64).

Martinez et al. conclude that "the perception of failure does more damage than low test scores" (2012, p. 64).

In-Text Citations for Sources That Contain Quoted Material

Give credit to the person who is being quoted by including his or her name in the signal phrase. Still provide the author of the source in the in-text citation, so your reader will be able to easily find the source on your Works Cited or References page.

MLA

Sarah Weber, marketing advisor for Kiser Permanente, proposed "a new campaign to show the company's focus is not on money, but on providing quality physicians and health care services" (qtd. in Patel 102).

APA

Sarah Weber, marketing advisor for Kiser Permanente, proposed "a new campaign to show the company's focus is not on money, but on providing quality physicians and health care services" (as cited in Patel, 2007, p. 102).

In-Text Citations for Sources with No Author

If no author is given, reference the work by the title.

MLA

Use a shortened version of the title. You may use the first few words. This may be helpful if you have two sources with similar titles that are also both lacking authors.

Researchers have found "the body image of young women is shaped long before they become teenagers" ("Advertisements" 134).

APA

Researchers have found "the body image of young girls is shaped long before they become teenagers" ("Advertisements Shape Our Reality," 2010, p. 134).

In-Text Citations for Sources with No Page Number

MLA

If the source does not have page numbers, MLA documentation does not require them. However, your instructor may still ask you to provide a paragraph number to help locate the material you have quoted in your paper. Other sources may provide paragraph numbers for readers; in this case you should also provide them in your citation. Abbreviate paragraph as "par." A comma is needed to separate the author's last name and the paragraph number.

> The author declares, "Television programming is not what we are given—spoon fed. Viewers get what they demand, and the more we watch, the more we get" (Cross, par. 17).

> Cross supports her argument with an interview with an average viewer who says that he "has not been tricked. I watch what I want. No one forces me" (par. 35).

APA

When page numbers are not available, use the paragraph number. Abbreviate paragraph as "para." A comma is needed to separate the author's last name and the paragraph number.

> The author declares, "Television programming is not what we are given—spoon fed. Viewers get what they demand, and the more we watch, the more we get" (Cross, 2014, para. 17).

> Cross supports her argument with an interview with an average viewer who says that he "has not been tricked. I watch what I want. No one forces me" (2014, para. 35).

Citations on the Works Cited or References Page

At the end of your paper, you will need to include citations that give your readers information about each source. The purpose of this information is to show your reader where the information you included in your paper was originally found and to allow them to look up your sources if necessary. Both MLA and APA format citations using a hanging indent. The first line of the citation begins at the margin. For citations that use more than one line of text, indent all subsequent lines a half-inch (.5") or by pressing the Tab button once.

Books

BASIC PATTERN FOR BOOKS

Last Name, First Name. *Book Title.* **Publisher, Year of Publication.**

Titles and degrees (Ph.D. and Dr.) should not be included.

Italicize book titles. Capitalize all words in the title except articles, conjunctions, and prepositions.

The publisher can be found on the title page or the copyright page.

If there have been several editions, there will be several copyright or publication dates. Use the most recent year given.

BOOK WITH ONE AUTHOR

Didion, Joan. *Blue Nights.* Knopf, 2011.

BOOK WITH TWO AUTHORS

When a book has two authors, you will need to give the names of both authors. For the first author, give the last name, and then his or her first name. For the other author, his or her name can be listed normally: first, then last. Separate the authors with a comma and an "and."

> Last Name of First Author, First Name, and First & Last Name of Second Author. *Book Title.* Publisher, Year of Publication.

A comma and an "and" separate the authors.

> Maddock, Richard, and Richard Fulton. *Marketing to the Mind: Right Brain Strategies for Advertising and Marketing.* Quorum Books, 1996.

BOOK WITH THREE OR MORE AUTHORS

When a book has three or more authors, you will only need to give the name of the first author listed by the source. Replace the names of the other authors with "et al."

Use the name of the first author given.

> Last Name, First Name, et al. *Book Title.* Publisher, Year of Publication.

> Brooks, Brian, et al. *News Reporting and Writing.* 10th ed., Bedford, 2010.

CHAPTER IN AN EDITED BOOK

List the name of the author of the essay or chapter first. Next, give the title of the chapter in quotation marks, and then the title of the book in italics. Give the editor's name after the title of the book, preceded by the words "edited by." Next, list the publication information. Remember to list the full range of page numbers for the essay or the chapter.

Last Name of Author, First Name. "Chapter Title." *Book Title*, edited by Editor's First and
    Last Name, Publisher, Year of Publication, Page Range of Chapter.

Wood, Fran. "Attacks on SUV Owners Are Driving Me Up the Wall." *Reading and Writing
    Short Arguments*, edited by William Vesterman, 5th ed., McGraw-Hill, 2005, pp.
    73–77.

E-BOOK

An e-book is a book you can read in an electronic format using software; it will not have a direct link to a website or a URL. For an e-book, start with the author and title. Then, give the type of e-book: Kindle ed., Nook ed., etc.

Last Name, First Name. *Book Title*. e-book ed., Publisher, Year of Publication.

Appleton, Dina, and Daniel Yankelevits. *Hollywood Dealmaking: Negotiating Talent
    Agreements for Film, TV and New Media*. Kindle ed., Allworth, 2010.

BASIC PATTERN FOR BOOKS

Last Name, First Initial. (Year of Publication). *Book title*. **Publisher.**

| Titles and degrees (Ph.D. and Dr.) should not be included. Give only the initials of the first and middle names. | If there have been several editions, there will be several copyright or edition dates. Use the most recent year given. | Italicize book titles. Capitalize only the first word, proper nouns, and the first word after a colon. | Include the name of the publisher as it appears on the copyright page. |

BOOK WITH ONE AUTHOR

Didion, J. (2011). *Blue nights*. Knopf.

BOOK WITH TWO TO TWENTY AUTHORS

When a book has two to twenty authors, you will need to give the names of all authors. Provide the names of the authors in the order they are shown in the source. For all authors, give the last name and then his or her initials, separated by a comma. Include an "&" before the last author.

Last Name of First Author, First Initial, & Last Name of Second Author, First Initial. (Year of Publication). *Book title*. Publisher.

EXAMPLE OF TWO AUTHORS

Commas separate each author. Add the "&" before the last author.

Maddock, R., & Fulton, R. (1996). *Marketing to the mind: Right brain strategies for advertising and marketing*. Quorum Books.

EXAMPLE OF THREE AUTHORS

Sider, R.J., Olson, P.N., & Unruh, H.R. (2002). *Churches that make a difference: Reaching your community with good news and good works*. Baker.

BOOK WITH TWENTY-ONE OR MORE AUTHORS

Use the names of the first nineteen authors, an ellipsis (…), and the final author's last name, and first initial. Finding a book with twenty-one authors or more is rare; however, you may find an article in a periodical that fits this description. For an example of a publication with twenty-one or more authors, please see page 275.

CHAPTER IN AN EDITED BOOK

List the name of the author of the essay or chapter first. Next, give the title of the essay or chapter, followed by "In" and the editor's name (first initial and last name). Mark the editor's name with the abbreviation "Ed." in parentheses. Then, give the title of the book in italics and the page numbers for the essay or the chapter. Next, list the publication information.

Last Name of Author, First Initial. (Year of Publication). Chapter title. In Editor's Name (Ed.), *Book title* (Page Range of Chapter). Publisher.

Wood, F. (2005). Attacks on SUV owners are driving me up the wall. In W. Vesterman (Ed.), *Reading and writing short arguments* (pp. 73–77). McGraw-Hill.

E-BOOK

For an e-book in APA style, start with the basic book citation and include the URL or DOI of the website where the book can be found.

Last Name, First Initial. (Copyright Year of Publication). *Book title*. Publisher. URL

Appleton, D., & Yankelevits, D. (2010). *Hollywood dealmaking: Negotiating talent agreements for film, tv and new media*. Allworth Press. http://www.amazon.com/Hollywood-Dealmaking-Negotiating-Agreements-ebook/dp/B003IN4AQ6/ref=tmm_kin_title_o?ie=UTF8&m=AG56TWVU5XWC2

EXAMPLE

MLA

Mackendrick, Alexander. *On Film-Making: An Introduction to the Craft of the Director*. Edited by Paul Cronin, Faber and Faber, 2004.

APA

Mackendrick, A. (2004). *On film-making: An introduction to the craft of the director*. (P. Cronin, Ed.). Faber and Faber.

Periodicals

BASIC PATTERN FOR PERIODICALS

Last Name, First Name. "Article Title." *Periodical Title*, vol. #, no. #, Date Published, Page Range.

If there is no author, start with the article title.	Give the full page range. Abbreviate page as "p." and pages as "pp."	Article titles should end in a period and be in quotation marks.	Italicize the title of the periodical. A comma is needed at the end of the periodical title.	Provide the volume and issue numbers as given by the source. Use the abbreviations "vol." and "no."	The date should be written with the day, month, and then the year. Some periodicals will give only the year, while others will provide the full date.

ARTICLE IN A JOURNAL OR MAGAZINE

Give the author's name first. If there is more than one author, follow the pattern for multiple authors shown earlier in this chapter. Provide the title of the article in quotation marks and the journal or magazine title in italics. Most journals have both a volume and issue number; however, you may find a source that does not have an issue number. If the issue number is not provided, skip to the date. Many journals and magazines will have a month (or season) in addition to the year. Give the full page range.

Last Name, First Name. "Article Title." *Journal Title*, vol. #, no. #, Date Published, Page Range.

Powell, Brett, et al. "Expenditures, Efficiency, and Effectiveness in U.S. Undergraduate Higher Education: A National Benchmark Model." *Journal of Higher Education*, vol. 83, no. 1, Jan./Feb. 2012, pp. 102–27.

ARTICLE IN A NEWSPAPER

After the author, article title, and newspaper title, give the date the article was published. Most newspapers are published daily, so the full date is needed. Page numbers in a newspaper often include letters and numbers. If the pages are also not sequential, or skip pages, give the first page followed by "+."

> Capitalize all words in article and periodical titles except articles, conjunctions, and prepositions.

Last Name, First Name. "Article Title." *Newspaper Title*, Date Published, Page Range.

For dates in MLA, give the day, month, and then the year: 4 Jan. 2011. Remember to abbreviate all months, except for May, June, and July.

Healy, Alison. "Cyber-bully Victims Can Be as Young as Six, Says Lecturer." *The Irish Times*, 20 Apr. 2012, p. 3+.

ARTICLE FROM A PERIODICAL IN A DATABASE

Start with the basic information for a journal or newspaper. After the page range, give the name of the database and either the DOI or URL for the source. Ask your instructor which he or she would prefer. Also ask your instructor if you should provide the date you accessed or found the article, as this is optional.

DOIs are not provided by all publishers. DOI is an abbreviation for digital object identifier.

Last Name, First Name. "Article Title." *Periodical Title*, vol. #, no. #, Date Published, Page Range. *Name of Database*, DOI or URL. Accessed Date.

While MLA doesn't require the date you accessed the source, your instructor may. If so, include it after the URL.

Westerman, David, and Ron Tamborini. "Scriptedness and Televised Sports: Violent Consumption and Viewer Enjoyment." *Journal of Language and Social Psychology*, vol. 29, no. 3, Sept. 2010, pp. 321–37. *EBSCOhost*, doi:10.1177/0261927X10368835. Accessed 15 June 2012.

See the example for citing a website for tips on how to properly format a URL.

Ngo-Ye, Thomas, et al. "Predicting the Helpfulness of Online Reviews Using a Scripts-Enriched Text Regression Model." *Expert Systems with Applications*, vol. 71, Apr. 2017, pp. 98–110. *EBSCOhost*, web.b.ebscohost.com.falcon.lib.edu/ehost/detail?vid=6&sid=b7f4od. Accessed 15 June 2017.

ARTICLE FROM AN ONLINE PERIODICAL

Start with the basic information for a journal or newspaper. Online periodicals usually don't provide page numbers for their articles, so if page numbers are not given, skip to the URL.

EXAMPLE FOR AN ONLINE JOURNAL

Last Name, First Name. "Article Title." *Periodical Title*, vol. #, no. #, Date Published, URL.

Karp, Regina. "Nuclear Disarmament: Should America Lead?" *Political Science Quarterly*, vol. 127, no. 1, Spring 2012, www.psqonline.org/volume.cfm?IDIssue=519.

EXAMPLE FOR AN ONLINE NEWSPAPER

Last Name, First Name. "Article Title." *Newspaper Title*, Date Published, URL.

Fulford, Robert. "Staying Thin Is Harder than Rocket Science." *National Post*, 12 May 2012, news.nationalpost.com/full-comment/robert-fulford-staying-thin-is-harder-than-rocket-science.

BASIC PATTERN FOR PERIODICALS

Last Name, First Initial. (Date Published). Article title. *Periodical Title*, *Volume* (Issue), Page Range.

If there is no author, start with the article title. Place the article title before the date.	The date should be written with the year first, then the month and day. Some periodicals will give only the year, while others will provide the full date.	Article titles should end in a period. Capitalize only the first word, proper nouns, and the first word after a colon.	Italicize the title of the periodical. Capitalize the first letter of each main word in this title because it is a proper name. Put a comma at the end of the periodical title.	Write the volume and issue numbers only. The volume number is italicized.

ARTICLE IN A JOURNAL OR MAGAZINE

Give the author's name first. If there is more than one author, follow the pattern for multiple authors described earlier. Give the date. Many journals and magazines will have a month (or season) in addition to the year. Provide the title of the article without quotation marks, and italicize the journal or magazine title. Most journals have both a volume and issue number; however, you may find a source that does not have an issue number. If the issue number is not provided, skip to the page range.

Last Name, First Initial. (Date Published). Article title. *Journal Title*, *Volume*(Issue), Page Range.

Spell out the full name of the month.

Powell, B., Gilleland, D. S., & Pearson, C. (2012, January/February). Expenditures, efficiency, and effectiveness in U.S. undergraduate higher education: A national benchmark model. *Journal of Higher Education*, *83*(1), 102–127.

ARTICLE WITH TWENTY-ONE OR MORE AUTHORS

Leung, W., Shaffer, C. D., Reed, L.K., Smith, S.T., Barshop, W., Dirkes, W., Dothager, M., Lee, P., Wong, J., Xiong, D., Yuan, H., Bedard, J. E. J., Machone, J. F., Patterson, S. D., Price, A. L., Turner, B. A., Robic, S., Luippold, E. K., McCartha, S. R., … Elgin, S. C. R. (2015, May 1). *Drosophila* muller F elements maintain a distinct set of genomic properties over 40 million years of evolution. *G3: Genes, Genomes, Genetics, 5*(5), 719–740.

ARTICLE IN A NEWSPAPER

After the author, give the date. Most newspapers are published daily, so the full date is needed. Then give the article title, newspaper title, and the page(s).

For dates in APA, give the year first, then the month and the day: 2011, January 4.

Last Name, First Initial. (Date Published). Article title. *Newspaper Title*, page(s).

Healy, A. (2012, April 20). Cyber-bully victims can be as young as six, says lecturer. *The Irish Times*, 3.

ARTICLE FROM A PERIODICAL IN A DATABASE

Start with the basic information for a journal or newspaper. APA does not require the name of the database, but your instructor may require that you add it to your citation. If your instructor requires the name of the database, add it after the page range. Your instructor may also require the date you found the source on the database. Include the DOI at the end of the citation. If the article does not have a DOI, end the citation with the page range.

Last Name, First Initial. (Date Published). Article title. *Journal Title, Volume*(Issue), Page Range. DOI

Westerman, D., & Tamborini, R. (2010, September). Scriptedness and televised sports: Violent consumption and viewer enjoyment. *Journal of Language and Social Psychology, 29*(3), 321–337. http://doi.org/10.1177/0261927X10368835

ARTICLE FROM AN ONLINE PERIODICAL

Start with the basic information for a journal or newspaper. Online periodicals usually don't provide page numbers for their articles, so if page numbers are not given, skip to the URL or DOI. If the article does not have a URL or DOI, end the citation with the page range.

EXAMPLE FOR AN ONLINE JOURNAL

Last Name, First Initial. (Date Published). Article title. *Journal Title, Volume*(Issue), Page Range. URL or DOI

Karp, R. (2012, Spring). Nuclear disarmament: Should America lead? *Political Science Quarterly*, *127*(1). http://www.psqonline.org/article.cfm?IDArticle=18878

EXAMPLE FOR AN ONLINE NEWSPAPER

Last Name, First Initial. (Date Published). Article title. *Newspaper Title*, Page Range. URL or DOI

Fulford, R. (2012, May 12). Staying thin is harder than rocket science. *National Post*. http://fullcomment.nationalpost.com/2012/05/12/robert-fulford-staying-thin-is-harder-than-rocket-science

EXAMPLE

The citation information needed for an article in a database can be found on the detailed record page.

MLA

Ngo-Ye, Thomas L., Atish P. Sinha, and Arun Sen. "Predicting the helpfulness of online reviews using a scripts-enriched text regression model." *Expert Systems with Applications*, vol. 71, Apr. 2017, pp. 98–110. *Academic Search Complete*, doi:10.1016/j.eswa.2016.11.029. Accessed 23 Sept. 2019.

APA

Ngo-Ye, T. L., Sinha, A. P., & Sen, A. (2017, April). Predicting the helpfulness of online reviews using a scripts-enriched text regression model. *Expert Systems with Applications*, 71, 98–110. https://doi:10.1016/j.eswa.2016.11.029

Websites

MLA

BASIC PATTERN FOR WEBSITES

Last Name, First Name. "Webpage Title." *Website Title*, **Publisher, Publication Date, URL. Accessed Date.**

If no author is given, start the citation with the webpage title.	Give the full URL for the webpage. Do not include http:// at the beginning of the URL.	The access date is optional but encouraged. Ask your instructor if you should include it. The access date is the date when you found the website.	The title of the webpage or article should be in quotation marks.	Put the title of the whole website in italics. Follow the title with a comma.	Give the company or organization that is associated or responsible for the website. If this is the same as the website title, it can be left out.	Give the most recent date listed. This may also be shown as the date when the site was last updated or as the copyright date. If there is no date, skip this part of the citation.

BASIC WEBSITE

"Values in Action." *McDonald's*, 2017, www.mcdonalds.com/us/en-us/about-us/values-in-action.html. Accessed 3 Feb. 2017.

> Word documents automatically make URLs into hyperlinks. You will need to remove this formatting unless your instructor specifically requests it.

BASIC PATTERN FOR WEBSITES

Last Name, First Initial. (Date). Webpage title. Website. URL

| If there is not an individual author, give the company or organization that is associated or responsible for the website. If this cannot be found, start the citation with the webpage title. | Give the most recent date listed. This may also be listed as when the site was last updated. If there is no date, put "n.d." instead. | The title of the webpage or article titles should end in a period. Capitalize only the first word, proper nouns, and the first word after a colon. | Provide the website name, unless the website name is used as the author. Capitalize all major words. Do not italicize the website name. |

BASIC WEBSITE

McDonald's. (2017). Values in action. http://www.mcdonalds.com/us/en-us/about-us/values-in-action.html

EXAMPLE

MLA

"Mission." *NBA Green*, NBA Cares, 2012, www.green.nba.com/mission/. Accessed 9 Jan. 2018.

APA

NBA Cares. (2012). Mission. http://www.green.nba.com/mission/

Media

Many of the essay prompts in this book require you to use a form of media as a source or reference. In this section, you will find the format for citing advertisements, television shows, songs, YouTube postings, and social media.

ADVERTISEMENTS

MLA

BASIC PATTERN FOR ADVERTISEMENTS

Name of Product or Company advertisement. Publication Information.

Begin with the name of the company or product in the advertisement. Include the word "advertisement." This will show your reader what kind of source it is.

Include the necessary publication information depending on where the advertisement was found, such as on a website, in a television commercial, or in print.

PRINT ADVERTISEMENTS

For printed advertisements, include the source title, the date it was published, and the page number.

Name of Company or Product advertisement. *Magazine* or *Newspaper Title*, Date, Page.

Lufthansa advertisement. *People*, Nov. 2006, p. 14.

ADVERTISEMENT OR COMMERCIAL ON TELEVISION

Give the name of the company or product and the word "advertisement." Then provide the television station the advertisement aired on in italics, the call letters, and the city. Next, give the date the ad or commercial was broadcast on television.

Name of Product or Company advertisement. *Television Station*, Call Letters, City, Date Shown.

Staples advertisement. *CBS*, **WBZ**, New York, 3 Dec. 2009.

ADVERTISEMENT OR COMMERCIAL ON THE WEB

If your ad comes from the Internet, you will add the website information. Provide the website title and the publisher, if different from the website title. You must provide the date it was published, but the date you accessed or found the advertisement is optional. If your ad is hard to find on the Internet, you may need to include the URL. Ask your instructor if he or she requires the URL or date accessed for sources found on the Internet.

Name of Product or Company advertisement. *Website Title*. Publisher, Date Published, URL. Accessed Date.

Milwaukee River Keepers advertisement. *AdsoftheWorld*. 11 Jan. 2010, adsoftheworld.com/media/ambient/milwaukee_river_keepers_a_fun_river. Accessed 30 May 2017.

APA

BASIC PATTERN FOR ADVERTISEMENTS

Name of Product by Company [Advertisement]. (Date). Publication Information.

| Give the name of the product and the company name. Include the word "Advertisement" in brackets. This will show your reader what kind of source it is. | Provide the publication date of the source. | Include the necessary publication information depending on where the advertisement was found, such as on a website, in a television commercial, or in print. |

PRINT ADVERTISEMENT

Begin with the product being advertised, the word "by," and the name of the company that the advertisement is for, followed by "Advertisement" in brackets. Then include the publication date of the magazine or newspaper in which you found the advertisement, followed by the magazine or newspaper title, volume (if available), and the page number(s).

Name of Product by Company [Advertisement]. (Date). *Magazine* or *Newspaper Title*, Page Number.

Airfare by Lufthansa [Advertisement]. (2006, November). *People*, 14.

ADVERTISEMENT OR COMMERCIAL ON TELEVISION

Give the name of the product and company. Then give the word "Advertisement" in brackets, followed by the date. Provide the television station in italics.

Name of Product by Company [Advertisement]. (Date). Advertisement. *Television Station*.

Back to school by Staples [Advertisement]. (2009, December 3). Advertisement. *CBS*.

ADVERTISEMENT OR COMMERCIAL ON THE WEB

If your ad comes from the Internet, you will add the website information. Provide the website title, as well as the full URL for the webpage.

Name of Product by Company [Advertisement]. (Date). *Website Title*. URL

Dos Equis beer [Advertisement]. (2012). *Lunch.com*. www.lunch.com/Reviews/online_video/ The_Most_Interesting_Man_in_the_World-Photos-1394828

EXAMPLE

MLA

Dos Equis advertisement. *Lunch*, 2012, lunch.com/Reviews/online_video/The_Most_Interesting_Man_in_the_World-Photos-1394828. Accessed 15 Feb. 2012.

APA

Cerveza by Dos Equis [Advertisement]. (2012). *Lunch*. http://www.lunch.com/Reviews/online_video/The_Most_Interesting_Man_in_the_World-Photos-1394828

TELEVISION EPISODES

The author's name should be preceded by "written by," and the director's name should come after the words "directed by."

MLA

"Episode Title." *Series Title*, written by Name, directed by Name, season #, episode #, Production Company, Release Date. *Network Name*, URL.

Provide the date the episode was released.

If the episode was watched online through a network like Netflix or Hulu, provide the name of the network in italics and the URL.

Provide the season and episode numbers, as well as the name of the production company.

Examples of Television Episodes

"Disneyland." *Modern Family*, written by Cindy Chupack, directed by Jason Winer, season 3, episode 22, Levitan/Lloyd, 20th Century Fox Television, 9 May 2012.

"Dr. Bogden Krilov." *The Blacklist*, written by Jon Bokenkamp, directed by Donald Thorin, season 4, episode 19, Davis Entertainment, 4 May 2017. *NBC*, www.nbc.com/the-blacklist/video/dr-bogdan-krilov/3509709.

"Chapter 1." *House of Cards*, written by Beau Willimon, directed by David Fincher, season 1, episode 1, Media Rights Capital, 1 Feb. 2013. *Netflix*, www.netflix.com/watch/70248289?trackId=15387182&tctx=0%2C0%2C5a770cc7-84d2-4d73-9b67-1ec1ae1d6f60-37542693.

Give the last name of the writer and director, and then his or her first initials.

Provide the date the episode was released.

Give the name of the single episode you are using as a source, followed by the season and episode numbers.

Writer's Name (Writer), & Director's Name (Director). (Date). Episode title. (Season #, Episode#) [Television series episode]. In Producer's Name (Producer), *Series Title.* **Production Company. URL**

Provide the name of the production company. If the episode was consulted online, include the URL.

Give the last name of the producer, and then his or her first initial.

The series title is the name of the show.

Examples of Television Episodes

Chupack, C. (Writer), & Winer, J. (Director). (2012, May 9). Disneyland. (Season 3, Episode 22) [Television series episode]. In J. Morton (Producer), *Modern Family.* Levitan/ Lloyd, 20th Century Fox Television.

Bokenkamp, J. (Writer), & Thorin, D. (Director). (2017, May 4). Dr. Bogdan Krilov. (Season 4, Episode 19) [Television series episode]. In L. Benson (Producer), *The Blacklist.* Davis Entertainment. http://www.nbc.com/the-blacklist/video/dr-bogdan-krilov/3509709

Willimon, B. (Writer), & Fincher, D. (Director). (2013, February 1). Chapter 1. (Season 1, Episode 1) [Television series episode]. In D. Brunetti (Executive Producer), *House of Cards.* Media Rights Capital. http://www.netflix.com/watch/70248289?trackId =15387182&tctx=0%2C0%2C5a770cc7-84d2-4d73-9b67-1ec1ae1d6f60-37542693

FILMS OR MOVIES

MLA

Italicize the title of the movie. Give the director. If important to your research, also add the three top billed actors, followed by the name of the studio or distributor and the year of the film's release. If the film is found online, also give the necessary website information.

Example of a Movie from a DVD or Online

Movie Title. Directed by Name, performances by Names, Distributor, Year, *Website if found online,* URL if found online.

The Godfather. Directed by Francis Ford Coppola, performances by Marlon Brando, Al Pacino, and James Caan, Paramount Pictures, 1972.

Footloose. Directed by Herbert Ross, performances by Kevin Bacon, Lori Singer, and John Lithgow, Paramount, 1984, *Netflix*, www.netflix.com/watch/21059770?trackId247 52380&tctx=1%2C0%2C25e614a5fa738ee24a633e65db22cfed98180c%3A82003.

Give the director in the position of author, followed by the date the movie was released. Then give the title of the film. The word "Film" should follow in brackets, followed by the production company or studio name. If the film is found online, also give the URL.

Director's Last Name, First Initial (Director). (Release Date). *Title of film* [Film]. Production Company or Studio. URL if found online

Example of a Movie from a DVD or Online

Coppola, F. F. (Director). (1972). *The Godfather* [Film]. Paramount Pictures.

Sanders, C., & DeBlois, D. (Directors). (2010). *How to train your dragon* [Film]. DreamWorks Animation. https://netflix.com/movie/How-to-Train-Your-Dragon/70109893

SONGS

MLA

Example of a Song from a CD
Give the artist first, then the song and album title. Provide the publisher or label and the year the CD was released.

Artist. "Song Title." *Album Title*, Publisher, Year Released.

Drake. "Over My Dead Body." *Take Care*, Cash Money. 2011.

Example of a Song Found Online
Give the artist first, then the song and album title. Provide the publisher or label and the year the song was released. Include the name of the website and URL where you found the song. The accessed date is optional, but may be requested by your instructor.

Artist. "Song Title." *Album Title*, Publisher, Year Released. *Website*, URL. Accessed Date.

Adele. "Rumour Has It." *21*, XL, 2011. *Spotify*, open.spotify.com/track/50yHVBbU6M4iIf qBI1bxWx. Accessed 2 Mar. 2011.

Example of a Song from a CD
Give the artist first, and then release date. Next, give the song title followed by the word "song" in brackets. Include "On" and the album title next, followed by the recording label.

Artist's Name. (Release Date). Title of the song [Song]. On *Title of the album*. Recording Label.

Drake. (2011). Over my dead body [Song]. On *Take care*. Cash Money.

Example of a Song Found Online
Start with the basic song recording and add the URL.

Artist's Name. (Release Date). Title of the song [Song]. On *Title of the album*. Recording Label. URL

Adele. (2011). Rumour has it [Song]. On *21*. XL. http://www.pandora.com/adele/rumour-has-it-radio-single/rumour-has-it

YOUTUBE POSTINGS

If the author and uploader are the same, include this information once, after the title of the video. The source, YouTube, should be in italics. Then provide the date it was posted. The direct URL and accessed date are optional but highly recommended. Ask your instructor to see if he or she requires them.

"Name of Video." *YouTube*, uploaded by Name, Date Uploaded, URL. Accessed Date.

"Energy Conservation." *YouTube*, uploaded by National Geographic, 6 Apr. 2009, www.youtube.com/watch?v=KlGoxk93J-E. Accessed 9 July 2017.

If the author and uploader of the video are different, include both names. Place the author's name before the title.

Pepsi. "Banned Kendall Jenner Pepsi Commercial." *YouTube*, uploaded by Dagbladet, 4 Apr. 2017, www.youtube.com/watch?v=73P9STckPLw. Accessed 19 May 2017.

APA

Give the author's username just as it is written on YouTube. Then give the date the video was posted and name of the video. Provide the words "YouTube." Lastly, give the URL.

Author/Uploader. (Date Uploaded). Name of video [Video]. YouTube. URL

National Geographic. (2010, September 29). Energy conservation [Video]. YouTube. http://www.youtube.com/watch?v=KlG0xk93J-E

TWEETS

MLA

Begin with the author's username instead of his or her real name. The tweet should be enclosed in quotation marks and end in a period. After the website name, Twitter, provide the date and time of the post, followed by the URL.

Username. "Tweet." *Twitter*, Date, Time, URL.

@stephenfry. "Without breath there is no Life. Brilliant charity, helping sick children, changing lives. Do support them http://fry.am/ITU3hD." *Twitter*, 9 May 2012, 5:34 a.m., twitter.com/#!/stephenfry/status/200202021272420352.

APA

Give the author's name followed by the author's username just as it is written on Twitter in brackets. Give the date of the post. Provide the full tweet up to the first 20 words in italics and the words "Tweet" in brackets. The word "Twitter" should precede the URL.

Author's Last Name, First Initial [@Username]. (Date). *Post* [Tweet]. Twitter. URL

Fry, S. [@stephenfry]. (2012, May 9). *Without breath there is no Life. Brilliant charity, helping sick children, changing lives. Do support them http://fry.am/ITU3hD* [Tweet]. Twitter. https://twitter.com/#!/stephenfry/status/200202021272420352

EXAMPLE

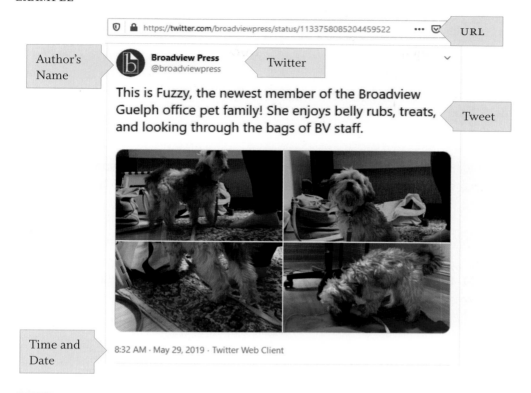

MLA

@broadviewpress. "This is Fuzzy, the newest member of the Broadview Guelph office pet
   family! She enjoys belly rubs, treats, and looking through bags of BV staff." *Twitter*,
   29 May 2019, 8:32 a.m., twitter.com/broadviewpress/status/1133758085204459522.

APA

Broadview Press. [@broadviewpress]. (2019, May 29). *This is Fuzzy, the newest member of
   the Broadview Guelph office pet family! She enjoys belly rubs, treats, and looking through
   bags of BV staff* [Image attached] [Tweet]. Twitter. http://twitter.com/broadviewpress/
   status/1133758085204459522

FACEBOOK POSTINGS AND UPDATES

MLA

Give the author's username as it appears on Facebook. Place the post in quotation
marks and italicize the website title, Facebook. Next, provide the date of the post. The

accessed date, or date you viewed the post, is optional, but strongly encouraged for this type of source.

Author Name. "Posting Title." *Facebook*. Date Posted, URL. Accessed Date.

Mark Zuckerberg. "Listed a Company on NASDAQ." *Facebook*. 18 May 2012, facebook.com/zuck. Accessed 23 Jan. 2013.

APA

Give the author's name followed by the date of the post. The title of the post in italics is followed by the words "Status update" in brackets. Lastly, the word "Facebook" followed by the URL.

Author's Last Name, First Initial. (Date). Post title [Status update]. Facebook. URL

Zuckerberg, M. (2012, May 18). *Listed a company on NASDAQ* [Status update]. Facebook. http://www.facebook.com/zuck

INTERVIEWS

MLA

Give the name of the person being interviewed in the author's position. If the interview is formal, provide the title of the interview. If it is untitled, use the general description "Interview."

Interviewed Person. Interview Title. Date.

Howard, Sarah. Interview. 8 Nov. 2008.

APA

APA instructions state that a personal interview should not be included on the References page since this type of source is not recoverable, meaning the reader cannot go back to the source of the interview and review it. If your instructor allows you to include a personal interview in your paper, it will only be cited in-text.

(Interviewed Person, personal communication, Date of Interview).

(S. Howard, personal communication, November 8, 2008).

Example Student Paper in MLA

In MLA, title pages are not always required, but if you need one, use the example to the left. Center the information on the title page. Include the following information:

Protecting the Internet

Anthony Jauregui
Dr. Coles
English 101
4 Nov. 2016

- Your title (approximately 1/3 down the page)
- Your name
- Your instructor's name
- The title of the class
- The essay's due date
- If no title page is required, include this information in the top, left-hand corner of your first page of text.

Use a 1-inch margin.

Double space your essay.

In the header, give your last name and the page number.

In today's world, piracy is a major problem. Piracy is the use of another's invention or idea, especially when it violates a copyright. The Stop Online Piracy Act (SOPA) was almost passed in an attempt to stop online piracy. This bill sought to destroy online piracy overseas as well as enforce copyrights; however, if SOPA or a similar bill is passed, it will harm the free flow of ideas through the Internet and would stop society from using free speech as well as the use/viewing of diverse websites on the Internet. Even though the government has a duty to protect our society and piracy costs the media industries millions of dollars in lost revenue each year, SOPA should not be passed because it interferes with the spread of knowledge through the Internet, shuts down major websites for infringement of copyright, and is an undeveloped bill that would cost the government millions of tax dollars.

Congress should be motivated to stop online piracy; however, SOPA is not the answer. SOPA will also censor our freedom of speech on the Internet. For example, websites that contain copyrighted content would be shut down or sued due to copyright infringement. Websites help spread knowledge and free-thinking as society progresses, and if this bill were passed, that would all be lost. On January 18, 2012, there was an Internet blackout to give the world, especially Congress, a taste of what the Internet would be like if it were censored. Michael Crowley argues in his article "Battlefield SOPA" that the Internet gives us the gift of freedom no longer present in other forms of media. The main objective of the online protests was to show that "none of us should take for granted the freedom and openness that have made the

Use ICE to introduce your quotes. See Chapter 15 for more information.

Keep quotes shorter than four lines in your essay. Long quotes are not usually appropriate in a short paper.

[m]ade it grow throughout the years. Crowley also [ha]ve unintended consequences. They would ensnare [in] expensive legal battles" (12). Instead of creating [... fosterin]g creative thought and information sharing. The [... rev]amped in order to be more specific and efficient. [... pi]racy. The fact of that matter is that piracy can never be completely stopped because there will always be someone out there that will pirate. This type of bill will stop some Internet criminals, but there will always be someone who finds a way around security measures. In the article "Don't Soft-Soap SOPA," Steve Forbes argues that previous anti-piracy acts haven't helped. He says there was another attempt at legislation in the "1998 act that makes copyright infringement illegal" (Forbes 15). There have been numerous attempts to protect original works of authorship, such as the Copyright Act of 1976 and the aforementioned act in 1998. Piracy is a major problem and should be stopped, but these bills are too extreme and could result in millions of people facing fines or prison time for downloading something illegally if it is fully enforced. More laws are not the answer. If the government's goal is to protect us, then they need to find an alternative method to reduce piracy.

Our society grows every day and every moment, and our innovations are fueled by the Internet. If SOPA were passed, this innovation and free flow of thought would be stopped because the Internet would be censored. According to David Carr in the works of a big machine on which we have all come to rely" (par. 4). Carr argues that if SOPA is passed, it could throw off the flow of innovation that flows through the Internet. Our society conducts business and learns through the Internet, and a bill with this amount of power could end this prosperity and growth. The disadvantages to passing a bill like SOPA outweigh the benefits. Laurence H. Tribe, a well-respected First-Amendment lawyer argues, "SOPA would 'undermine the openness and free exchange of information at the heart of the Internet. And it would violate the First Amendment" (qtd. in Carr, par. 15). The First Amendment reflects on freedom; freedom of religion, and freedom of speech. SOPA is violating the First Amendment by censoring the Internet, therefore making it unconstitutional. In her book Internet Censorship: Protecting Citizens or Trampling Freedom?, Christine Zuchora-Walske presents the dangers associated with both too much and too little control over the Internet. She, however, believes that SOPA is a little too close to censorship, which she defines as "suppressing (forbidding, s

(Zuchora-Walske 46). Despite these issues, SOP

The reason there is so much political sup

serving in Congress weren't raised with the Intern

those who rely on the Internet and those who do

booming for the past decade and a half, and most

a part of this cultural Internet boom. Carr states, '

> Use a paragraph number for sources that offer paragraph numbers rather than page numbers.

Works Cited

"Accessories after the Fact." *Economist*, vol. 401, no. 8761, Nov. 2011, p. 21. *EBSCOhost*,
  falcon.lib.csub.edu:2048/login?url=http://search.ebscohost.com/login.aspx?direct=tru
  e&db=buh&AN=67469716&login.asp&site=ehost-live. Accessed 30 Sept. 2016.

Carr, David. "The Danger of an Attack on Piracy Online." *New York Times*, vol. 161, no.
  55638, 2 Jan. 2012, p. B1. *Global Newsstream*, search.proquest.com/docview/913244294?
  accountid=10345. Accessed 15 Oct. 2016.

Crowley, Michael. "Battlefield SOPA." *Time*, vol. 179, no. 4, Jan. 2012, p. 12. *EBSCOhost*,
  falcon.lib.csub.edu:2048/login?url=http://search.ebscohost.com/login.aspx?direct=tru
  e&db=a9h&AN=70569723&login.asp&site=ehost-live. Accessed 1 Oct. 2016.

Forbes, Steve. "Don't Soft-Soap SOPA." *Forbes*, vol. 189, no. 2, Feb. 2012, pp. 15–16.
  EBSCOhost,falcon.lib.csub.edu:2048/login?url=http://search.ebscohost.com/login.asp
  x?direct=true&db=buh&AN=70744506&login.asp&site=ehost-live. Accessed 12 Oct.
  2016.

Goldberg, Jonah, and Nick Schulz. "Gated or X-Rated?" *National Review*, vol. 62, no. 13, July
  2010, pp. 35–36.

Matter, Ulrich, and Alois Stutzer. "Does Public Attention Reduce the Influence of
  Moneyed Interests? Policy Positions on Sopa/Pipa Before and After the Internet
  Blackout." *Economic Inquiry*, vol. 57, no. 4, Oct. 2019, pp. 1879–1895. *EBSCOhost*.
  doi:10.1111/ecin.12812.

Zuchora-Walske, Christine. *Internet Censorship: Protecting Citizens or Trampling
  Freedom?* Twenty-First Century Books, 2010.

> Start your Works Cited page on a new page.

> Use a hanging indent. Any line after the first line of the citation is indented.

> Double space the sources. There should be no large gaps.

Example Student Paper in APA

APA has specific requirements for a title page. Start your page numbers on the title page in the top right. All of the information on your title page should be double spaced. Center the following information three to four lines from the top of the page:

1

Protecting the Internet

Anthony W. Jauregui

Department of English, Knox College

ENG 101: Freshman Composition

Dr. George Coles

November 4, 2016

- Your title typed in bold font
- Your first name, middle initial, and last name
- The name of the department and the school's name separated by a comma
- The course number followed by a colon and the title of the course
- The first and last name of the instructor
- The due date of the assignment
- Some instructors may also require an abstract between the title page and the first page of the essay text.

Use 1-inch margins

Your title should be in the header on the left on every page.

Page numbers go in the header on the right.

Double space your essay.

Use ICE to introduce your quotes. See Chapter 15 for more information.

Protecting the Internet

In today's world, piracy is a major problem. Piracy is the use of another's invention or idea, especially when it violates a copyright. The Stop Online Piracy Act (SOPA) was almost passed in an attempt to stop online piracy. This bill sought to destroy online piracy overseas as well as enforce copyrights; however, if SOPA or a similar bill is passed, it will harm the free flow of ideas through the Internet and would stop society from using free speech as well as the use/viewing of diverse websites on the Internet. Even though the government has a duty to protect our society and piracy costs the media industries millions of dollars in lost revenue each year, SOPA should not be passed because it interferes with the spread of knowledge through the Internet, shuts down major websites for infringement of copyright, and is an undeveloped bill that would cost the government millions of tax dollars.

Congress should be motivated to stop o[...]
answer. SOPA will also censor our freedom o[...]
websites that contain copyrighted content w[...]
right infringement. Websites help spread k[...]
progresses, and if this bill were passed, that [...]
there was an Internet blackout to give the wo[...]
the Internet would be like if it were censored [...]
"Battlefield SOPA" that the Internet gives us t[...]

Internet for granted because we have made it beneficial to our lives and have made it grow throughout the years. Crowley also says, "The bills are too broad and would have unintended consequences. They would ensnare small sites that have done nothing wrong in expensive legal battles" (2012, p. 12). Instead of creating a culture of fear, we should be encouraging creative thought and information sharing. The bill is underdeveloped and need to be revamped in order to be more specific and efficient.

The role of SOPA is to stop online piracy. The fact of that matter is that piracy can never be completely stopped because there will always be someone out there that will pirate. This type of bill will stop some Internet criminals, but there will always be someone who finds a way around security measures. In the article "Don't Soft-Soap SOPA," Steve Forbes argues that previous anti-piracy acts haven't helped. He says there was another attempt at legislation in the "1998 act that makes copyright infringement illegal" (Forbes, 2012, p. 15). There have been numerous attempts to protect original works of authorship, such as the Copyright Act of 1976 and the aforementioned act in 1998. Piracy is a major problem and should be stopped, but these bills are too extreme and could result in millions of people facing fines or prison time for downloading something illegally if it is fully enforced. More laws are not the answer. If the government's goal is to protect us, then they need to find an alternative method to reduce piracy.

Our society grows every day and every moment, and our innovations are fueled by the internet. If SOPA were passed, this innovation and free flow of thought would be stopped social networking to change without hurting several industries. Carr claims that "the open consumer Web has been a motor of American innovation and the attempt to curtail some of its excesses could throw sand in the works of a big machine on which we have all come to rely" (2012, para. 4). Carr argues that if SOPA is passed, it could throw off the flow of innovation that flows through the Internet. Our society conducts business and learns through the Internet, and a bill with this amount of power could end this prosperity and growth. The disadvantages to passing a bill like SOPA outweigh the benefits. Laurence H. Tribe, a well-respected First-Amendment lawyer argues, "SOPA would 'undermine the openness and free exchange of information at the heart of the Internet. And it would violate the First Amendment'" (as cited in Carr, 2012, para. 15). The First Amendment reflects on freedom; freedom of religion, and freedom of speech. SOPA is violating the First Amendment by censoring the Internet, therefore making it unconstitutional. In her book *Internet Censorship: Protecting Citizens or Trampling Freedom?*, Christine Zuchora-Walske presents the dangers associated with both too much and too little control over the Internet. She, however, believes that SOPA is a little too close to censorship, which she defines as "suppressing (forbidding, silencing, or punishing) communications" (Zuchora-Walske, 2010, p. 46). Despite these issues, SOPA still has political support.

The reason there is so much political support for SOPA is because those currently serving in Congress weren't raised with the Internet, causing a major

> Keep quotes shorter than 40 words. Long quotes are not usually appropriate in a short paper.

> Use a paragraph number for sources without page numbers.

...ates, "It's people who grew up on the Web versus ...n, they simply don't see the way that the Web has ...asses. The Internet isn't real to them yet" (Carr, ...has not lived with the Internet their whole lives ...not just put a damper on our freedom of speech,

...it is expensive. Our government is millions of ...dollars in debt, and if SOPA were passed, it would only increase our monetary problems: SOPA is a multi-million-dollar legislation. According to Michael Crowley, supporters "exaggerate their economic losses, and imposing new regulations on the Internet is sure to create new costs. That's why so many of the country's top dotcom companies, from Google to Facebook to Twitter, are protesting this move" (2012, p. 12). Although Crowley's comments are biased, they are true. The government and media companies are exaggerating their losses; however, "piracy threatened 19 million American jobs" (Carr, 2012, para. 7). Because piracy has threatened so many jobs, the government feels it is their obligation to stop it by passing this legislation. However, there is no evidence to support the argument that SOPA will solve our piracy problems or save jobs. The strict rules and punishments it contains are not the kind of protection that we need.

SOPA is a bill meant to stop online piracy, and it intends to do it in an inefficient

Start your References page on a new page.

References

Accessories after the fact. (2011, November). *The Economist.* https://www.economist.com/
    leaders/2011/11/26/accessories-after-the-fact

Carr, D. (2012, January 1). The danger of an attack on piracy online. *New York Times.* http://
    www.nytimes.com/2012/01/02/business/media/the-danger-of-an-attack-on-piracy-
    online.html?pagewanted=all&_r=0

Crowley, M. (2012, January). Battlefield SOPA. *Time, 179*(4), 12.

Forbes, S. (2012, February). Don't soft-soap SOPA. *Forbes, 189*(2), 15–16.

Goldberg, J., & Schulz, N. (2010, July). Gated or x-rated? *National Review, 62*(13), 35–36.

Matter, U., & Stutzer, A. (2019). Does public attention reduce the influence of moneyed
    interests? Policy positions on SOPA/PIPA before and after the internet blackout.
    Economic Inquiry, 57(4), 1879–1895. https://doi.org/10.1111/ecin.12812

Zuchora-Walske, C. (2010). *Internet censorship: Protecting citizens or trampling freedom?*
    Twenty-First Century Books.

Double space the sources. There should be no large gaps.

Use a hanging indent. Any line after the first line of the citation is indented.

Assessing Your Knowledge

KEY POINTS	REMINDER	HOW WELL DID YOU UNDERSTAND THIS MATERIAL?	PAGE(S)
Use MLA or APA to cite books	This chapter provides sample citations for variations in the book citation format.	☐ I've Got It! ☐ Almost There ☐ Need More Practice	pp. 268–71
Use MLA or APA to cite periodicals	This chapter provides sample citations for a variety of periodicals: journals, magazines, and newspapers.	☐ I've Got It! ☐ Almost There ☐ Need More Practice	pp. 272–77
Use MLA or APA to cite websites	This chapter provides sample citations for websites.	☐ I've Got It! ☐ Almost There ☐ Need More Practice	pp. 277–79
Use MLA or APA to cite forms of media	This chapter provides sample citations for various forms of media: advertisements, television episodes, YouTube postings, tweets, Facebook posts, movies, and songs.	☐ I've Got It! ☐ Almost There ☐ Need More Practice	pp. 279–88
Recognize a paper written in MLA or APA	Papers documented in **MLA** and **APA** may initially look the same, but there are specific requirements for each style.	☐ I've Got It! ☐ Almost There ☐ Need More Practice	pp. 289–95

Deepening Your Understanding

If you would like to go beyond the material in this chapter, explore additional connections, and get more practice, check out these related topics:

- **Quotation Marks**: Quotation marks are an essential part of citing in your essay. Using quotation marks effectively will help you distinguish between your ideas and the ideas of others.

- **Editing the Essay**: Documenting your sources means paying attention to many details. Editing is the perfect time to check that you have used MLA or APA correctly.

- **Abbreviations and Numbers**: Both MLA and APA require the use of abbreviations and numbers; make sure you are using them properly. Formatting them incorrectly can be confusing for your readers.

- **Developing and Organizing a Paragraph**: Including sources is a nice way to help develop a paragraph. Readers will appreciate a paragraph that fully incorporates a source.

PART IV
Polishing Your Writing

AS YOU'VE LEARNED in previous chapters, editing is an important part of the writing process. Editing allows us to polish our work to make sure it is as good as possible. When we edit, we check for spelling, grammar, and mechanical errors in our paper. We do this to ensure that our paper makes sense and reads well to our audience.

When you polish your writing, here are some tips:

1. Read your paper through for one type of error at a time.

2. Review your graded writing from the past, to see what types of error you commonly make.

3. Take a break. Make sure you put some distance between yourself and your paper before you go back to edit.

4. Read your paper backwards sentence by sentence.

5. Read your paper aloud to yourself, or have someone read it aloud to you. Listen for errors that you hear, and mark them.

6. Enlist the help of a friend, family member, or fellow classmate. Sometimes, a fresh pair of eyes will help the editing process.

7. Use a ruler or piece of paper to guide yourself as you read, focusing on one line at a time.

8. Print out your paper. Often, it is hard to read for errors on a computer screen.

9. Make sure a dictionary and handbook are handy, in case you need to check spelling or look up grammar rules.

In Part IV, there are ten chapters covering some of the most common grammar problems. It is important to recognize that Part IV is not an exhaustive list of all grammar problems. You'll find the following chapters:

- Parts of Speech, Phrases, and Clauses
- Subject-Verb Agreement
- Pronoun-Antecedent Agreement
- Fragments
- Run-Ons
- Commas
- Semicolons, Colons, Dashes, and Parentheses
- Apostrophes
- Quotation Marks
- Easily Confused Words

Before You Read

Before you read the chapters in Part IV, answer the following questions:

1. Why is using your word processing program's grammar and spelling check not enough to edit your papers?

2. Make a list of the grammar and mechanics items that you personally feel you need the most help with. Why did you choose these items?

3. Search online for Weird Al Yankovic's "Word Crimes" music video. Which do you think is the best reason he gives for using proper grammar?

Parts of Speech, Phrases, and Clauses

17

"Language is not merely a set of unrelated sounds, clauses, rules, and meanings; it is a total coherent system of these integrating with each other, and with behavior, context, universe of discourse, and observer perspective."
—Kenneth L. Pike

FACT OR FICTION?
Dependent clauses have both a subject and a verb.

FACT.
The word dependent may make us think that a dependent clause would be missing something as crucial as a subject or a verb, but clauses, independent and dependent, contain both subjects and verbs.

Discovering Key Points

⊙ Identify the use of parts of speech, phrases, and clauses

⊙ Apply knowledge of and correct errors in parts of speech, phrases, and clauses within the context of a sentence

⊙ Apply knowledge of and write to demonstrate knowledge of parts of speech, phrases, and clauses

For more information about fragments, see Chapter 20. For run-ons, see Chapter 21.

Parts of speech are defined by the job that they do or the function that they have in the sentence. This chapter will cover the following parts of speech: **nouns**, **verbs**, **pronouns**, **adjectives**, **adverbs**, **prepositions**, and **conjunctions**. This chapter also includes **phrases** and **clauses**, which are groups of words that work together. Using them both can help you vary your sentence structure and communicate more effectively. Learning to identify the differences between the types of phrases and clauses is an important step toward avoiding costly grammatical errors like **run-ons** and **fragments**.

How many independent clauses are in this sign?

Nouns

Nouns identify people, places, things, ideas, and emotions. Nouns are sometimes referred to as naming words.

PEOPLE	PLACES	THINGS	IDEAS	EMOTIONS
Ana	ball park	bowl	gravity	anger
Mr. Smith	sauna	homecoming dance	patriotism	love
students	campground	cannon	dream	greed

Mitch got to work late because the buses were not running.

Pronouns

Pronouns take the place of nouns and help us vary our word choice so that we don't sound repetitive. There are several types of pronouns: personal, demonstrative, relative, and indefinite.

Personal Pronouns

Tip #1: Personal pronouns take the place of nouns.

Personal pronouns can be divided into first, second, and third person. Pronouns can also be either singular, representing one person or item, or plural, representing more than one person or several items.

To learn about pronouns and the nouns they replace, see Chapter 19.

	SINGULAR	PLURAL
First Person	I, me, my, mine, myself	we, us, our, ours, ourselves
Second Person	you, your, yours, yourself	you, your, yours, yourselves
Third Person	he, she, it, him, her, his, hers, its, himself, herself, itself	they, them, their, theirs, themselves

The students hoped they would find an empty table on the fourth floor of the library.

Demonstrative Pronouns

Tip #2: Demonstrative pronouns point to or draw attention to someone or something.

SINGULAR	PLURAL
this, that	these, those

These need to be moved toward the far wall.

Relative Pronouns

Tip #3: Relative pronouns start dependent clauses.

You will learn more about dependent clauses later in this chapter.

who
whoever
whom
whomever
whose

whosever
which
whichever
that

My sister, who owns a large car, will be giving us a ride.

Indefinite Pronouns

Tip #4: Indefinite pronouns are used when you are referring to someone or something that is very general or unknown.

SINGULAR	PLURAL	SINGULAR OR PLURAL
another, anybody, anyone, anything, each, either, everyone, everything, little, much, neither, nobody, none, no one, nothing, one, other, somebody, someone, something	both, few, many, others, several	all, any, more, most, some

No one knows who took the last cookie.

Verbs

You may have heard verbs called action words, but verbs can show more than actions. Sometimes they tell us how someone feels or what something looks like.

Action Verbs

Tip #1: Action verbs explain what a person or thing is doing.

We started the Color Run in white, and finished covered in paint.

Linking Verbs

Tip #2: Linking verbs explain a state of being, feeling, or appearance.

You look really nice today.

Helping Verbs

Tip #3: Helping verbs offer additional information to an action or linking verb.

HELPING VERB   LINKING OR ACTION VERB

I will be ready to go in about ten minutes; we must leave on time.

Adjectives

Adjectives describe or modify nouns and pronouns. Adjectives make our writing more vibrant and detailed by giving more specific information, such as color, amount, and even type.

ADJECTIVES   NOUNS   PRONOUNS
We didn't make a reservation, so we were seated in a dark corner at the last table.

Adverbs

Adverbs describe or modify adjectives, verbs, and other adverbs. While these words often end in –ly, they don't always. Generally, adverbs answer the questions *how*, *when*, *where*, *how often*, and *to what extent*.

ADVERBS   VERBS   ADJECTIVES
I always make it a point to hold the door for other people; it is very polite.

Prepositions

Prepositions show or define a relationship between ideas or other nouns in a sentence. Prepositions are always followed by a noun or pronoun. Below is a list of prepositions.

about	before	during	of	to
above	behind	except	off	toward
across	below	following	on	under
after	beneath	for	onto	underneath
against	beside	from	outside	until
along	between	in	over	up
among	beyond	inside	past	upon
around	but	into	plus	with
as	by	like	since	within
at	down	near	through	without

PREPOSITION   NOUN
We have extra storage under the stairs.

Conjunctions

Conjunctions connect and show a relationship between groups of words, ideas, and parts of sentences. There are two types of conjunctions: coordinating and subordinating.

Coordinating Conjunctions

Tip #1: Coordinating conjunctions are used to join parts of a sentences and independent clauses that are of equal importance.

To find out more about using commas with conjunctions, see Chapter 22.

These words are also sometimes called **FANBOYS**, because the initials of the coordinating conjunctions can be rearranged to spell **FANBOYS**. Below is a list of coordinating conjunctions.

for   and   nor   but   or   yet   so

It rained today, so it was cloudy, humid, and dreary.

Subordinating Conjunctions

Tip #2: Subordinating conjunctions are used to join two ideas; however, they also show that one idea is less important or dependent on the other.

Below is a list of subordinating conjunctions.

after	even though	that	where
although	if	though	whereas
as	once	unless	wherever
because	provided that	until	whether
before	since	when	while
even if	than	whenever	why

I am working on my lab report, even though I would much rather be playing rugby.

Clauses

A clause is a group of words that contains both a **subject** and a verb. A subject is the main noun in the sentence plus any modifiers or descriptive words. A verb provides the subject's action or state of being.

SUBJECTS	VERBS
The greatest party	provided
My grandmother	is
Lola	sang

There are two types of clauses: independent and dependent.

Independent Clauses

An **independent clause** contains a subject and verb and expresses a complete thought.

SUBJECT   VERB
My neighbor never locks his front door.
Greg has the largest video game collection.
The bus left on time.

    Because this kind of clause expresses a complete thought, it can express meaning on its own, independent of other clauses and phrases. An independent clause can stand alone as a sentence.

Dependent Clauses

A **dependent clause** also contains a subject and a verb, but it doesn't express a complete thought and can't be used alone. Dependent clauses begin with subordinating conjunctions or relative pronouns.

SUBORDINATING CONJUNCTION   RELATIVE PRONOUN   SUBJECT   VERB
since he lives in a safe area
that I have seen
even though the weather was bad

For a list of subordinating conjunctions and relative pronouns, see the appropriate section earlier in this chapter.

When dependent clauses are found on their own, they are called fragments. A dependent clause must be connected to an independent clause. When attached to an independent clause properly, a dependent clause can add additional information or further define a word.

SUBORDINATING CONJUNCTION	RELATIVE PRONOUN	SUBJECT	VERB

(INDEPENDENT CLAUSE)   [DEPENDENT CLAUSE]

[Since he lives in a safe area,] (he didn't think to lock his car doors.)

(Cameron hasn't done anything to earn an award) [that I have seen.]

(I had to walk to school,) [even though the weather was bad.]

Phrases

A **phrase** is a group of words that may define, describe, or clarify information. A phrase, however, is missing a subject and/or a verb and therefore cannot stand alone as an independent thought. In your writing, phrases must be connected to an independent clause. There are many types of phrases. However, they are all similar in that they are missing a subject or a verb; sometimes, they are missing both. Noun, verb, and prepositional phrases are three common types you may recognize.

VERB PHRASES	NOUN PHRASES	PREPOSITIONAL PHRASES
should build	her backpack	on the table
did eat	my favorite necklace	after the earthquake
would have seen	the dirty mop	against my better judgment
could be	Owen's laugh	throughout his career

Practice the Skills 1

Identify various parts of speech in the sentences below. Label the nouns (N), pronouns (PN), verbs (V), and prepositions (PP) in each sentence by writing the initials above the part of speech.

Example:
       PN   **V**   **PP**   **N**
       I usually get really sleepy during long movies.

1. We should go to the Harry Potter theme park in Florida.

2. Most people don't get the newspaper; they read the news online instead.

3. My grandmother lives 3000 miles away, so we Skype once a week.

4. Even though our school email should be secure, I still get spam.

5. Mark always changes the channel during commercials.

Practice the Skills 2

Correct the following sentences by circling the correct adjectives and adverbs. Then underline the part of speech that the adjective or adverb modifies.

Example: Her piano recital was a huge success; she played (beautiful / beautifully).

1. The movie was (incredible / incredibly) long and lasted almost three hours.

2. Some newspapers allow journalists to use (anonymous / anonymously) or unnamed sources.

3. The star of the reality television show I watch just went into rehab, so it won't be as interesting without him and his (wild / wildly) behavior.

4. Samantha decided to help her friend create a website (quick / quickly), since he was on a short deadline.

5. I (accident / accidentally) broke my new phone by dropping it into the pool.

Practice the Skills 3

Write your own sentence using conjunctions, phrases, and clauses correctly by following the instructions below.

Example: Write a sentence using a coordinating conjunction to connect parts of a sentence of equal importance.

> The *Titanic* had its own newspaper called *The Atlantic Daily Bulletin*; it provided passengers with news, advertisements, and gossip.

1. Write a sentence using a coordinating conjunction to connect two independent clauses.

2. Write a sentence using a subordinating conjunction.

3. Write a sentence using two independent clauses.

4. Write a sentence using one independent and one dependent clause.

5. Write a sentence using a prepositional phrase.

Assessing Your Knowledge

KEY POINTS	REMINDER	HOW WELL DID YOU UNDERSTAND THIS MATERIAL?	PAGE(S)
Identify the use of parts of speech, phrases, and clauses	There are seven parts of speech covered in this chapter along with phrases and clauses. ◦ **Nouns** identify people, places, things, ideas, and emotions. ◦ **Pronouns** take the place of a noun and help us vary our word choice. ◦ **Verbs** show us actions, how someone feels, or what something looks like. ◦ **Adjectives** describe or modify nouns and pronouns. ◦ **Adverbs** describe or modify adjectives, verbs, and other adverbs. ◦ **Prepositions** show or define a relationship between ideas or nouns in a sentence. ◦ **Conjunctions** connect and show a relationship between groups of words, ideas, and parts of sentences. ◦ **Clauses** are groups of words that contain both a subject and a verb. ◦ **Phrases** are groups of words that work together, but they are missing a subject and/or a verb.	☐ I've Got It! ☐ Almost There ☐ Need More Practice	pp. 300–06
Apply knowledge of and correct errors in parts of speech, phrases, and clauses within the context of a sentence	Parts of speech are defined by the job that they do or the function that they have in the sentence. Understanding how to use the parts of speech correctly in your writing can help you avoid confusing mistakes and be more effective at revising and editing.	☐ I've Got It! ☐ Almost There ☐ Need More Practice	pp. 300–04
Apply knowledge of and write to demonstrate knowledge of parts of speech, phrases, and clauses	Phrases and clauses combine the parts of speech in meaningful ways to create complex ideas. Showing awareness of how these are created and how to identify them will help you to write clear and coherent sentences.	☐ I've Got It! ☐ Almost There ☐ Need More Practice	pp. 300–07

Deepening Your Understanding

If you would like to go beyond the material in this chapter, explore additional connections, and get more practice, check out these related topics:

➔ **Commas**: Using commas correctly makes sentences easier to read by breaking up information. Commas are sometimes needed when connecting independent and dependent clauses.

➔ **Sentence Structure**: Understanding how sentences are put together will help you to use a variety of phrases and clauses correctly. Once you are comfortable with these rules, you can develop a style of your own.

➔ **Fragments**: Readers find it difficult to understand writing that contains fragments. Incomplete ideas, like phrases and dependent clauses, can't serve as sentences.

Subject-Verb Agreement

18

"Only in grammar can you be more than perfect."
—William Safire

FACT OR FICTION?
To make a verb plural, I just add an s on the end of the word.

FICTION.
You may be tempted to "add an s" to the end of a verb to make it plural; however, this is not correct. We often can add an s to the end of most nouns to make them plural, but when we add an s to the end of a verb, it can also make the verb singular.

Discovering Key Points

- Identify singular and plural subjects and verbs
- Apply knowledge of and correct subject-verb agreement errors in the context of a sentence
- Apply knowledge of and write to demonstrate knowledge of subject-verb agreement

Subject-verb agreement occurs when the subject and verb match in number. This means that when we use a singular subject, we also use a singular verb; when we use a plural subject, we use a plural verb.

Singular refers to one, while plural refers to two or more.

Can you find and fix the subject-verb agreement error in this sign?

Subjects

A **subject** is often called the naming part of a sentence. The subject of a sentence shows what the sentence is about and who performs the action in the sentence.

The subject may be one word, or it may be several words. Here are some examples of subjects:

1. A single word as a subject:

`Jeffrey` sat down.

For more information on pronouns, see Chapter 17.

Here, the subject is a proper noun—the name of a person: Jeffrey.

2. A pronoun as a subject:

`He` sat down.

3. Several words or a phrase as a subject:

`The group of boys` sat down.

Here, *The group of boys* is a noun phrase. A **noun phrase** is a grouping of words that serve as one noun/subject. A noun phrase is made up of a head word and modifiers, complements, and/or determiners.

`Jeffrey and his friends` sat down.

Jeffrey and his friends is considered a compound subject. A **compound subject** is when two nouns, pronouns, or noun phrases are combined by using the word "and."

For more information on helping verbs, see Chapter 17.

In Chapter 17, you learned about verbs. As a reminder, a **verb** is a word that shows action or state of being. Every sentence needs a main verb that shows action. Sometimes, however, this main verb is preceded by a helping verb, such as *be*, *do*, or *have*. Here are some examples:

The actor `walked` across the movie set to hit his mark.

The actor `had been walking` across the movie set to hit his mark when he received the call from his agent.

Tips for Subject-Verb Agreement

Tip #1: A singular subject always has a singular verb, just as a plural subject always has a plural verb.

SINGULAR SUBJECT   SINGULAR VERB
`The cat drinks` from her bowl.

PLURAL SUBJECT   PLURAL VERB
`The cats drink` from their bowls.

Tip #2: The indefinite pronouns *anyone, someone, no one, nobody,* and *everyone* are always treated as singular. The indefinite pronouns *all* and *some* can be singular or plural.

SINGULAR SUBJECT   SINGULAR VERB
`No one was` available to help today at the main desk.

SINGULAR SUBJECT   SINGULAR VERB
`All of the water has evaporated`.

PLURAL SUBJECT   PLURAL VERB
`Some of the students were` absent the day of the test.

Tip #3: When combining two singular subjects with *or*, *either/or*, or *neither/nor*, the verb will always be singular.

SINGULAR SUBJECT   SINGULAR VERB
The hamburger or the chicken sandwich is your choice for lunch.

SINGULAR SUBJECT   SINGULAR VERB
Either a cat or a dog offers friendship to lonely people.

SINGULAR SUBJECT   SINGULAR VERB
Neither Frederik nor Jacen was eligible to play football.

Tip #4: When combining two subjects (a combination of plural and singular) with *or*, *neither/nor*, or *either/or*, the verb will agree with the subject closest to it.

SINGULAR SUBJECT   PLURAL SUBJECT   PLURAL VERB
Neither Jane nor her sisters were able to attend the beauty pageant.

PLURAL SUBJECT   SINGULAR SUBJECT   SINGULAR VERB
Either the students or course instructor writes evaluations for TAs.

Tip #5: When combining two subjects connected by *and*, use a plural verb.

PLURAL SUBJECT   PLURAL SUBJECT   PLURAL VERB
The dogs and the horses walk the trail each morning with their owner.

SINGULAR SUBJECT   SINGULAR SUBJECT   PLURAL VERB
Hard work and time management are important skills for students to have.

Practice the Skills 1

Underline the subject in each sentence. In the blank, write whether the subject is plural or singular.

Example: The coffee was too hot.   _____singular_____

1. Hulias and his friends enjoy going to the theater.   _____

2. My paper is going to be about global warming.   _____

3. My biology and history classes are quite difficult this semester. _____

4. The dishes fell from the rack onto the floor. _____

5. The pirates are sick with scurvy. _____

Practice the Skills 2

Circle the correct verb for each sentence.

Example: The extended cut of the film (was) / were) too long.

1. The television show (was canceled / were canceled) after only three episodes.

2. Jonathon (hate / hates) waking up early.

3. Anne and her family (is planning / are planning) to throw me a bridal shower.

4. The elevators (is / are) broken in the library.

5. The brothers and their mother (is going / are going) to the graduation on Sunday.

Practice the Skills 3

Underline the subject(s) in each sentence. Then rewrite each sentence by fixing the verbs to make sure they agree with each other.

Example: Marcus run anchor for his university's track team.

                Marcus runs anchor for his university's track team.

1. Everybody have difficulty with learning new languages.

2. Neither Iona nor Shauna wear fur or leather.

3. The manager and the staff plays softball in the adult softball league.

4. Jacques and his parents travels to Puerto Rico each summer.

5. No one believe his alibi.

Assessing Your Knowledge

KEY POINTS	REMINDER	HOW WELL DID YOU UNDERSTAND THIS MATERIAL?	PAGE(S)
Identify singular and plural subjects and verbs	**Singular** refers to one, while **plural** refers to two or more. When we use a singular subject, we also use a singular verb; when we use a plural subject, we use a plural verb.	☐ I've Got It! ☐ Almost There ☐ Need More Practice	pp. 312–14
Apply knowledge of and correct subject-verb agreement errors in the context of a sentence	Learning the tips for subject-verb agreement will ensure your writing is direct and clear: ▪ Tip #1: A singular subject always has a singular verb, just as a plural subject always has a plural verb. ▪ Tip #2: The indefinite pronouns *anyone*, *someone*, *no one*, *nobody*, and *everyone* are always treated as singular. The indefinite pronouns *all* and *some* can be singular or plural. ▪ Tip #3: When combining two singular subjects with *or*, *either/or*, or *neither/nor*, the verb will always be singular. ▪ Tip #4: When combining two subjects (a combination of plural and singular) with *or*, *neither/nor*, or *either/or*, the verb will agree with the subject closest to it. ▪ Tip #5: When combining two subjects connected by *and*, use a plural verb.	☐ I've Got It! ☐ Almost There ☐ Need More Practice	pp. 313–14
Apply knowledge of and write to demonstrate knowledge of subject-verb agreement	If your subjects and verbs do not agree, it can cause confusion for your readers. Taking what you learn about subject-verb agreement and applying it to your own writing is important for clear and effective communication.	☐ I've Got It! ☐ Almost There ☐ Need More Practice	pp. 314–15

Deepening Your Understanding

If you would like to go beyond the material in this chapter, explore additional connections, and get more practice, check out these related topics:

- ⟳ **Subjects and Verbs**: Before you delve into subject-verb agreement, it is important to know the basics. Knowing what a subject and verb are and how they interact will help you form a context to build upon.
- ⟳ **Regular and Irregular Verbs**: Once you know what a verb is, learning the patterns for verb formation will help you better grasp subject-verb agreement.
- ⟳ **Pronoun Case**: Sometimes, your subject will be a pronoun. Understanding the different pronoun cases will help you be clear in your writing, but it will also help you choose the right verb to agree with your pronoun subject.

Pronoun-Antecedent Agreement

19

"Grammar is a piano I play by ear. All I know about grammar is its power."

—Joan Didion

Discovering Key Points

⊙ Identify pronoun-antecedent agreement errors

⊙ Apply knowledge of and correct pronoun-antecedent agreement errors in the context of a sentence

⊙ Write to demonstrate knowledge of avoiding pronoun-antecedent agreement errors

You may remember from Chapter 17 that pronouns can take the place of nouns. When you use pronouns, you must make sure that the pronouns match their **antecedents**, the words they refer to, in number and gender. This is called **pronoun-antecedent agreement**. If the pronouns and antecedents don't match, your readers may become confused, and your meaning may become unclear.

Can you find and fix the pronoun-antecedent error in this sign?

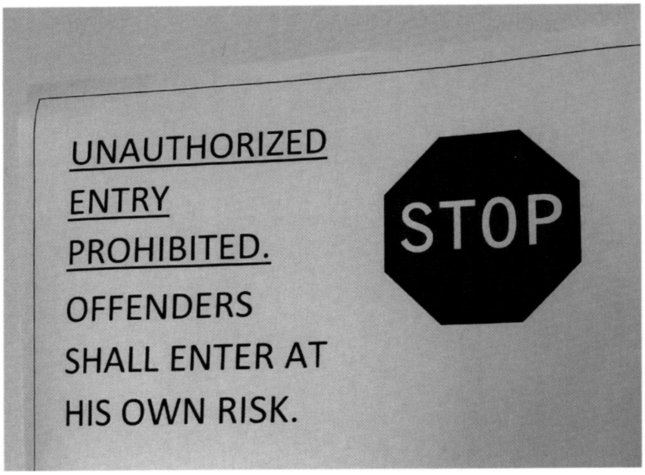

Tips for Pronoun-Antecedent Agreement

Pronouns and their antecedents should agree in number and gender.

For more information on pronouns, see Chapter 17.

Tip #1: Use pronouns and antecedents that agree in number.

Pronouns can be singular, representing one person or item, or plural, representing more than one person or several items. While some pronouns are easily identifiable as singular or plural, such as *he* (singular) or *them* (plural), others, like indefinite pronouns, such as the ones in the chart below may require more practice to identify.

SINGULAR	PLURAL	SINGULAR OR PLURAL
another, anybody, anyone, anything, each, either, everyone, everything, little, much, neither, nobody, none, no one, nothing, one, other, somebody, someone, something	both, few, many, others, several	all, any, more, most, some

If the antecedent is singular, meaning that there is only one person or thing, then the pronoun should match. Similarly, if the antecedent is plural, meaning that there is more than one, then the pronoun should also be plural.

SINGULAR ANTECEDENT   SINGULAR PRONOUN
Mark left his textbook on the desk after class.
Sarah feels she needs one good friend to help her through hard times.

PLURAL ANTECEDENT   PLURAL PRONOUN
Many would assume that they would be happier if they made more money.
Others also have the right to express their political views.

Tip #2: Use pronouns and antecedents that agree in gender or are gender neutral.

Gender-specific pronouns identify a subject as being either male or female. Gender-neutral pronouns do not. These pronouns can be used regardless of whether the subject is male or female.

	SINGULAR	PLURAL
GENDER SPECIFIC	he, she, him, her, himself, herself	
GENDER NEUTRAL	I, me, my, mine, myself, it, its, you, your	we, us, our, ourselves, they, them, their, theirs, themselves, you, your

Note: While *you* and *your* are always gender neutral, they can be either singular or plural depending on the context of your sentence.

GENDER SPECIFIC   GENDER NEUTRAL
Gretta was able to put on her SCUBA gear by herself.
I would like my cupcake without frosting.
Here at the University, we pride ourselves on hard work and dedication.

Using the right pronoun is not usually a problem when you know exactly who the subject of your sentence is. However, when the subject could be male or female, you should be careful to avoid sexist language. MLA and APA now recognize the use of plural pronouns with singular antecedents when the gender is unknown.

SINGULAR ANTECEDENT   SINGULAR PRONOUN
PLURAL ANTECEDENT   PLURAL PRONOUN
One should always be aware of their surroundings. = CORRECT
One should always be aware of one's surroundings. = CORRECT

People should always be aware of their surroundings. = CORRECT
Every medical doctor should work on their bedside manner. = INCORRECT
Medical doctors should work on their bedside manner. = CORRECT

Practice the Skills 1

Underline the pronouns and antecedents in each sentence. In the blank, write whether the pronouns are plural or singular.

Example: Richard gave his driver's license to the bartender.   _____singular_____

1. Did Anika give them their money back?   _____

2. All of my friends want to have a party when they graduate.   _____

3. You should get your girlfriend flowers for every anniversary.   _____

4. We need to find the best location for our photo shoot.   _____

5. Noah did his homework last night.   _____

Practice the Skills 2

Correct the pronoun-antecedent errors below by rewriting the following sentences. Change the pronoun to match the antecedent.

Example: Artists should find joy in his or her work.

                Artists should find joy in their work.

1. All children should bring his or her toys inside to play.

2. One should check their tire pressure before going on a long trip.

3. A cashier needs to move quickly in order to keep her line short.

4. Matt requested that his or her paper be reviewed.

5. Many people like taking his pets on vacation.

Practice the Skills 3

Write your own sentences using pronouns and antecedents that agree by following the instructions below.

Example: Write a sentence using singular pronouns and antecedents.

> I have a hard time saving my money.

1. Write a sentence using plural pronouns and antecedents.

2. Write a sentence using gender-neutral pronouns and antecedents.

3. Write a sentence using pronouns and antecedents that are singular and gender specific.

4. Write a sentence using pronouns and antecedents that are plural and gender neutral.

5. Write a sentence using pronouns and antecedents that are singular and gender neutral.

Assessing Your Knowledge

KEY POINTS	REMINDER	HOW WELL DID YOU UNDERSTAND THIS MATERIAL?	PAGE(S)
Identify pronoun-antecedent agreement errors	When you have correct **pronoun-antecedent agreement**, the pronouns match the people or items they refer to, called antecedents, in both number and gender.	☐ I've Got It! ☐ Almost There ☐ Need More Practice	pp. 318–20
Apply knowledge of and correct pronoun-antecedent agreement errors in the context of a sentence	Pronouns can be classified in several ways, as singular, plural, gender neutral, and gender specific. These distinctions are important because the pronouns you use must match the antecedent in order for the sentence to make sense.	☐ I've Got It! ☐ Almost There ☐ Need More Practice	pp. 318–20
Write to demonstrate knowledge of avoiding pronoun-antecedent agreement errors	Many pronoun-antecedent agreement errors are overlooked in casual conversation, making it hard for us to spot them in our own writing. Pronoun-antecedent agreement is incredibly important to your readers, however. Without correct agreement, you can confuse your readers.	☐ I've Got It! ☐ Almost There ☐ Need More Practice	pp. 320–21

Deepening Your Understanding

If you would like to go beyond the material in this chapter, explore additional connections, and get more practice, check out these related topics:

→ **Parts of Speech, Phrases, and Clauses**: Sometimes pronouns and their antecedents are separated by other parts of speech that can distract us. Knowing all the parts of speech can help you determine if your sentence has good pronoun-antecedent agreement.

→ **Pronouns**: Understanding pronouns thoroughly will help you to create sentences with correct pronoun-antecedent agreement. Using pronouns properly will also help you clearly communicate your message to your readers.

→ **Pronoun Reference and Point of View**: Identifying an antecedent may be difficult if you have never tried it before. Practice finding and writing clear antecedents in pronoun reference and point of view.

Fragments

"The greater part of the world's troubles are due to questions of grammar."

—Michel de Montaigne

Discovering Key Points

- Identify fragments
- Apply knowledge of and correct fragments in context
- Write to demonstrate knowledge of avoiding fragments

A full sentence, or independent clause, must have a subject and a verb and must communicate a full thought. A **fragment** can be missing any one of these crucial parts. A fragment may be missing a subject or a verb, and, in some cases, it can be missing both. Even if it does have both a subject and a verb, it cannot be a full sentence if it begins with a word that makes it dependent on more information, like a subordinating conjunction.

Can you find and fix the fragment in this advertisement?

For more information on independent clauses, see Chapter 17.

There are five common types of fragments that you should look for and eliminate in your writing. There are two ways to correct a fragment. You can turn the fragment into an independent clause or connect it to another independent clause.

Tips for Identifying and Correcting Fragments

Tip #1: Identify *-ing* fragments.

These fragments are made up of verb phrases that start with *-ing* words. They show that something is happening, but they do not contain a main subject.

FRAGMENT   INDEPENDENT CLAUSE
Getting to the phone when it rang.

CORRECTIONS
I stubbed my toe on the couch getting to the phone when it rang.
I stubbed my toe on the couch. I tried to get to the phone when it rang.

Tip #2: Identify *to* fragments.

These fragments are made up of verb phrases that start with *to*. These give the reader more information, but do not contain a main subject.

<u>FRAGMENT</u>   <u>INDEPENDENT CLAUSE</u>
<u>To entertain the children she was babysitting</u>.

CORRECTIONS
To entertain the children she was babysitting, <u>Opal decided to play hide and seek</u>.
<u>Opal wanted to entertain the children she was babysitting</u>. <u>She decided to play hide and seek</u>.

Tip #3: Identify afterthought fragments.

These fragments are usually meant to help finish a thought and add information to a sentence that comes directly before or after. Often, these fragments are missing a subject or a verb.

For more information on subjects and verbs, see Chapters 17 and 18.

<u>FRAGMENT</u>   <u>INDEPENDENT CLAUSE</u>
<u>Including three corndogs, funnel cake, and a deep-fried Twinkie</u>.

CORRECTIONS
<u>I ate a ton at the fair</u>, including three corndogs, funnel cake, and a deep-fried Twinkie.
<u>I ate a ton at the fair</u>. <u>I had three corndogs, funnel cake, and a deep-fried Twinkie</u>.

Tip #4: Identify dependent clause fragments.

While these fragments contain a subject and a verb, they don't express a complete thought and can't be used alone. Look for dependent clauses that start with subordinating conjunctions, such as *after*, *although*, *if*, *unless*, or *while*.

For more information on and examples of subordinating conjunctions, see Chapter 17.

<u>FRAGMENT</u>   <u>INDEPENDENT CLAUSE</u>
<u>Although I had the money</u>.

CORRECTIONS
Although I had the money, <u>my aunt insisted on buying my ticket</u>.
<u>I had the money</u>. <u>My aunt insisted on buying my ticket</u>.

For more information and examples of relative clauses, see Chapter 17.

Tip #5: Identify relative clause fragments.

These fragments are dependent clauses that start with relative pronouns: *who, whoever, whom, whomever, whose, whosever, which, whichever,* and *that.*

<u>FRAGMENT</u>   <u>INDEPENDENT CLAUSE</u>
Which taught me to be patient.

CORRECTIONS
My first job was working in retail, which taught me to be patient.
My first job was working in retail. That job taught me to be patient.

Practice the Skills 1

Identify the fragments below by underlining them.

Example: My cat likes to wake me up at night. <u>When she is out of food</u>.

1. To find other people who have similar interests. I am joining a club.

2. Smashing all pumpkins in our apartment complex. The boys ruined our festive decorations.

3. The Internet in my dorm isn't working, so I am going to do homework somewhere else. Like a coffee shop or Internet café.

4. Since I am moving to a new house. My commute to work will be shorter.

5. We refused to go back to the restaurant. Which gave us horrible service.

Practice the Skills 2

Correct the fragments below by rewriting the sentences. Correct each one by connecting it to the independent clause. You may need to add or change the punctuation.

Example: I never make New Year's resolutions. Although this year I should try.

                I never make New Year's resolutions, although this year I should try.

1. I am going to try to get backstage passes. To see my favorite band.

2. Sadie will spend most of Saturday helping her friends. Setting up for the party.

3. Now that I have a DVR. I hate to watch live television because I don't want to sit through commercials.

4. Because I studied so hard for the test. My tutor expects me to get a good grade.

5. At dinner, we all stared at the man in the corner booth. Who ate with his fingers.

Practice the Skills 3

Write your own fragment. Then fix the fragment by connecting it to an independent clause or by turning it into an independent clause. Use the instructions below to practice correcting different types of fragments.

Example: Write and correct a dependent clause fragment.
Fragment: Despite the fact that he fell off three times.
Correction: My little brother is determined to learn to ride his bike today despite the fact that he fell off three times.

1. Write and correct a *to* fragment.

2. Write and correct an *-ing* fragment.

3. Write and correct an afterthought fragment.

4. Write and correct a dependent clause fragment.

5. Write and correct a relative clause fragment.

Assessing Your Knowledge

KEY POINTS	REMINDER	HOW WELL DID YOU UNDERSTAND THIS MATERIAL?	PAGE(S)
Identify fragments	A **fragment** is an incomplete sentence because it is missing one or more of the following parts: a subject, a verb, or a complete thought.	☐ I've Got It! ☐ Almost There ☐ Need More Practice	pp. 324–26
Apply knowledge of and correct fragments in context	There are five common types of fragments that you should learn to correct in your writing: **-ing fragments**, **to fragments**, **afterthought fragments**, **dependent clause fragments**, and **relative clause fragments**.	☐ I've Got It! ☐ Almost There ☐ Need More Practice	pp. 324–26
Write to demonstrate knowledge of avoiding fragments	Eliminating fragments from your writing is important, as they are distracting for readers. Because fragments lack necessary information, they make it very difficult for readers to understand what you are trying to say.	☐ I've Got It! ☐ Almost There ☐ Need More Practice	pp. 326–27

Deepening Your Understanding

If you would like to go beyond the material in this chapter, explore additional connections, and get more practice, check out these related topics:

⊙ **Subjects and Verbs**: Independent clauses require both a subject and a verb. Knowing how to identify the subject and the verb of a sentence can help you to avoid writing fragments.

⊙ **Parts of Speech, Phrases, and Clauses**: The parts of speech are the foundation of grammar and sentence structure. The more you understand the parts of speech and how they work together, the easier it will be to construct well-written sentences.

⊙ **Commas**: Some fragments are dependent clauses that need to be connected to an independent clause. Understanding how these properly connect and whether to use a comma is important.

Run-Ons

"It is well to remember that grammar is common speech formulated."

—Somerset Maugham

FACT OR FICTION?
Run-on sentences are just long sentences. If I write short sentences, I won't create a run-on.

FICTION.
Run-on sentences don't have much to do with length. Whether a sentence is a run-on is determined by how it is punctuated. Even relatively short sentences can be run-ons. It is better to understand how to avoid run-ons and vary your sentence structure than to decide to write only short sentences.

Discovering Key Points

- Identify run-on sentences as fused sentences or comma splices
- Apply knowledge of and correct run-on sentences within the context of a sentence
- Write to demonstrate knowledge of avoiding run-on sentences

When we speak, we use pauses, hand gestures, and voice inflection to help our listeners understand when one idea ends and another begins. When we write, we must separate our ideas using punctuation. **Run-on sentences** occur when two or more ideas or independent clauses are presented without being separated correctly.

Can you find and fix the run-on sentence in this sign?

Types of Run-On Sentences

There are two types of run-on sentences: **fused sentences** and **comma splices**. A fused sentence occurs when two independent clauses are joined together without punctuation. Below each independent clause is highlighted.

Fused Sentence

I couldn't find a parking spot ( ) I was late to class.

Both *I couldn't find a parking spot* and *I was late to class* are independent clauses. Notice there is no punctuation between them.

A comma splice occurs when two independent clauses are joined with only a comma. A comma, however, is not enough to connect two independent clauses correctly.

Comma Splice

I couldn't find a parking spot (,) I was late to class.

The only difference between a fused sentence and a comma splice is a comma.

For more information on independent clauses, see Chapter 17.

Tips for Fixing Run-On Sentences

A run-on sentence can be corrected in several ways.

Tip #1: Separate the independent clauses with a period.

I couldn't find a parking spot (.) I was late to class.

Tip #2: Separate the independent clauses with a semicolon.

I couldn't find a parking spot (;) I was late to class.

For more information on semicolons, see Chapter 23.

Tip #3: Separate the independent clauses with a comma and a coordinating conjunction.

I couldn't find a parking spot (, so) I was late to class.

Coordinating conjunctions are sometimes called FANBOYS: for, and, not, but, or, yet, so. For more information, see Chapter 17.

Tip #4: Separate the independent clauses by turning one into a dependent clause.

Create a dependent clause by adding a subordinating conjunction (e.g., *after, although, if, unless, while*) or relative pronoun (e.g., *that, which, who,* or *whom*). In the examples below, the dependent clauses are highlighted in green, while the independent clauses are highlighted in yellow. The subordinating conjunctions are circled.

For more examples of subordinating conjunctions and relative pronouns, see Chapter 17.

Since I couldn't find a parking spot (,) I was late to class.

I couldn't find a parking spot (, which) is the reason I was late to class.

Practice the Skills 1

Identify each of the sentences below as a comma splice (CS) or a fused sentence (FS).

Example: __FS__ The air conditioning in my car is broken I have to get it fixed.

1. _____ I could have afforded to go to the first Academy Awards ceremony, tickets were only five dollars.

2. _____ You won't see an Oscar statue for sale on eBay the statuettes must be offered back to the Academy for a dollar.

3. _____ Shirley Temple was the youngest person to win an Oscar, a junior Oscar was given to her when she was six years old.

4. ____ The original rules stated a movie must be shown in Los Angeles to be eligible for an Oscar, this rule has now been changed.

5. ____ Oscar statues are made in Chicago all are plated in gold.

Practice the Skills 2

Rewrite the following run-on sentences by correcting them. Refer to the four tips on how to fix run-ons if you need help.

Example: Harrison has trouble understanding HTML he needs to learn to manage his new website.

Harrison has trouble understanding HTML, but he needs to learn to manage his new website.

1. My favorite blog asked me to contribute most blogs encourage knowledgeable readers to participate.

2. Music is incredibly helpful as therapy, it can be used to help people with stressful jobs relax after work.

3. I lost the remote, I have to get up to turn off the television.

4. Many current movies are adaptations of movies from the 1980s I like to watch both the new and old versions to see the differences.

5. Childhood obesity is on the rise companies still advertise sugary cereals to children.

Practice the Skills 3

Write your own sentence by correctly separating either two independent clauses or an independent and dependent clause to avoid run-ons by following the tip indicated.

Example: **Tip #1:** Separate the independent clauses with a period.

My favorite show was canceled. I plan to watch all three seasons again online.

1. **Tip #1**: Separate the independent clauses with a period.

2. **Tip #2**: Separate the independent clauses with a semicolon.

3. **Tip #3**: Separate the independent clauses with a comma and coordinating conjunction.

4. **Tip #4**: Separate the independent clauses by turning one into a dependent clause.

Assessing Your Knowledge

KEY POINTS	REMINDER	HOW WELL DID YOU UNDERSTAND THIS MATERIAL?	PAGE(S)
Identify run-on sentences as fused sentences or comma splices	A **fused sentence** occurs when two independent clauses are joined together without punctuation. A **comma splice** occurs when two independent clauses are joined with only a comma.	☐ I've Got It! ☐ Almost There ☐ Need More Practice	pp. 330–31
Apply knowledge of and correct run-on sentences within the context of a sentence	Fused sentences and comma splices can be corrected using a period, a semicolon, a comma with a coordinating conjunction, or by creating a dependent clause.	☐ I've Got It! ☐ Almost There ☐ Need More Practice	pp. 331–32
Write to demonstrate knowledge of avoiding fragments	Learning to write without fused sentences and comma splices takes practice and diligence. If this is a common error in your writing, review your work specifically for run-ons.	☐ I've Got It! ☐ Almost There ☐ Need More Practice	pp. 332–33

Deepening Your Understanding

If you would like to go beyond the material in this chapter, explore additional connections, and get more practice, check out these related topics:

- **Commas**: Proper comma placement is important. If used wisely, commas can help you express yourself more clearly by separating ideas. While not all comma rules deal with run-ons, understanding commas will allow you to use a variety of sentence types.

- **Sentence Structure**: There are four sentence types in English: simple, compound, complex, and compound-complex. Understanding how these sentence types are constructed will help you avoid run-ons.

- **Combining Sentences**: We all want to express ourselves through our writing. Learning a variety of ways to combine sentences will enable you to communicate effectively and create your own style.

Commas

"I have been fighting over commas all my life."
—Mark Helprin

FACT OR FICTION?
Any time I take a breath or pause while reading a sentence aloud, I place a comma.

FICTION.
While this "tip" may seem true, it is hardly foolproof. Each writer has his or her own speech pattern, and a group of people may speak the same sentence multiple ways—each with a different pause. When in doubt about commas, follow the comma tips.

Discovering Key Points

- Identify the seven comma tips
- Apply knowledge of and correct comma errors in the context of a sentence
- Apply knowledge of and write to demonstrate knowledge of commas

The comma is a piece of punctuation that many people have difficulty using. While there are many tips about using commas, this chapter will delve into the seven comma tips most often applied in student writing.

Can you find and fix the comma error in this sign?

Tips for Using Commas

Tip #1: Use commas to separate items in a list.

Use a comma to separate items in a series or a list of three or more items.

> Fred enjoys gardening, traveling to new places, meeting new people, singing karaoke, and eating wild blueberries.

> I went to the store to buy milk and cookies.

For more information on adjectives, see Chapter 17.

In the second sentence, there is no comma needed, as there are only two items in the list.

Tip #2: Use commas to separate adjectives describing the same noun.

When there is a group of adjectives describing the same noun, we must use two tests to see if a comma is required.

> The young silly boy was a troublemaker.

Test 1—Place "and" between the adjectives.

> The young and silly boy was a troublemaker.

Test 2—Switch the placement of the adjectives.

> The silly young boy was a troublemaker.

If the sentence still makes sense and sounds correct after both tests, a comma is required.

> The young, silly boy was a troublemaker.

Let's look at another example.

> They live in the big blue house on the corner.

Test 1—Place "and" between the adjectives.

> They live in the big and blue house on the corner.

Test 2—Switch the placement of the adjectives.

> They live in the blue big house on the corner.

Here, the sentence does not pass the tests. It sounds unclear and incorrect to our ears to say *big and blue house* or *blue big house*. Therefore, we do not need a comma in this sentence.

Tip #3: Use commas to separate introductory or opening clauses.

An introductory or opening clause is found at the beginning of a sentence. If the clause can be taken out of the sentence, and it still makes sense, a comma can be used.

> While the UFC is a dangerous sport, the fighters would not hurt anyone outside of the octagon.

> In 2004, Lysa married Arturo.

> Frank, what are you wearing tonight?

Here, we can take out the introductory clauses (*While the UFC is a dangerous sport, In 2004,* and *Frank*) and the sentences still make sense to the readers.

Tip #4: Use commas to separate two independent clauses and a coordinating conjunction.

If you want to combine two independent clauses (independent clauses have both a subject and verb and can stand on their own as a full sentence) with a coordinating conjunction (*for, and, nor, but, or, yet, so*), you'll need a comma before the coordinating conjunction.

> For more information about how to use coordinating conjunctions to combine sentences, see Chapter 21.

Brice's home was ransacked, yet nothing was taken.

Remember to choose the correct coordinating conjunction for what you want to say. Not all coordinating conjunctions are equal!

Lauren went to the party, and it was boring.

This sentence means that Lauren went to the party, only to find out it was boring.

Lauren went to the party, so it was boring.

This sentence means that because Lauren went to the party, it became boring. Lauren was the cause of the boring party.

Tip #5: Use commas to set off nonessential information from the rest of a sentence.

This tip is similar to Tip #3, except Tip #3 occurs only at the beginning of a sentence. Nonessential information in the sentence can be taken out, and the sentence still makes sense.

I am telling you, citizens of this good city, we must prepare for the upcoming festival.

Samuel, my brother-in-law, loaned us his truck for the afternoon.

When we set off information in commas as nonessential, we are telling the readers that it is not vital to the meaning of the sentence. Here is another example:

INCORRECT: Students, who are absent, will not be eligible to take the test.

The commas in this sentence are incorrect because without the information set off in commas, the sentence does not have the same meaning. If we were to leave the commas here, the meaning of the sentence would be that all students are not able to take the test.

Tip #6: Use commas with dates, cities, and numbers.

When writing a date, the comma is placed between the day and year.

David met his wife on May 5, 1992.

In regard to places, the comma is placed between a city and country or city and state.

> Noah is originally from Bilbao, Spain.

With numbers, a comma is placed every three numbers from the right.

> My hometown is 1,203 years old.

> He has been playing polka music for 73 years.

Tip #7: Use commas to set off quotations or dialogue.

This example is in MLA formatting. For more information about in-text citations, see Chapter 16.

> Germano argues, "Parents should ensure they know what their children are doing online" (38).

> Mark said, "The gnomes presented in Harry Potter are incredibly inaccurate."

> "Cloning," Irma insisted, "is a messy practice and should be stopped."

Practice the Skills 1

Identify which comma tip (1–7) is being used in the sentence.

Example: ___1___ My favorite subjects are math, English, and French.

1. _____ We all had fun at Disneyland, and we went home tired.

2. _____ Armin said, "Why does my dog keep chasing her tail?"

3. _____ Loki is a cunning, crafty trickster.

4. _____ My maid of honor, Renee, wore a blue dress to the wedding.

5. _____ At a job interview, it is important to make a good first impression.

Practice the Skills 2

Rewrite the following sentences by using commas correctly. Some sentences may require more than one comma.

Example: Marta my best friend has two dogs and she lives at 1294 West Buchanan Street.
            Marta, my best friend, has two dogs, and she lives at 1294 West Buchanan Street.

1. Ernest said "Gerome please pass the cookies."

2. Excuse me but there are many items to consider when we cast our vote today.

3. The ingredients for the recipe include chocolate chips peanut butter and vanilla ice cream.

4. Pete was born in Davenport Iowa on January 3 1995.

5. Lil Jon also known as Jonathan Smith is featured on the song "Turn Down for What."

Practice the Skills 3

Write your own sentence using commas correctly by following the tips below.

Example: Tip #2: Use commas to separate adjectives describing the same noun.

            Pete has stylish, inexpensive tastes when it comes to clothes.

1. **Tip #1**: Use commas to separate items in a list.

2. **Tip #3**: Use commas to separate introductory or opening clauses.

3. **Tip #4**: Use commas to separate two independent clauses and a coordinating conjunction.

4. **Tip #5**: Use commas to set off nonessential information from the rest of a sentence.

5. **Tip #6**: Use commas with dates, cities, and numbers.

Assessing Your Knowledge

KEY POINTS	REMINDER	HOW WELL DID YOU UNDERSTAND THIS MATERIAL?	PAGE(S)
Identify the seven comma tips	There are seven comma tips: - **Tip #1**: Use commas to separate items in a list. - **Tip #2**: Use commas to separate adjectives describing the same noun. - **Tip #3**: Use commas to separate introductory or opening clauses. - **Tip #4**: Use commas to separate two independent clauses and a coordinating conjunction. - **Tip #5**: Use commas to set off nonessential information from the rest of a sentence. - **Tip #6**: Use commas with dates, cities, and numbers. - **Tip #7**: Use commas to set off quotations or dialogue.	☐ I've Got It! ☐ Almost There ☐ Need More Practice	pp. 336–39
Apply knowledge of and correct comma errors in the context of a sentence	Being able to find comma errors is important, as they can sometimes impede the meaning of your sentences, thus confusing your readers.	☐ I've Got It! ☐ Almost There ☐ Need More Practice	pp. 339–40
Apply knowledge of and write to demonstrate knowledge of commas	When you read a sentence (or even a paragraph or a paper), you'll want to be able to identify the types of comma errors. This is helpful not only for your own writing but also when you peer edit in class. Once you know the comma tips, you can show this awareness in your own writing. This will also allow you to fix your own comma errors when you go back to edit your own writing.	☐ I've Got It! ☐ Almost There ☐ Need More Practice	p. 340

Deepening Your Understanding

If you would like to go beyond the material in this chapter, explore additional connections, and get more practice, check out these related topics:

- **Run-ons**: There are two types of run-ons: comma splices and fused sentences. In order to avoid comma splices, you'll need to know how to use commas properly.

- **Sentence Structure**: There are four sentence types in English: simple, compound, complex, and compound-complex. When you write these types of sentences, you will often require commas.

- **Combining Sentences**: Having an assortment of ways to write your sentences is important so that you can vary your writing. Sometimes, we want to use a comma to combine parts of a sentence; other times, we decide to use a semicolon or a period.

Semicolons, Colons, Dashes, and Parentheses

"The art of the parentheses is one of the greatest secrets of eloquence in Society."
—Sébastien-Roch Nicolas de Chamfort

FACT OR FICTION?
A colon can be used any time I want to make a list.

FICTION.
While colons are a great way to vary your sentence structure and introduce a list, there are a few restrictions on how they are used. A colon must be used after an independent clause. In addition, the colon cannot be used after verbs and prepositions.

Discovering Key Points

- Identify semicolons, colons, dashes, and parentheses
- Apply knowledge of semicolons, colons, dashes, and parentheses within the context of a sentence
- Write to demonstrate knowledge of semicolons, colons, dashes, and parentheses

Semicolons, **colons**, **dashes**, and **parentheses** are punctuation marks that writers often say they avoid because they don't know how to use them. Fear shouldn't keep you from using these punctuation marks. If you know how to use them, you will feel more comfortable stretching your grammar wings and trying them out more often. Semicolons, colons, dashes, and parentheses are a wonderful way to vary your sentence structure and develop your style. Each of these pieces of punctuation can assist you in expressing your thoughts more clearly.

Can you find and fix the error in this sign with a semicolon?

Tips for Using Semicolons

Semicolons are sometimes mistakenly compared to commas or periods; however, they function differently. Semicolons have two main purposes. They (1) can join two independent clauses and (2) can be used to separate items in a list that already contains commas. Semicolons look like this: **;**.

Want more practice with independent clauses? See Chapter 17.

Tip #1: Semicolons join together two closely related independent clauses.

In this case, a semicolon connects two independent clauses, or sentences, together. The semicolon is special because it has the strength to show the relationship between ideas on its own. A semicolon is unlike a period, which can only separate ideas. A semicolon is also stronger than a comma, which needs the help of a coordinating conjunction (also known as **FANBOYS**) to connect two independent clauses.

> My husband wants to add a second story to our house (**;**) I dread chaos and construction.

> Lolita, my dog, loves to go on walks (**;**) I enjoy taking her during the evening.

Tip #2: A semicolon can be used with a conjunctive adverb to help clarify the relationship between independent clauses.

Conjunctive adverbs connect ideas and provide a smooth transition from one independent clause to another. Below are a few commonly used conjunctive adverbs. Some of the conjunctive adverbs show contrast, while others demonstrate a sequence, a cause and effect, or even an agreement. Think carefully about the meaning of any conjunctive adverb you use, as it can change the meaning of your sentence.

also	indeed	otherwise
consequently	likewise	similarly
finally	meanwhile	still
furthermore	moreover	therefore
hence	namely	thus
however	nevertheless	undoubtedly
incidentally	nonetheless	

Using conjunctive adverbs allows you to help the reader better understand the connections between your ideas. Always add a comma after the conjunctive adverb. The conjunctive adverb is highlighted below.

> I want to go to Jamaica for my vacation this year (;) thus, I am willing to give up other luxuries to save more money.

> Every Sunday, we all gather to watch TV (;) undoubtedly, it is a nice way to end the weekend with my family.

Tip #3: Semicolons can be used to separate items in a list that already contains commas.

Semicolons, in this instance, will help create a clear break between items in a list. Semicolons are used in a list only if there are commas already being used by the items in the list. In the example below, the items in the series are highlighted. The semicolons are circled and the commas are marked with squares.

> I learned the most from Mr. Anton [,] my high school English teacher (;) Mrs. Letlo [,] my junior high math teacher (;) and Mr. Walker [,] my 4th grade science teacher.

> I had to wait in one line to get my picture taken [,] which looks horrible (;) in another to pay the fee (;) and in a third to receive my completed ID card.

Tips for Using Colons

Colons have two main uses in your writing. They can (1) link two independent clauses together and (2) introduce an idea or list. Colons look like this: :.

Tip #1: Colons can connect two independent clauses.

Unlike a semicolon that links two balanced independent clauses, a colon tells a reader that more information will be provided. After a colon, readers expect to get a further explanation of the information they have just learned. Below, the colons are circled. The additional information or explanation is highlighted.

Last spring, my teacher had strep throat (:) she had to cancel class twice.

The situation at school this morning made me think of that opening line of *A Tale of Two Cities* (:) "It was the best of times, it was the worst of times."

For more information on prepositions and verbs, see Chapter 17.

Tip #2: Colons can introduce an idea, example, or list.

In academic writing, colons should be used only after an independent clause. In addition, colons cannot follow a verb or a preposition. While there are several restrictions as to what comes before a colon, the information that comes afterward is unrestricted and can be given as a word, phrase, or list.

When I dropped my purse, everything fell out onto the classroom floor (:) lipstick, pens, change, receipts, and a parking pass.

There is only one thing that makes me feel better when I am depressed (:) jogging.

Tip for Using Dashes

Dashes are used only one way: to set off additional information that you would like to call attention to. The em dash (or a longer dash, or double dash) is used for this purpose. Dashes are considered informal and should be used only occasionally. The em dash looks like this: ——. In the examples below, the additional information is highlighted and the em dashes are circled.

Tip #1: Dashes separate information you want to emphasize.

My favorite celebrity—Luis Guzmán—won the reality television competition he was in.

I really want to be successful in my classes—I need more time.

Tips for Using Parentheses

Parentheses can be used for a couple of purposes. They are helpful (1) to number items in a list and (2) to include added information. Parentheses look like this: **( )**.

Tip #1: Parentheses can be used to mark items in a numbered list.

All lists do not require numbers, but if you are describing a process or focusing on each step, numbering can be helpful. The parentheses are circled.

When I sprained my ankle, my doctor told me to (1) get lots of rest, (2) apply ice, (3) wrap it in a bandage, and (4) elevate my foot.

Animal Crossing: New Horizons should (1) make the wetsuit clothing, (2) allow the player to customize every item catalogued, and (3) bring back the megaphone from previous versions.

Tip #2: Parentheses can provide additional information.

Parentheses de-emphasize information, and while the information provided in parentheses is generally helpful, it is not necessary for the basic meaning of the sentence and can be taken out. Even though commas or dashes can be used instead of parentheses, parentheses put less emphasis on the information. Parentheses make the writing a bit more informal, so use them sparingly in your papers. The additional information in parentheses below is highlighted. The parentheses are highlighted in blue.

> For more information on using commas with nonessential information, see Chapter 22.

Since my car broke down, I am now forced to take the bus (the red route) to school.

My brother owes me money (ten dollars) because I won the bet on the soccer game last weekend.

Practice the Skills 1

Identify the underlined part of the sentence that should be surrounded by parentheses. Add parentheses around the correct underlined section in each sentence.

Example: My best friend (Zack) is good enough to compete in the X Games on his snowmobile.

1. Movie nights are my favorite events to plan especially in the summer; they are special for all who come.

2. To have a successful movie night, start with a theme like a city.

3. Then, you will need to pick out 1 invitations, (2) decorations, and (3) food.

4. Telling everyone about the theme before they come will allow people to dress up if they want.

5. Make sure you have something for the guests to go home with themed party favors are a must.

Practice the Skills 2

Rewrite the following sentences by adding semicolons and colons where they are necessary. You may need to change some of the existing punctuation.

Example: In *The Wizard of Oz*, Dorothy meets three friends, the lion, the tin man, and the scarecrow.

In *The Wizard of Oz*, Dorothy meets three friends: the lion, the tin man, and the scarecrow.

1. Marco lives in Oregon, however, he was born in Puerto Rico.

2. In the movie *Pulp Fiction*, all of the clocks are set to one time 4:20.

3. I have roommates from Denver, Colorado, Franklin, Pennsylvania, and Paris, France.

4. I need coffee, to stay awake, snacks, so I don't get hungry, and a miracle, because I have to cram for a test.

5. He says my favorite line in the movie "Here's lookin' at you, kid."

Practice the Skills 3

Write your own sentence correctly following the specific tip or guideline given above for using semicolons, colons, dashes, and parentheses.

Example: The em dash can be used to show emphasis.

Stewart has worked in the movie industry for many years—30 years, in fact.

1. **Semicolons Tip #1:** Semicolons join together two closely related independent clauses.

2. **Colons Tip #1:** Colons can connect two independent clauses.

3. **Dashes Tip#1:** Use the em dash to show emphasis.

4. **Parentheses Tip #1:** Parentheses can be used to mark items in a numbered list.

5. **Semicolons Tip #3:** Semicolons can be used to separate items in a list that already contains commas.

Assessing Your Knowledge

KEY POINTS	REMINDER	HOW WELL DID YOU UNDERSTAND THIS MATERIAL?	PAGE(S)
Identify semicolons, colons, dashes, and parentheses	**Semicolons** can be used to connect two closely related independent clauses, can be used with a conjunctive adverb to help clarify the relationship between two independent clauses, or can be used to separate items with commas in a list. **Colons** can be used to elaborate or provide additional information. **Dashes** are used to highlight information in a sentence. **Parentheses** can be used to number items in a list or to de-emphasize additional information.	☐ I've Got It! ☐ Almost There ☐ Need More Practice	pp. 344–47

Apply knowledge of semicolons, colons, dashes, and parentheses within the context of a sentence	Many students avoid using other forms of punctuation because they are unfamiliar with them or because they don't understand how to use them properly. Practice using semicolons, colons, dashes, and parentheses regularly, so you will feel confident.	☐ I've Got It! ☐ Almost There ☐ Need More Practice	p. 348
Write to demonstrate knowledge of semicolons, colons, dashes, and parentheses	While you don't want to overuse semicolons, colons, dashes, and parentheses in your writing, varying your punctuation will make your writing interesting and offer you more options for clear communication.	☐ I've Got It! ☐ Almost There ☐ Need More Practice	p. 349

Deepening Your Understanding

If you would like to go beyond the material in this chapter, explore additional connections, and get more practice, check out these related topics:

- **Parts of Speech, Phrases, and Clauses**: The most common uses of semicolons and colons require the use of independent clauses. Being able to identify independent clauses will help you use colons and semicolons properly.

- **Commas**: Semicolons, colons, and parentheses can be found in sentences with other punctuation marks, like commas. Commas are important in lists and for setting off nonessential information.

- **Varying Sentence Structure**: There are many ways to create interest when you write: one is through your sentence structure. Using a variety of punctuation and sentence structures can help hold your reader's attention.

Apostrophes

"To those who care about punctuation, a sentence such as 'Thank God its Friday' (without the apostrophe) rouses feelings not only of despair but of violence."

—Lynne Truss

FACT OR FICTION?
If a word ends in s, in order to make it possessive, I should always add 's at the end of the word.

FICTION.
This often taught "rule" is not always true. If the word is singular and ends in s, then adding 's is appropriate; however, if the word is plural and ends in s, only an apostrophe is required.

Discovering Key Points

- Identify the use of an apostrophe to form both singular and plural possessive nouns and contractions
- Apply knowledge of and correct apostrophe errors within the context of a sentence
- Apply knowledge of and write to demonstrate knowledge of apostrophes

The apostrophe is a commonly used punctuation mark that looks like this: '.

The **apostrophe** can be used in two ways: (1) to show possession and (2) to omit letters in order to make a contraction. When apostrophes are used incorrectly, they can make your writing unclear and confusing to your readers.

The most common error regarding apostrophes is to add one to a plural word when not needed. Be sure you read your sentences carefully to decide whether a word should be possessive (and therefore use an apostrophe).

Plural Noun
The carolers sang Christmas songs door to door.

Possessive Noun
The carolers' favorite song was "Little Drummer Boy."

Can you find and fix the apostrophe error in this sign?

Tips for Using Apostrophes to Indicate Possession

Tip #1: Use apostrophes to indicate possession or ownership.

The van belongs to Steve. ➜ Steve's van

Even if the word ends in *s* already, if the word is singular, just add *'s* to the end of the word to make it possessive.

Yuri's bicycle
the hamster's ball
Jess's paper
yesterday's forecast

Tip #2: Use 's for possessives of plural nouns that do not end in an *s*.

If the word is plural and does not end in an *s*, add 's to the end of the word to make it possessive.

```
the men's workplace
the children's toys
the cacti's flowers
the deer's antlers
```

Tip #3: Use ' (*without the s*) for possessives of plural nouns that end in *s* already.

If the word is plural and ends in *s*, just add ' at the end of the word to make it possessive.

```
the boys' baseball game
the classes' finals
the Reynoldses' house
the bottles' filters
```

Tip #4: Don't use an apostrophe with possessive pronouns.

Possessive pronouns, such as *yours*, *his*, *hers*, *its*, *ours*, and *theirs*, are already possessive; therefore, they do not need an apostrophe or an *s* at the end of the word.

```
The check is yours.
Those keys are his.
```

Tip #5: Use 's when two or more nouns possess the same thing.

If you have two or more nouns that possess the same thing, add 's to the end of the *last* word to make them both possessive.

```
Jenn and Erma's outfits (they both share the same outfits)
the cat and dog's water bowl (the animals share a water bowl)
```

If both nouns possess the item separately, add 's to the end of *both* nouns to make them possessive.

```
Jenn's and Erma's outfits (each girl has her own outfit)
the cat's and dog's water bowls (each animal has its own water bowl)
```

Using Apostrophes to Create Contractions

The second way in which apostrophes can be used is to omit letters by creating a contraction. Notice that the apostrophe is placed where the letters have been omitted, not where the two words are combined.

do not ➜ don't

Here are some common contractions:

I	+	am	=	I'm
she	+	is	=	she's
he	+	is	=	he's
it	+	is	=	it's
who	+	is	=	who's
you	+	are	=	you're
they	+	are	=	they're
we	+	are	=	we're
is	+	not	=	isn't
do	+	not	=	don't
will	+	not	=	won't
can	+	not	=	can't
could	+	not	=	couldn't

It is easy to confuse *its/it's* and *whose/who's*. However, these words have very different meanings. If you're ever confused about which to choose, substitute the words the contractions stand for to see if the sentence makes sense with the word you've chosen.

The dog licked it's/its bowl clean.
The dog licked it is bowl clean. = INCORRECT
The dog licked its bowl clean. = CORRECT

Whose/Who's that woman with the red hair?
Whose that woman with the red hair? = INCORRECT
Who is that woman with the red hair? = CORRECT

Practice the Skills 1

Identify whether the apostrophe is being used for possession (P) or as a contraction (C).

Example: __P__ That house on the corner is Jack's.

1. _____ It's good that we all ate lunch before going to the park.

2. _____ Why are the posters' fonts so small?

3. _____ Mjölnir, Thor's hammer, is only to be wielded by those found worthy.

4. _____ Don't you want to get a latte before class?

5. _____ You're going to be tired if you don't take a nap before we leave tonight.

Practice the Skills 2

Rewrite the following sentences by using apostrophes correctly. Some sentences may require more than one apostrophe.

Example: Who's turn is it in Cards Against Humanity?
Whose turn is it in Cards Against Humanity?

1. Canadas national anthem is Kiernans favorite song.

2. Getting a college degree in English is helpful for teacher's, lawyer's, and writer's.

3. The smog was so thick today that we couldnt see the mountain's clearly.

4. The Johnsons family parrots name is Birdie.

5. Blueberries's are very healthy foods; were supposed to eat them frequently to get antioxidants.

Practice the Skills 3

Write your own sentence using apostrophes correctly by following the tips below.

Example: **Tip #6**: Use ' to omit letters and create a contraction.
We're going to Hollywood Studios this weekend to see Muppet Vision 3D.

1. **Tip #1**: Use apostrophes to indicate possession or ownership.

2. **Tip #2**: Use 's for possessives of plural nouns that do not end in an *s*.

3. **Tip #3**: Use ' (*without the s*) for possessives of plural nouns that end in *s* already.

4. **Tip #4**: Don't use an apostrophe with possessive pronouns.

5. **Tip #5**: Use 's when two or more nouns possess the same thing.

Assessing Your Knowledge

KEY POINTS	REMINDER	HOW WELL DID YOU UNDERSTAND THIS MATERIAL?	PAGE(S)
Identify the use of an apostrophe to form both singular and plural possessive nouns and contractions	There are two ways in which apostrophes are used: ▪ to indicate possession in singular and plural nouns ▪ to omit letters or words by creating a contraction	☐ I've Got It! ☐ Almost There ☐ Need More Practice	pp. 352–54
Apply knowledge of and correct apostrophe errors within the context of a sentence	Once you know the ways that apostrophes can be used, you can show this awareness in your own writing. This will also allow you to fix your own apostrophe errors when you go back to edit your writing. If you are ever unsure whether the apostrophe is needed, substitute the words the contraction stands for to see if the sentence makes sense with the word you've chosen.	☐ I've Got It! ☐ Almost There ☐ Need More Practice	pp. 354–55
Apply knowledge of and write to demonstrate knowledge of apostrophes	Apostrophes can help simplify your writing. They help shorten awkward phrases like "the pen that belongs to Aria" down to "Aria's pen." They can also help shorten by creating contractions.	☐ I've Got It! ☐ Almost There ☐ Need More Practice	p. 355

Deepening Your Understanding

If you would like to go beyond the material in this chapter, explore additional connections, and get more practice, check out these related topics:

⊙ **Nouns**: In order to decide what apostrophe tip to use in your writing, you must first learn the difference between singular and plural nouns.

⊙ **Spelling**: When you use apostrophes to form contractions or possessives, you should also make sure you are spelling the words correctly. Remember that plural words that don't end in s are irregular and should be checked carefully for spelling.

⊙ **Easily Confused Words**: Words like its/it's and whose/who's are also known as easily confused words. Being aware of the definition of each word is important, so you can ensure you are using the right one.

Quotation Marks

"Quotations offer one kind of break in what the eye can see, the ear can hear."

—Ihab Hassan

FACT OR FICTION?
The titles of all sources I use in my papers will be put in quotation marks.

FICTION.
Titles of shorter works (articles, essays, songs, etc.) will be put in quotation marks; however, titles of longer works (books, magazines, films, etc.) will be italicized. A full list of those works that should be in quotation marks can be found in this chapter.

Discovering Key Points

- Identify the use of quotation marks with direct quotes, dialogue, and titles of short works
- Apply knowledge of and correct quotation mark errors in the context of a sentence
- Apply knowledge of and write to demonstrate knowledge of quotation marks

Like the apostrophe, the quotation mark is another commonly used punctuation mark. It looks like this and comes in a pair or set: " " .

The **quotation mark** is a punctuation mark used to indicate a direct quotation, dialogue, or titles of short works. Quotation marks should not be used for emphasis.

> All employees "must wash hands" before returning to work. = INCORRECT
> All employees must wash hands before returning to work. = CORRECT

Can you find and fix the quotation mark error in this sign?

There are three ways in which quotation marks are used. We use quotation marks with direct quotations, dialogue, and titles of short works.

Quotation Marks with Direct Quotations

For more information on in-text citations, see Chapter 16.

Quotation marks are used to set off any direct quotation. Therefore, you will use quotation marks most often in research papers or essays in which you quote from sources. An in-text citation will also come after the quotation.

> Smith argues, "We've been living in a fool's paradise" (2007, p. 28).
> "Many politicians use mudslinging to gain the popular vote," the author claims (Jones 192).

Quotation Marks with Dialogue

To learn more about the modes of writing, see Chapter 6.

Quotation marks can also be used to show dialogue or a conversation. You might write dialogue if you were writing a short story or composing a description or narrative piece of writing. In this case, the quoted material is not followed by an in-text citation, as it is not taken directly from a source, such as an essay or book.

"I felt," Alton said, "the salmon was unnecessary in this dish."
He was clearly angry: "Stop apologizing for everything!"

Quotation Marks with the Titles of Short Works

The last use of quotation marks is when punctuating the titles of short works. Refer to the chart below to find out when to use quotation marks with titles:

ITEM	EXAMPLE
Essays from journals, anthologies, etc.	"The Language of Advertising"
Articles from magazines, newspapers, etc.	"The Seven Deadly Ways to Kiss"
Short stories	"The Body"
Short poems	"The Raven"
Songs	"Always"
Television program episodes	"The One Who Got Away"

My favorite song is "Hallelujah" sung by Jeff Buckley.
"Baelor" is the most shocking episode of *Game of Thrones*.

Tips for Using Punctuation with Quotation Marks

When using punctuation with quotation marks, refer to these three tips:

Tip #1: When quoted material ends with a period or comma, the punctuation goes inside the quotation marks, except when an in-text citation follows the quotation.

"My favorite cereal," Harold said, "is Fruit Loops."
Cunningham described milk toast as "Nourishing and soul-satisfying" (32).

Tip #2: When quoted material ends with a colon or semicolon, the punctuation goes outside of the quotation marks.

At the beginning of the study, the participants "showed no significant change with Drug X"; however, two years into the study, "87% of the participants were cured of their illness" (Paulson & Tobin, 2003, p. 116).

San-ha said, "He got exactly what he deserved": a sentence of life without parole.

Tip #3: When quoted material ends with an exclamation point or question mark, the punctuation goes inside the quotation marks, unless the exclamation point or question mark applies to the whole sentence.

> Velma screamed, "You can't just kick me out!"
> Why don't you like Iggy Azalea's song "Fancy"?

Here, the question mark goes after the quotation marks because the sentence itself is a question.

> I love Pink Floyd's song "Is Anybody Out There?"

In this example, the quotation mark goes inside the quotation marks because the song title is a question.

Practice the Skills 1

Identify whether the quotation marks are being used to indicate a direct quotation (DQ), dialogue (D), or the title of a short work (S).

Example: __D__   Nikolas said, "I'm surprised to see you here!"

1. _____ At our wedding, my mother read the poem "Dear Heart."

2. _____ Seifer stated, "Tesla's patron saint Nicholas was a fourth-century god who protected sailors" (2).

3. _____ "Please," the attendant said, "prepare for landing by making sure your seat backs and tray tables are in their full upright position."

4. _____ The author argues, "Like Stults, others have suffered because P&G controls Cincinnati" (Swasy, 1993, p. 97).

5. _____ *Cat Fancy*'s article titled "Buyer Beware!" really helped me understand more about buying medicine for my cat online.

Practice the Skills 2

Rewrite the following sentences by using quotation marks correctly. Pay close attention to the punctuation required for the sentence. Refer to the three punctuation tips if you need help.

Example: Silas asked, Are you going to just admit you're wrong?
             Silas asked, "Are you going to just admit you're wrong?"

1. Is Resentment your favorite episode of *Wilfred*, too?

2. You really shouldn't sneak up on me like that! Jocelyn exclaimed.

3. O'Grady asks, But what could you do with a tool like that? (2009, p. xi).

4. In the article titled Things You Need to Know about Student Loans, the author clarifies many of the myths about paying for education.

5. Rafael thought, It is just an ordinary day; that was true until he went to work.

Practice the Skills 3

Write your own sentence using quotation marks correctly by following the directions below.

Example: Write a sentence using quotation marks to indicate a direct quotation.

             The author is quite informative, stating that "The magnolias are some of the oldest types of hardwood that we still have around" (Thomas 5).

1. Write a sentence using quotation marks to indicate a direct quotation.

2. Write a sentence using quotation marks to indicate dialogue.

3. Write a sentence using quotation marks to indicate titles of short works.

Assessing Your Knowledge

KEY POINTS	REMINDER	HOW WELL DID YOU UNDERSTAND THIS MATERIAL?	PAGE(S)
Identify the use of quotation marks with direct quotes, dialogue, and titles of short works	There are three ways to use quotation marks: ▪ to indicate a direct quotation, which would be found in an essay that uses and cites sources formally ▪ to indicate dialogue ▪ to indicate titles of short works, such as essays, articles, song titles, etc.	☐ I've Got It! ☐ Almost There ☐ Need More Practice	pp. 358–59

Apply knowledge of and correct quotation mark errors in the context of a sentence	Whenever you use quoted material, you have to use quotation marks. Do not use quotation marks to emphasize a word or phrase. When using punctuation with quotation marks, refer to three tips:	☐ I've Got It! ☐ Almost There ☐ Need More Practice	pp. 359–61

- **Tip #1**: When quoted material ends with a period or comma, the punctuation goes inside the quotation marks, except when an in-text citation follows the quotation.
- **Tip #2**: When quoted material ends with a colon or semicolon, the punctuation goes outside of the quotation marks.
- **Tip #3**: When quoted material ends with an exclamation point or question mark, the punctuation goes inside the quotation marks, unless the exclamation point or question mark applies to the whole sentence.

Apply knowledge of and write to demonstrate knowledge of quotation marks	You must set off direct quotations or dialogue with quotation marks in your research paper to show your reader who is speaking. Without the quotation marks, your reader can become con-fused about who is speaking and what is being said.	☐ I've Got It! ☐ Almost There ☐ Need More Practice	p. 361

Deepening Your Understanding

If you would like to go beyond the material in this chapter, explore additional connections, and get more practice, check out these related topics:

- **Verbs**: When you are using quotation marks for a direct quotation, you'll want to use a signal phrase. Signal phrases include a subject (who is saying the quote) and a verb (how the quote is being said). It is important to make sure your verb choice fits the context of the quotation.

- **Commas**: Often when you use quotation marks, you'll also need to use commas to properly punctuate your sentences. Commas will help you better integrate sources and dialogue into your writing.

- **End Punctuation Marks**: In this chapter, the three tips for using punctuation with quotation marks were presented. Knowing what these punctuation marks are and how to use them is essential to being a good writer. These punctuation marks will also help you vary your writing.

Easily Confused Words

26

"How often misused words generate misleading thoughts."
—Herbert Spencer

FACT OR FICTION?
When I misuse or confuse a word, spell check will fix it for me.

FICTION.
Unfortunately, because the words are merely confused, and not misspelled, the spell check in your word processing program will not catch easily confused words.

Discovering Key Points

- Identify easily confused words
- Apply knowledge of and correct easily confused words in the context of a sentence
- Apply knowledge of and write to demonstrate knowledge of easily confused words

Easily confused words are words that are often mistaken and misused by writers and readers. Many times, the confusion comes from the words sounding alike. Words that sound alike but have different meanings or spellings are called homophones.

By now, you have probably realized that a dictionary is an important weapon in every writer's arsenal. A dictionary can help you increase your vocabulary or even to learn a new language, and when it comes to easily confused words, the dictionary serves an equally important role. If you are ever confused about which word to use in a sentence, look up the definitions of both words in a dictionary. This will help you discern which word you want to use.

Can you find and fix the easily confused word error in this sign?

List of Easily Confused Words

Below are two charts of the most common easily confused words, along with their definitions.

WORD 1	PART OF SPEECH	DEFINITION	WORD 2	PART OF SPEECH	DEFINITION
accept	verb	means "to take or receive"	**except**	preposition	refers to something being left out
advice	noun	means "a recommendation or suggestion"	**advise**	verb	refers to the act of making a recommendation or suggestion
affect	verb	means "to influence"	**effect**	noun	usually means "a result of"
beside	preposition	means "close to or next to"	**besides**	preposition or adverb	refers to an exception or an addition
coarse	adjective	means "rough"	**course**	noun	refers to a path or a class
compliment	noun or verb	means "flattery"	**complement**	noun or verb	means "something that completes"

desert	noun	refers to a dry, sandy region	**dessert**	noun	refers to the final course in a meal			
farther	adverb	refers to a greater point or distance	**further**	adverb	means "to a greater extent or depth"			
few	adjective	means "small in number" (used only with countable nouns)	**less**	adjective	means "small in amount" (used only with uncountable or mass nouns)			
figuratively	adverb	means "symbolically or metaphorically"	**literally**	adverb	means "actually"			
it's	pronoun/ verb contraction	contraction meaning "it is" or "it has"	**its**	pronoun	possessive form of "it"			
laid	verb	past tense of "lay"	**lay**	verb	past tense of "lie"			
lose	verb	means "to misplace or fail"	**loose**	adjective	means "not tight"			
passed	verb	past tense of "pass"	**past**	noun or adjective	refers to time having gone by			
precede	verb	means "to come before"	**proceed**	verb	means "to move forward"			
then	adverb or noun	refers to time	**than**	conjunction or preposition	is a comparison between two things			
who's	pronoun/ verb contraction	contraction meaning "who is"	**whose**	pronoun	possessive form of "who"			
your	pronoun	possessive form of "you"	**you're**	pronoun/ verb contraction	contraction meaning "you are"			

This second chart highlights groups of three words that are easily confused.

WORD 1	PART OF SPEECH	DEFINITION	WORD 2	PART OF SPEECH	DEFINITION	WORD 3	PART OF SPEECH	DEFINITION
cite	verb	means to quote	**sight**	noun	refers to vision	**site**	noun	refers to a piece of land or place on the Internet
to	preposition	preposition that indicates movement or infinitive used with a verb	**too**	adverb	means also or excessively	**two**	adjective	refers to a number
they're	pronoun/ verb con- traction	contraction meaning "they are"	**their**	pronoun	possessive form of "they"	**there**	adverb	refers to a place or location

Here are examples of easily confused words used in context.

I always lose things in my purse, especially loose change.
Their house is over there. That's where they're living currently.
Ivy is more prepared than Donald for the marathon. If he doesn't practice,
   then he may not be able to keep up.
I advise that you take my advice about the breakup.

Practice the Skills 1

Circle the correct word for each sentence.

Example: I am currently taking a summer school (course) / coarse) in math.

1. Each time Steph receives a (complement / compliment), she blushes.

2. The phone is (beside / besides) my bed.

3. Although I hate to admit it, I (accept / except) that I am always late.

4. When she gets mad, steam (literally / figuratively) comes out of her ears.

5. My favorite (dessert / desert) is strawberry cheesecake.

Practice the Skills 2

Rewrite the following sentences by using easily confused words correctly. Some sentences
may have more than one easily confused word to correct.

Example: Whose going to the party beside me?
            Who's going to the party **besides** me?

1. I really hope I past the Chemistry test; I studied really hard for it.

2. I need advise about my old car. It can't go further than 25 miles without breaking down.

3. Dr. Christensen requires our research papers to site five sources, including one scholarly
   sight from the Internet.

4. Before we precede with the meeting, we should first discuss the history of the issue at
   hand.

5. Jasmine went too the park with to of her friends.

Practice the Skills 3

Write multiple sentences of your own using the correct easily confused words by following the directions below. After you have written each sentence, underline the easily confused word.

Example: Write two sentences, one using its, and the other using it's.

> **It's** important to remember healthy eating habits.
> The ant took the cookie crumb back to **its** hill.

1. Write two sentences, one using affect, and the other using effect.

2. Write two sentences, one using few, and the other using less.

3. Write three sentences, one using to, one using too, and the last using two.

4. Write two sentences, one using laid, and the other using lay.

5. Write two sentences, one using your, and the other using you're.

Assessing Your Knowledge

KEY POINTS	REMINDER	HOW WELL DID YOU UNDERSTAND THIS MATERIAL?	PAGE(S)
Identify easily confused words	**Easily confused words** are words that are often mistaken and misused by writers and readers. Many times, the confusion comes from the words sounding alike. When the words sound alike, but have different meanings or spellings, these words are called homophones.	☐ I've Got It! ☐ Almost There ☐ Need More Practice	pp. 364–66
Apply knowledge of and correct easily confused words in the context of a sentence	Because some words sound so similar, it is easy to confuse them. When in doubt, use a dictionary to look up the words. This way, you can make sure you are using the correct word each time you write.	☐ I've Got It! ☐ Almost There ☐ Need More Practice	p. 366

| Apply knowledge of and write to demonstrate knowledge of easily confused words | Identifying easily confused words is important because misusing words can impair your meaning and confuse your readers. Being aware of the differences between easily confused words is also important because it can help enhance your spoken and written vocabulary. | ☐ I've Got It! p. 367
☐ Almost There
☐ Need More Practice |

Deepening Your Understanding

If you would like to go beyond the material in this chapter, explore additional connections, and get more practice, check out these related topics:

- **Vocabulary**: As a reader, speaker, and writer, you must improve your vocabulary. Think of your vocabulary as your appearance. Each and every word you choose to write or say tells people quite a bit about you. Building your vocabulary will also help make you a more confident reader, speaker, and writer.

- **Standard and Non-Standard English**: Non-standard English refers to dialect, slang, and improper English. When you write formal essays, you should not only use the correct words but avoid non-standard English as well.

- **Using Precise Language**: When you write, you must choose your words carefully. This ensures your meaning is clear and coherent.

Permissions Acknowledgments

Alexrod, Joshua. "*South Park* Is Still Our Most Consistently Fair Political Satire," *Fansided*, © 2019 Fansided.

Bachman, Katy. "Study: Industry's Found Sneaky Way to Keep Advertising Junk Food to Kids," *Adweek*, © 2020 Adweek. Reprinted by permission.

Hartley, Matt. "Social News Site Reddit the 'Groundskeepers' of the Internet," *The Financial Post*, © 2012 Financial Post, a division of Postmedia Network Inc. Reprinted by permission.

Hine, Thomas. From *The Total Package: The Secret History and Hidden Meanings of Boxes, Bottles, Cans and Other Persuasive Containers*, copyright © 1995, 1997. Used with permission of Little, Brown and Company, an imprint of Hachette Book Group, Inc., and of The Karpfinger Agency.

Jones, Carolyn. "Out of the Retail Rat Race: Consumer Group Doesn't Buy Notion that New Is Better," *The San Francisco Chronicle*, © 2006 The San Francisco Chronicle. Used with permission obtained through Copyright Clearance Center, Inc.

Klass, Perri. "When Social Media Is Really Problematic for Adolescents," *The New York Times*, © 2019 The New York Times Company. All rights reserved. Reprinted by permission.

Linn, Susan. "Commercializing Childhood: The Corporate Takeover of Kids' Lives," *Multinational Monitor*, © 2008 Susan Linn. Reprinted by permission.

Parker, James. "Our Zombies, Ourselves: Why We Can't Get the Undead Off Our Brains," *The Atlantic*, © 2011 The Atlantic Monthly Group, LLC. All rights reserved. Reprinted by permission.

Scaife, Steven Nguyen. "*Crazy Rich Asians* Has Survived Impossible Representation Standards," *The Verge*, © 2018 Vox Media. Reprinted by permission.

Schmuhl, Robert. "That's News to Me," *Notre Dame Magazine*, © 2005 Robert Schmuhl. Reprinted by permission.

Spake, Amanda. "Hey, Kids! We've Got Sugar and Toys," *US News and World Report*, © 2003. Reprinted by permission.

Tate, Christine. "My Daughter Asked Me to Stop Writing about Motherhood. Here's Why I Can't Do That," *The Washington Post*, © 2019 The Washington Post. All rights reserved. Reprinted by permission.

Wang, Amy. "McDonald's Pulls Ad about a Grieving Boy and His Dead Father after Criticism," *The Washington Post*, © 2017 The Washington Post. All rights reserved. Reprinted by permission.

Watercutter, Angela. "Pepsi's Kendall Jenner Ad Was So Awful It Did the Impossible: It United the Internet," *Wired*, © 2017 Condé Nast. Reprinted by permission.

Image Credits

Page 10: Harvey Weinstein Tweet from *The New York Times*, © 2017 The New York Times Company. All rights reserved. Reproduced by permission.

Page 11: Matej Kastelic/Shutterstock.com.

Page 91: Pool, Smiley. Hurricane Katrina aftermath, © 2018 The Dallas Morning News, Inc. Reproduced by permission.

Page 103: PRESSLAB/Shutterstock.com.

Page 130: DBSOCAL/Shutterstock.com.

Page 139: Planned Parenthood. Website screen capture. Reproduced by permission.

Page 140: No Kid Hungry, a campaign of Share our Strength. Website screen capture. Reproduced by permission.

Page 141: US Forest Service. US Forest Service website screen capture. Reproduced by permission.

Page 160: National FFA Organization. Facebook post. Reproduced by permission.

Page 172: MITstudio/Shutterstock.com.

Page 230: Tannen, Deborah. *That's Not What I Meant!* cover, © 1986 by Deborah Tannen. Used with permission of HarperCollins Publishers.

Page 231: *Journal of Marketing Management* cover, © Westburn Publishers Ltd. and Taylor & Francis.

Page 231: Greenburg, Jill. *Wired* cover, © The Condé Nast Publications Ltd. Reproduced by permission.

Page 271: Mackendrick, Alexander. *On Film-Making: An Introduction to the Craft of the Director* cover and colophon, © 2005 Faber & Faber.

Page 276: EBSCO. Website screen capture. Reproduced by permission.

Page 278: NBA Cares. Website screen capture.

Page 281: STIR. Milwaukee Riverkeeper ad. Reproduced by permission.

Page 287: Tweet used with permission of Broadview Press.

Page 300: Stephen Barnes/Shutterstock.com. Montage by Elizabeth Broes.

Page 312: Andrey Bayda/Shutterstock.com, Shawna and Damien Richard/Shutterstock.com. Montage by Elizabeth Broes.

Page 324: HstrongART/Shutterstock.com.

Page 330: feelphoto2521/Shutterstock.com. Montage by Elizabeth Broes.

Page 336: lil-mo/Shutterstock.com. Montage by Elizabeth Broes.

Page 344: Hekla/Shutterstock.com, Thaspol Sangsee/Shutterstock.com. Montage by Elizabeth Broes.

Page 352: Photograph by Don LePan.

Page 358: Cagkan Sayin/Shutterstock.com. Montage by Elizabeth Broes.

Page 364: Photograph by Don LePan.

Index

----

talking back, when reading, 29. *See also* annotation

From the Publisher

A name never says it all, but the word "Broadview" expresses a good deal
of the philosophy behind our company. We are open to a broad range of
academic approaches and political viewpoints. We pay attention to the
broad impact book publishing and book printing has in the wider world;
for some years now we have used 100% recycled paper for most titles.
Our publishing program is internationally oriented and broad-ranging.
Our individual titles often appeal to a broad readership too; many are
of interest as much to general readers as to academics and students.

Founded in 1985, Broadview remains a fully independent
company owned by its shareholders—not an imprint
or subsidiary of a larger multinational.

For the most accurate information on our books (including
information on pricing, editions, and formats) please
visit our website at www.broadviewpress.com. Our print
books and ebooks are available for sale on our site.

broadview press
www.broadviewpress.com